Victorian Shakespeare, Volume 2

Other books by the editors:

GAIL MARSHALL:

ACTRESSES ON THE VICTORIAN STAGE: Feminine Performance and the Galatea
  Myth
VICTORIAN FICTION
GEORGE ELIOT (ed.)

ADRIAN POOLE:

GISSING IN CONTEXT
TRAGEDY: Shakespeare and the Greek Example
SHAKESPEARE: Coriolanus
HENRY JAMES
THE OXFORD BOOK OF CLASSICAL VERSE IN TRANSLATION (ed. with Jeremy
  Maule)
SHAKESPEARE AND THE VICTORIANS

Victorian Shakespeare, Volume 2

Literature and Culture

Edited by

Gail Marshall
Senior Lecturer in Victorian Literature
School of English
University of Leeds

Adrian Poole
Reader in English and Comparative Literature
University of Cambridge

Foreword by

Nina Auerbach

Published in association with the Institute of English Studies, School of Advanced Study, University of London

First published 2003 by
PALGRAVE MACMILLAN
Houndmills, Basingstoke, Hampshire RG21 6XS and
175 Fifth Avenue, New York, N. Y. 10010
Companies and representatives throughout the world

PALGRAVE MACMILLAN is the global academic imprint of the Palgrave Macmillan division of St. Martin's Press, LLC and of Palgrave Macmillan Ltd. Macmillan® is a registered trademark in the United States, United Kingdom and other countries. Palgrave is a registered trademark in the European Union and other countries.

ISBN 1-4039-1117-7 hardback

This book is printed on paper suitable for recycling and made from fully managed and sustained forest sources.

A catalogue record for this book is available from the British Library.

Library of Congress Cataloging-in-Publication Data

Victorian Shakespeare / edited by Gail Marshall, Adrian Poole.
    p. cm.
  Includes bibliographical references and index.
  Contents: –v. 2. Literature and culture
  ISBN 1-4039-1117-7 (v. 2)
    1. Shakespeare, William, 1564-1616–Criticism and interpretation–History–19th century. 2. Shakespeare, William, 1564-1616–Appreciation–Great Britain. 3. Shakespeare, William, 1564-1616–Stage history–1800-1950. 4. Criticism–Great Britain–History–19th century. I. Marshall, Gail, 1965- II. Poole, Adrian.

PR2969.V47 2003
822.3'3–dc21
                                                          2003046950

10 9 8 7 6 5 4
12 11 10 09 08 07 06 05

Printed and bound in Great Britain by
Antony Rowe Ltd, Chippenham and Eastbourne

Contents

List of Illustrations

All illustrations are reproduced by permission of the Syndics of
Cambridge University Library.

Foreword

Nina Auerbach

Many of our contemporaries assume that the Victorian Shakespeare was a bully, an Imperialist insignia, an apologist for Anglo-Saxon supremacy, a particularly grandiose nineteenth-century ideal of Britannia. To actual Victorians, however, at least for those who were writers, Shakespeare was often a thorn in the Establishment side, as the essays in this stunning collection show. Far from being a triumphant vessel of unilateral Bardolatry, implicitly belittling cultural outsiders, the Victorian Shakespeare spoke in opaque language for the silenced dispossessed.

The tragic star of this collection is not royal. Kings Macbeth and Lear appear only incidentally, while Prince Hamlet sweeps in largely to be mocked by Dickens in his populist persona. It is Othello who stars in three of the most striking essays, but he is not the luminous black champion we are familiar with from Laurence Fishburne's 1995 film performance. Victorian Shakespearean productions featured a hero critics now paradoxically call 'the white Othello', an aggressively non-black husband who was both a concession to British racial taboos and a reminder of its denied voices.

Diana Henderson's 'Othello Redux?' refracts *Othello* through Walter Scott's *Kenilworth*, whereby Othello's suppressed blackness implicitly evokes the suppressed Scottish nation, recently absorbed by the English crown. In the same vein, John Glavin's rich 'To make the situation natural' transmutes this non-black black man through Trollope's devious novel, *He Knew He Was Right*. Trollope and Glavin's combined wizardry turns Othello's repressed colour into a conduit for the voices of women who have no power over their stories. In both readings, a troubling hero becomes, not a symbol of imperial homogenisation as we might think, but an emissary for the excluded.

Pascale Aebischer's startling account of George Vandenhoff's *Leaves from an Actor's Notebook* finds in the despised genre of theatrical memoirs an anecdote about *Othello* that speaks for actors' tainted lives. Embellishing the legend of a mad actor who begins to live his Othello, a legend Ronald Colman's Oscar-winning performance in *A Double Life* (1947) immortalised in American film, Aebischer unravels a memorable parable about performers' hybrid natures, at once pure and whores, artists and mountebanks, cynosures and outcasts. Othello, who, it might seem, epitomised Victorian exclusions, becomes a vehicle for uncomfortable identities beyond simulated whiteness.

Other essays focus similarly on Shakespearean discomfort. Clare Pettitt shows that even in the 1851 Great Exhibition, that spectacle of British technological supremacy, the welter of Shakespearean artefacts coalesced into an icon more fragile than imperial, whose original genius dissipates in cheap copies. As Francis O'Gorman's Ruskin grows old, he denounces as fraudulent Shakespeare's heroic influence on England's broken manhood. For Juliet John, Hamlet exists only so that democratic Dickens can laugh his outdated Romantic elitism off the stage.

In the same aggressively modern spirit, Victorian poets who seemed to celebrate Shakespeare relegated him in their imagery to opacity or the grave. Robert Douglas-Fairhurst's Tennyson plants his Shakespearean allusions in weediness, decay, things rank and gross in nature; Danny Karlin reads a particularly convoluted sonnet by Browning in which Shakespeare dissolves into the lost esoterica of Hebraic religion. In all these readings, Bards shun Bardolatry. Their Shakespeare is an outgrowth of the lost, the putrid, the arcane. Perhaps, like King Hamlet, he should remain underground.

The only wholehearted celebrants in this collection are two woman writers: Mary Cowden Clarke and George Eliot. Ann Thompson and Sasha Roberts's testimonial to Mary Cowden Clarke shows that through her prolific Shakespeare scholarship, alone and in collaboration with her husband, she became that Victorian rarity, a wife with a voice of her own. In her own time if not in ours, Shakespeare (along with her encouraging husband) lent her the prestige that made her welcome in the men's club of scholarship. With seeming ease, she slid into an inclusion for which most diligent Victorian women struggled vainly.

In a voice almost as shrewd and subtle as its subject's, Philip Davis's 'Implicit and Explicit Reason: George Eliot and Shakespeare' teases out the Shakespearean echoes, not only in George Eliot's wise saws, but in her penetration of her characters' secret, shameful thoughts. For Davis, George Eliot is Shakespearean not in her theatricality, but in her secrecy; through Shakespearean empathy, she constructs the pervading persona of 'George Eliot', who lives both within and beyond her characters. Davis's is not the bombastic Shakespeare of 'what ho's' and trumpet fanfares, but the obscure creeper into unacknowledged places to which, centuries later, he leads a psychological novelist for her penetration.

For the most part women were beyond the pale of Victorian eminence. It is appropriate for this surprising collection that only women,

Mary Cowden Clarke and George Eliot, find unambiguous authorisation in Shakespeare. The subject of this volume is an uncomfortable figure who arouses, not the dread and fear of kings, but the greater dread and fear of unacknowledged voices.

Acknowledgments

We would like to thank Warwick Gould, Director of the Institute of English Studies at the School of Advanced Studies, University of London, for the invitation to hold the conference on which the papers gathered in these volumes are based, and both him and his colleagues, especially Joanne Nixon and Michael Baron, for their support in making arrangements for it. We are very grateful to all the contributors who helped to make this conference such a success, and to the British Academy for a grant that supported it. We thank Josie Dixon and Emily Rosser at Palgrave Macmillan for the initial encouragement they gave this project. To our editor Emily Rosser we owe particular thanks for her firm guidance and warm co-operation throughout its development, and to Paula Kennedy for her work in seeing it through to completion.

Notes on the Contributors

Pascale Aebischer is a Lecturer in Shakespeare and Renaissance Literature at the University of Leicester. She is the author of *Shakespeare's Violated Bodies: Stage and Screen Performance* (forthcoming 2004), and the co-editor of *Remaking Shakespeare: Performance across Media, Genres and Cultures* (2003) and *Personation and Performance: Staging the Early Modern Subject* (2003). She has published essays on drama theory, Restoration comedy and Henry Green.

Philip Davis is a Professor in the English Department at the University of Liverpool. His most recent publications include *Sudden Shakespeare* (1996) and *The Victorians 1830–1880*, published in 2002 as one of the first volumes in the new Oxford English Literary History series.

Christopher Decker is Assistant Professor of English at Boston University. He was a Research Fellow at Trinity College, Cambridge, from 1994 to 1998. He has written on eighteenth- and nineteenth-century English poetry, and his critical edition of Edward FitzGerald's *Rubáiyát of Omar Khayyám* was published by the University Press of Virginia in 1997.

Robert Douglas-Fairhurst is Fellow and Tutor in English at Magdalen College, Oxford. He is the author of *Victorian Afterlives: the Shaping of Influence in Nineteenth-Century Literature* (2002), and is currently researching a book on Victorian magic.

John Glavin is Professor of English at Georgetown University in Washington, DC, where he also directs the John Carroll Scholars Program. He is the author of *After Dickens: Reading, Adaptation and Performance* (1999) and editor of the forthcoming *Dickens on Screen* (2003). He is currently at work on a study of Shakespeare's 'Italian' plays.

Diana Henderson, Associate Professor of Literature at MIT, is the author of *Passion Made Public: Elizabethan Lyric, Gender, and Performance* (1995), and numerous essays on early modern drama, poetry, and domestic culture. Recent articles include contributions to *Shakespeare: the Movie, 2*; *Shakespeare After Mass Media*; *Shakespeare and his Contemporaries in Performance*; *Virginia Woolf: Reading the Renaissance*; and several of

Blackwell's *Companion* anthologies. She is currently editing Blackwell's *Concise Companion to Shakespeare on Screen* and completing her book *Uneasy Collaborations: Working with Shakespeare across Time and Media*.

Philip Horne is Professor of English at University College London. He has written and published extensively on Henry James, most notably *Henry James and Revision* (1990), and *Henry James: a Life in Letters* (1999).

Juliet John is Senior Lecturer in English at the University of Liverpool. She is author of *Dickens's Villains: Melodrama, Character, Popular Culture* (2001), editor of *Cult Criminals: the Newgate Novels* (1998) and co-editor (with Alice Jenkins) of *Rethinking Victorian Culture* (2000) and *Rereading Victorian Fiction* (2000). She is currently working on a book entitled *Dickens and Popular Culture*.

Danny Karlin is Professor of English at University College London. He is the author of numerous books and articles about Robert Browning, including *The Courtship of Robert Browning and Elizabeth Barrett* (1985) and *Browning's Hatreds* (1993). He is the editor of the *Penguin Book of Victorian Verse* (1997).

Gail Marshall is Senior Lecturer in Victorian Literature at the University of Leeds. She is the author of *Actresses on the Victorian Stage: Feminine Performance and the Galatea Myth* (1998) and *Victorian Fiction* (2002), and editor of *George Eliot* (2003). Her research interests include the novel, women's writing, and Victorian theatrical culture, and she is currently writing a monograph on the relationships between Shakespeare and Victorian women.

Francis O'Gorman is Lecturer in Victorian Literature at the University of Leeds. His books include *John Ruskin* (1999), *Late Ruskin: New Contexts* (2001), and a collection, edited with Dinah Birch, *Ruskin and Gender* (2002). Forthcoming books include the *Blackwell's Annotated Anthology of Victorian Poetry* (2004) and a study of *Ruskin, Venice, and the Idea of Influence*.

Clare Pettitt is a Fellow of Newnham College, Cambridge, and author of a monograph on the Great Exhibition of 1851 (forthcoming 2004).

Adrian Poole is Reader in English and Comparative Literature at the University of Cambridge, and a Fellow of Trinity College. His books include *Gissing in Context* (1975), *Tragedy: Shakespeare and the Greek Example* (1987), *Henry James* (1991), and *Shakespeare and the Victorians* (2003). He has edited novels by Dickens, Stevenson and James, and co-edited (with Jeremy Maule) *The Oxford Book of Classical Verse in Translation* (1995). He is currently working on a book on 'Witnessing Tragedy'.

Sasha Roberts is Lecturer in English at the University of Kent. She is the author of *Reading Shakespeare's Poem in Early Modern England* (2003), and *Writers and their Work: Romeo and Juliet* (1998), co-editor with Ann Thompson of *Women Reading Shakespeare 1660–1900: an Anthology of Criticism* (1997), and has published numerous articles on Shakespeare, the history of reading, and early modern visual culture. She is currently working on a book on *The Formation of Literary Taste in Early Modern Manuscript Culture*.

Ann Thompson is Professor of English Language and Literature at King's College London. She is a General Editor of the Arden Shakespeare (third series), for which she is co-editing *Hamlet* with Neil Taylor (forthcoming 2004). Her publications include *Shakespeare's Chaucer* (1978), *Shakespeare, Meaning and Metaphor* (co-authored with John O. Thompson, 1987), an edition of *The Taming of the Shrew* (1984, second edition 2003) and an anthology of criticism, *Women Reading Shakespeare 1660–1900*, co-edited with Sasha Roberts (1997).

A Note on References

All references to Shakespeare are to *The Riverside Shakespeare*, general and textual editor, G. Blakemore Evans, with the assistance of J. J. M. Tobin, 2nd edn (Boston: Houghton Mifflin, 1997).

Introduction

Adrian Poole

Is Shakespeare better read than seen and heard? Is it better think of him as a poet or a dramatist? Is the afterlife of his works and words an inspiration to later artists or an inhibition? Is his continued popularity a sign of cultural health or stagnation? Is he an honest ghost? Are these good questions?

The answer to the last may well be 'no'. Many of the essays in this and its companion volume contest the assumptions on which such questions are based: that writing and reading are entirely distinct from performance, or that the influence of artists on each other, if they are any good, can ever be purely tonic or toxic, or that our ancestry, personal and collective, should be embraced or rejected in its totality. As for the relations between writing and performance, all the writers discussed here had Shakespeare's words more or less by heart, but they were also keen to hear them spoken and see them enacted. The young Robert Browning thrilled to Edmund Kean and the young Henry James to Fanny Kemble. Dickens, Tennyson, Ruskin, Eliot – they all watched with the keenest attention the leading players of the time, Macready and Faucit, Salvini and Rossi, Irving and Terry. Writers could themselves be performers. In 1848 Dickens put on *The Merry Wives of Windsor* with a cast that included himself as Justice Shallow and Mary Cowden Clarke (the remarkable woman of letters admired by Ann Thompson and Sasha Roberts in Chapter 10) as Mistress Quickly (Dickens addressed her as 'My dear Concordance'). Christopher Decker gives us a telling glimpse of Tennyson in 1874 regaling Irving and his company with an impromptu masterclass on *Hamlet* (Chapter 9).

Shakespeare is in turn constantly being performed in Victorian writing. As writers can perform, so performers can write and they did: Macready, Fanny Kemble, Helen Faucit, Ellen Terry and many other

1

lesser lights, George Vandenhoff, for example. Pascale Aebischer has a highly suggestive discussion (Chapter 11) of the role played in his memoirs by the strange tale of an actress who fatally identifies with the tragic roles she plays – Juliet, Ophelia, Desdemona. Meanwhile numerous fictional characters perform Shakespeare, from Dickens's Nicholas Nickleby and Smike to Wopsle, from Eliot's Gwendolen Harleth to James's Miriam Rooth. In Charlotte Brontë's *Shirley* (1849) two of the leading characters read *Coriolanus* together, and in Hardy's *A Laodicean* (1881) a jealous lover watches his girl and his rival playing together in *Love's Labour's Lost*. In prose and verse, in fiction, history, life-writing, memoirs, speeches, sermons, diaries, and private correspondence, Victorians quote and allude to Shakespeare so frequently you wonder how they would have managed without him. Fanny Kemble was not the only one of whom it might have been said, to borrow the words James lyrically murmured on her death in 1893: 'She was so saturated with Shakespeare that she had made him, as it were, the air she lived in. . . . '[1]

This might be oppressive, always to breathe the Shakespearean air, never to utter any words of your own. Is there magic in the very web of Shakespeare's words, for good or ill? Or is it mere superstition to suppose that any words, even Shakespeare's, carry blessing or bane in themselves, independent of how they are heard and read? 'The web of our life is of a mingled yarn, good and ill together', remarks a nameless French lord in *All's Well that Ends Well* (IV. 3. 71–2). It's the kind of sententious saying that found a natural niche in the commonplacebooks of which the Victorians were fond, over which it's all too easy to imagine them complacently murmuring 'how true, how true'. The complacency might well be ours rather than theirs. For we must also imagine Victorian readers asking themselves exactly *how* it is true – how is it true in this particular web, of my life or yours? For George Eliot story-telling was itself a mingled yarn of lives interwoven with good and ill and ravelled with each other. Words that are tossed off on the spur of the moment by a minor character in performance can be dwelt on, pondered and pursued by the writer into the most intimate details of conduct, feeling and thought, as experienced by a Lydgate or a Dorothea, and reflected on by their narrator. How much more so, then, the words of a Hamlet or a Macbeth that are not lightly uttered but forced violently into existence by the very pressure of circumstance. This is Philip Davis's emphasis in his essay here (Chapter 5), and in his book *Sudden Shakespeare* (1996). At a different but complementary level, in 'Shakespeare's Weeds' (Chapter 7) Robert Douglas-Fairhurst meditates on the mingled yarn of allusion, as we hear it in Tennyson's poetry. What does it mean to repeat old words? Every time we do so there is a double possibility: we may be breathing new life into them, or we may be draining yet another vital drop from them, like Chekhov's 'Three Sisters' and their fading cries of 'To Moscow, to Moscow'. At many different levels the essays in this volume argue that the legacy of 'Shakespeare', to the Victorians as to us, was complex and ambivalent, and that the posing of questions as sharp either/ors is a way of dodging or denying this complexity.

Of course ripped out of context Shakespeare's words can be put to any old use or new that one cares to think of. It was often in bits and pieces that the Victorians encountered their Shakespeare, in anthologies such as the durable Dodd's (first published in 1752) or the brand new Palgrave's *Golden Treasury* (first published in 1861, and still going, in its fifth edition, a century later). There were less respectful pickers and stealers. By the time some fundraisers held a 'Shaksperean Show' in aid of the Chelsea Hospital for Women at the Royal Albert Hall in May 1884, the firms advertising their wares in the brochure knew a thing or two about lifting lines from Shakespeare (see Danny Karlin's paper on Browning's 'The Names', Chapter 9). Shakespeare could be made to blow hot and cold in support of Keen's Mustard and – with the help of a distinctly risqué phrase from the brothel-scene in *Pericles* – an ice-making machine. This is the era when Shakespeare becomes serious business. His name, his words, his characters get attached to durables and consumables from crockery and clocks to mustard and, in due course, a cigar called Hamlet. All this commercial enterprise had powerful ramifications for notions of originality, authenticity and cultural property with which we now still wrestle, as Clare Pettitt demonstrates in her discussion of the Great Exhibition of 1851 (Chapter 4). Many Victorians express a deep anxiety at the prospect of poetry being suffocated by prose, spirit consumed by matter, art overtaken by technology. Ruskin was horrified by the Great Exhibition. But Dickens and Collins were not. And we regularly find an elation, however circumspect, at the discovery that the creative spirit can renew itself even in the most unpromising circumstances. Philip Horne takes as the title for his essay (Chapter 6) the incredulous exclamation of a character in James's *The Tragic Muse*, when he realises that a previously unpromising young actress has found the real thing in herself, the spirit, the poetry: 'Where did she get hold of that?' he asks. Readers of Danny Karlin's paper might correspondingly murmur: 'Where did he get hold of that?' Browning's extraordinary sonnet 'The Names' has lain largely neglected, even by Browning himself, from the time it first saw the light of day in the ephemeral pages of *The Shaksperean Show Book*. To borrow some phrases from the end of *Middlemarch*, we might think of Browning's poem as an unhistoric act which has lived faithfully a hidden life, and of Karlin's reading as an act of revelation and revival.

Back in the 1830s Macready had thought the young Browning might prove a new Shakespeare for the English theatre. But when it came to writing drama in the conventional sense, Shakespeare *was* an inhibiting model for the Victorians rather than a liberating one. We can take an historical interest in the verse dramas of Sheridan Knowles ('the Victorian Shakespeare'),[2] and we can find interest in Browning's plays *Strafford* and *Luria* and Tennyson's *The Cup* and *The Foresters* because of everything else that they wrote, but it would be absurd to claim for them a creative value equal to that of *In Memoriam A. H. H.*, 'Caliban upon Setebos', *Great Expectations* or *Middlemarch*. These four very diverse texts demonstrate an active collaboration with Shakespeare in which the later writer is not cowed by excessive respect. *The Sonnets* and *Hamlet* were vividly present in Tennyson's mind as *In Memoriam* accumulated, along with other Shakespearean bits and pieces. So was a particular moment from *Cymbeline*, the public and personal reverberations of which Christopher Decker ponders to moving effect in 'Shakespeare and Tennyson's Death' (Chapter 8). The partnership between Tennyson's mind and Shakespeare's, and the complicity between their words, are fluid, fluctuating, and unpredictable, as far as possible from the rigid protocols of master and servant. But then there is good precedent in Shakespeare's own works for the creative upsetting of formulae, when clowns and fools and servants and women refuse to know their place, when people and scenes and whole plays insist on behaving badly. 'Transgression' is a lumpen word for the various ways in which people and things can cross boundaries, break rules and fool around with distinctions. But in this very general sense, which may after all be just another way of describing what it is to be creative, 'transgressive' would apply to all the Victorian writers who make good use of Shakespearean matter by displaying a mind and creative intent of their own.

Simply put, it means finding new ways of making writing dramatic *outside* the theatre. This does not mean a brute rejection of drama, theatre and performance, but a critical engagement with the last and most elusive of these terms. For writing is itself a performance. This is true not only for the kind of writing for which Dickens is best known, full of speech that clamours to be voiced and heard, that lends itself to performance on stage, as it did in his life-time, long before the solo readings by the author himself (and long after now on film, television and radio). There's a cunning proximity to a conventional idea of performance in Browning's great dramatic monologues, and in the astonishing 'monodrama' that Tennyson created in *Maud* (his 'little *Hamlet*', as he called it). The very presence of such voices seems to demand auditors, to mourn their absence, to half-conjure them into existence. But in less obvious ways, the notion of performance is also highly germane to Browning's explosive 'The Names' and to Tennyson's protracted story of mourning, *In Memoriam A. H. H.* These poems raise questions about who might be listening to them, in this world or another, with what kinds of understanding, passion and insight. And the same is true of story-tellers less blatantly 'dramatic' than Dickens, of Hallam Tennyson as he composes in writing the scene of his own father's death, for example. And of novelists such as Trollope and George Eliot, who expose the innumerable ways in which men and women – such as Louis Trevelyan in *He Knew He Was Right* and Gwendolen Harleth in *Daniel Deronda* – get attached to the characters they perform, fail to listen to themselves and each other, and refuse to recognise that there may be more ways of performing than one, even something that is not performance at all.

Shakespeare was not the Victorians' only resource for ideas of performance. The French were always available to demonstrate a style so extravagant that it helped English audiences feel that perhaps it was only foreigners who perform while we just, well, behave. In the second half of the nineteenth century the great Italian performers start to arrive – Ristori, Salvini, Rossi, Duse – and partly to confirm such convenient distinctions between 'us' and 'them'. But the reassurance is precarious because amongst other things these foreigners can play our Shakespeare, unforgettably. What's more they play him with such passion that it's hard to know where performance begins and ends. This is the trouble with all performance, except those so incompetent, like the Hamlet of Dickens's Wopsle, that an audience can simply relax in derision. Performance can cast a spell. It can stage the doubleness and fluidity of selfhood, its potential infinity and endless fugitivity. This is where Shakespeare stood the Victorians in such wonderful stead. He provided them with an immense repertoire of characters and stories and verbal expressions, through which to explore and against which to measure the possibilities of knowing who everyone was and might be, including yourself. Hence the role played by Shakespeare in many kinds of story-telling, from Trollope's *He Knew He was Right* (Glavin, Chapter 2) and Dickens's *David Copperfield* (John, Chapter 3) and Mary Cowden Clarke's *The Girlhood of Shakespeare's Heroines* (Thompson and Roberts, Chapter

10) to Hallam Tennyson's *Memoir* of his father (Decker, Chapter 8) and Vandenhoff's *Leaves from an Actor's Notebook* (Aebischer, Chapter 11) and the autobiography strewn through Ruskin's whole writing life (O'Gorman, Chapter 12).

In her generous Foreword Nina Auerbach has identified some of the leading emphases in the essays which follow, but it may be helpful to indicate the logic governing the sequence in which they appear here. The first six essays are predominantly engaged with novels and novelists: Scott, Trollope, Collins, Dickens, Eliot and James. The volume opens with a pair of papers by Diana Henderson and John Glavin that address the uses to which *Othello* was put by Scott and Trollope. Scott is a crucial figure for the understanding of what Shakespeare meant to the Victorians in so far as he emulates the representation of social, political and cultural crisis at the heart of Shakespeare's Histories and Tragedies. Glavin sees Trollope as consciously engaging with Scott's project, and Philip Davis rightly notes the importance of Scott to George Eliot. Though *Kenilworth* (first published in 1821) does not qualify as a Victorian novel according to the strict letter of chronological law, and although it has long suffered from critical neglect, Diana Henderson establishes its high popularity through the nineteenth century, not only in its first fictional form but also in the astonishing number of dramatic productions, burlesques and operas that it generated. Its example serves to remind us how thick was the traffic between texts and performance, and how multiple and oblique were the forms in which 'Shakespeare' reached Victorian audiences and readers. Shakespearean stories, characters, sayings were being constantly, as we would now say, re-cycled, often misremembered or turned deliberately to novel effect, both serious and parodic.

Henderson and Glavin are particularly interested in what it meant for the nineteenth century to whiten Othello, to erase or deny the racial otherness that is integral to the Shakespearean source. In performance, after Edmund Kean, Othello becomes an impossible role, at least for the anglophone actor. But outside the theatre the play's central configuration of characters becomes for the novelist highly generative. Thackeray and Dickens are drawn to it, and Mrs Braddon's *Aurora Floyd* (1863) represents an ingenious, mischievous re-working, for instance. For Scott and Trollope racial conflict is largely re-figured in terms of gender, but its presence is still detectable. If Scott is concerned with the racial composition of contemporary Britain, especially the position of the Celt, he initiates a large argument about nationhood and Englishness that threads its way through the volume as a whole to emerge in the final chapter – completing a circle – with the Ruskin who began his autobiography *Præterita* with the defiant declaration that he was 'a violent Tory of the old school; – Walter Scott's school, that is to say, and Homer's'.

John Glavin pursues many of the same issues as Henderson through a reading of Trollope's *He Knew He Was Right*. The 'He' of the title, Louis Trevelyan, explicitly sees himself as Othello, in a way that eerily complements the fatal identification of the actress Coralie Wilton with Desdemona, as recounted by the actor George Vandenhoff (Chapter 11). In Trollope's ingenious re-writing, the white Othello comes to represent a catastrophic will-to-power inherent both in the English class-system at home and its colonial ambitions abroad. Trollope's novel is not just a re-working of Shakespeare's play, but an active critique that makes its author, Glavin claims, 'for the nineteenth century, the play's most capable reader, and at the same time an extraordinary reader of that century'.

This suggests a thought that applies to many of the authors discussed in this volume, that so far from reposing inertly on the prestige the invocation of Shakespeare might be thought to confer on themselves – the sure mark of the wholly forgettable, of which the Victorian age indisputably boasts its fair share – their best dealings with plots, scenes, characters, passages and verbal expressions from Shakespeare invariably constitute just such *positive* readings as Glavin proposes – strong, subtle, searching, interrogative.

This is how Juliet John characterises Dickens in his dealings with Hamlet (Chapter 3). The melancholy, meditative prince may have been an approved role model for the Romantic artist, and he may go on to sponsor an idea of 'character' integral to the development of the nineteenth-century novel. But this was not an idea of the self or of the artist – individualistic, introspective, self-centered – of which Dickens approved. On the contrary, so John argues: Dickens saw in the Hamlet his generation inherited from the Romantics something distinctly baneful, 'a model of intellectual and aristocratic disengagement from the public sphere'. John helps to remind us, as Richard Schoch does in the companion volume, what lively derision Shakespeare's leading characters could arouse, as the massive outpouring of travesties and burlesques testifies. From a popular perspective – a gravedigger's, for example – Hamlet could seem ridiculously self-absorbed, posturing, 'theatrical'. Such performers could be fascinating, loveable, dangerous – like Steerforth. But it is David Copperfield who is Dickens's artist, the quiet, unobtrusive onlooker.

In 'Shakespeare at the Great Exhibition of 1851' (Chapter 4) Clare Pettitt continues some lines of thought opened up by John about the claims to 'exclusiveness' associated with the iconic status of Shakespeare's most famous character, and that of his author. The figure of Shakespeare conferred prestige on all sorts of artefacts at the greatest show on earth (so far), on tables, salvers, plates and clocks. This was a prestige qualified by his appearance alongside other iconic figures such as Newton and Watt, and of course, in the dawning age of mechanical reproduction, by sheer repetition. Pettitt shrewdly fastens on the symbolic role that Shakespeare takes on in debates about the rival claims of art and technology, of aesthetic and commercial 'value', of 'autonomous authorship' and the 'common patrimony of English culture'. Who does Shakespeare belong to? Does *any* Tom, Dick or Harry have the right to read and understand him, own a copy of his works, perform him? We may note how the arguments here connect up with those discussed by Newey and Swindells in the companion volume, about the right to perform 'legitimate drama'. Pettitt finds some of the issues raised by the Great Exhibition concentrated in a tale of Wilkie Collins, in which a super-annuated actor finds his whole identity bound up with the cast of Shakespeare's bust that he has secretly taken from the church at Stratford. Is this a crime? How much should you charge? Pettitt suggests that the tale 'eloquently bespeaks the bewilderment of this period', uncertain whether culture is priceless, or costs a guinea.

Some Victorians were troubled by the thought that the man who wrote *Hamlet* might also have enjoyed putting money in his purse. They did not include the author who wrote to her publishers: 'You know how important this money question is to me. I don't want the world to give me anything for my books except money enough to save me from the temptation to write *only* for money.'[3] George Eliot was level-headed about the material circumstances in the midst of which we create or fail to, and in which our creations go on to thrive or wane. These include, for the artist, the circumstances in which a play or a novel is produced – that is, in the case of the latter, printed and published and read. In his essay on George Eliot (Chapter 5), Philip Davis is concerned not only with the difference between such circumstances – the suddenness, the once-only-ness of live performance, as against the protractedness and repeatability of writing and reading – but also the relation between them. What Shakespeare achieves in the pressured conditions of dramatic performance cannot be simply repeated in the different space-and-time of writing. Macaulay thought the progress of civilisation entailed the decline of poetry and the dominance of prose, and to the Victorians

Shakespeare could seem to stand for something irrecoverable, a 'lost dynamic of creative thinking', as Davis calls it. With the help of Newman, however, he makes a bold claim for the power of prose narrative, in the hands of George Eliot, to delve beyond the immediacy of drama, into the spaces behind and between Shakespearean speech. If this entails loss, it also brings gain, a new kind of dramatic excitement in exploring, alongside the developing thought of psychologists such as Lewes, Spencer and Myers, the invisible structures of consciousness. But the terms of loss and gain are beside the point as we contemplate the creative achievement of *Middlemarch* and *Daniel Deronda*. This, so Davis contends, is where we should look, first and last, for 'Victorian Shakespeare'.

In the last of the papers that takes a novel as its prime focus (Chapter 6), Philip Horne ponders the frustrations confronting an ardent and discerning theatre-goer towards the end of the century. Henry James figures quite frequently in both volumes here as a theatre critic (the first international theatre-critic, Jane Moody suggests), and in *The Tragic Muse* he projects some of his ideals into the rising diplomat Peter Sherringham. Into the young actress Miriam Rooth who intrigues and excites Sherringham, James may be thought to have poured some of his own ferocious ambitions for theatrical success. But if the source of Miriam's genius is a mystery – 'where did she get hold of that?' – it is also a mystery where she will find the roles or plays that will be a match for her. She can do Constance in *King John*, one of Sarah Siddons's great parts, and at the end she conquers the London audience – 'the great childish audience' – in the role marked out for every aspiring young actress: Juliet. Good luck to her, the novel seems to say, but if you call this triumph. . . . For all the massive differences he had with Shaw, James breathes a comparable weariness, a sense that by the 1890s we have had more than enough of Shakespeare in performance – certainly as he's been canonised, institutionalised, and in due course royally recognised, at Irving's Lyceum and Beerbohm Tree's Her Majesty's. As a portrait of a fictional actress, Miriam may be the real thing that Eliot's Gwendolen Harleth so signally wasn't. But in *Daniel Deronda* 'Shakespeare' had figured as a dynamic force against which Gwendolen's shallowness could be measured, whether in passing allusion to 'Macbeth's rhetoric' (the end of Chapter 4) or explicit invocation of the great tableau-scene from *The Winter's Tale* (Chapter 6). By contrast Shakespeare helps to get Miriam launched, as Constance and Juliet – but then what?

The next three chapters (7–9) are devoted to the two major poets who most often seemed to their contemporaries to challenge comparison with Shakespeare: Tennyson and Browning. (There is of course no pretence in this volume at anything like comprehensive coverage of Shakespeare's presence in Victorian poetry – or prose· the Brontës, for instance, or George Meredith, who seemed to his admirers near the end of the century the nearest thing to a modern Shakespeare. Nor does it seek to address all aspects of Victorian culture in which Shakespeare featured, as for example in the visual arts, a huge topic in its own right.) Robert Douglas-Fairhurst reflects on what it might mean to hold 'communion with the dead' when their words live on and can pass into our own (Chapter 7); Christopher Decker studies the scene of Tennyson's own dying, for the way some particular words of Shakespeare's help to mark its passage, and for the way his son's *Memoir* composes the personal memory for all to read (Chapter 8). Memory, memorial, memoir, commemoration, monument: Decker and Douglas-Fairhurst are both concerned with the verbs that animate these nouns (or might, or should), in the hands and mouths of poets who make memory happen again, and help each other to do so. Tennyson summons the lines from *Cymbeline* and his son, remembering the scene of their remembering, impresses them into his reader's memory. Encouraged by Shakespeare's *Sonnets*, Tennyson strives through the long sequence of *In Memoriam A. H. H.* to achieve the great ambition expressed in sonnet 55: 'The living record of your memory'. Yet there stirs through the Tennysons' engagement with Shakespeare, both father's and son's, a restless sense of the difficulty and dread surrounding such communion, no matter how strong the awe and love, between the living and the dying and the dead.

'Awe', 'love' and 'dread' all feature in the poem that takes centre-stage in the paper by Danny Karlin that's already been glanced at: Browning's 'The Names' (Chapter 9). Karlin recovers the paraphernalia with which it was surrounded on its first appearance in a Charity Show brochure, 'the Shakespearean babble of the Victorian age', as he puts it. Looking back, he relates 'The Names' to other key moments in Browning's writing on which Shakespeare has featured, in the exchange between the worldly Bishop Blougram and the idealistic Gigadibs, for example. If all poetry is 'a putting the infinite within the finite', as Browning told Ruskin, then there is more than enough of the 'finite' around us – or as George Eliot has it: 'the quickest of us walk about well wadded with stupidity' (*Middlemarch*, Chapter 20). So a poem as quick as 'The Names' is surrounded and wadded with babble. In proposing that it is 'only by the very gaps and flaws' resulting from its 'gesture *towards* transcendence' that Browning's poetry can hope to 'succeed', Karlin makes suggestive contact with images that recur elsewhere in this volume: with 'the cracks of thought and speech' on which Douglas-Fairhurst dwells, with the 'borders' so prominent in Henderson's discussion of Scott, with the 'space between' essential to Davis's characterisation of George Eliot.

The last three chapters (10–12) may seem to deal with more disparate material than their predecessors, but the figures and texts addressed represent a fair sample of the enormous range of literary activity and cultural performance that does *not* fall under the brute categories of 'novel' and 'poetry'. In fact the previous nine chapters have included a good deal about cultural productions other than novels and poems, performances within which literary acts are embedded and on which in turn they reflect: to take some obvious examples, the Great Exhibition (Chapter 4), the funeral of the Poet Laureate (Chapter 8), and the Albert Hall charity show (Chapter 9). Mary Cowden Clarke was one of the many scholars and critics who contributed to the massive diffusion of 'Shakespeare' in the nineteenth century (especially the second half), through affordable editions of the works, learning aids, commentaries, anthologies and so on. But she was one of the first women in this field, and the nature of her partnership with her husband adds a further dimension to the topic of collaboration on which this introduction has laid some stress, principally until now on the collaboration between the living and the dead.

Whether it was collaboration between the living and the dead when the actor George Vandenhoff came to write his memoirs and thought of 'Coralie Walton' it's impossible to say, as Aebischer persuasively demonstrates (Chapter 11). Whether we're reading fact or fiction, Vandenhoff's is certainly one of the eeriest texts under discussion. The antidote to Coralie's fatal identification with Desdemona would have been a good reading of Mary Cowden Clarke's *Girlhood of Shakespeare's Heroines*. Not that Cowden Clarke seeks to deflect the bad ends that Desdemona and Ophelia have coming to them. But the reader can see *why* they are coming, and she can decide to perform or behave otherwise, because she can take comfort and inspiration from all the much better role models on display, such as Portia, Isabella, Rosalind and Beatrice. If you *must* identify with a Shakespeare role – and John Glavin notes, with help from Macready, how the old point-seeking extrovert style of acting was being superseded in the Victorian era by a new kind of inwardness – then for goodness sake take care whom you choose, and don't get stuck with it.

Ruskin brings this short sequence of exemplary narratives to a chastening close (Chapter 12). Like Cowden Clarke and Anna Jameson before her, but far more extravagantly, Ruskin admired most (though not all) of Shakespeare's women. It was the men that worried him, especially the kings. The story told by Francis O'Gorman is one which itself borders on tragedy. Ruskin was as close and passionate a reader of Shakespeare as any of the writers studied in this volume. In his youth he began by identifying in Shakespeare a love of fathers and kings that he wished to share, but he came to feel that 'the master of tragedy' had betrayed him by failing to uphold the image of the noble hero the modern world so badly needed. Ruskin's growing apprehension of conflicting meanings in the plays, and of the unknowability of the authorial intentions that lay behind them, bring him to the edge of a modernist sense of unavailable origins. But he reaches this extreme verge through trauma – the man who lost his faith in Shakespeare.

The Victorian age testifies to the massive cultural authority invested in the figure crowned by Carlyle as 'King Shakespeare', an authority no less evident in the commercial products on show at the Great Exhibition of 1851 than in allusions to *Hamlet* and *Othello* in novels by Dickens and James or poems by Tennyson and Browning. But this authority does not go uncontested – any more than does that of Shakespeare's own kings. (Why couldn't he have chosen some really *good* kings to write about, groaned Ruskin? Why not Richard I instead of Richard III?) Victorian writers wrest new meanings from Shakespeare's plots and language even as they wrestle to be free from the ghost of the Royal Bard himself. Carlyle might try to crown him 'King Shakespeare' but in the main the voice they listen to is not that of the king, let alone of his deputies and counsellors. It is the voice of the dissident, questioning prince, of the rebel, the clown and the misfit. With such a voice you can have a conversation, an argument, perhaps even a friendship – until seized by dread at the thought of listening to a ghost.

But this too is to misrepresent 'Shakespeare', whose voice is not singular but carnival, teeming, multitudinous. This is exactly what so disturbed Ruskin, as he searched for some principle of unity, consistency, singleness of purpose, and failed. What would it mean to listen to all those conflicting, dissonant voices? That way madness lies. Or a new voice, new voices.

Notes

1. 'Frances Anne Kemble' (1893), in *Literary Criticism: Essays on Literature, American Writers, English Writers*, ed. by Leon Edel, Library of America (Cambridge: Cambridge University Press, 1984), p. 1079.

2. See Christopher Murray, 'James Sheridan Knowles: the Victorian Shakespeare?', in *Shakespeare and the Victorian Stage*, ed. by Richard Foulkes (Cambridge: Cambridge University Press, 1986), pp. 164–79.
3. *The George Eliot Letters*, ed. by Gordon S. Haight, 9 vols (New Haven: Yale University Press, 1954–78), III, 152.

1

Othello Redux?: Scott's *Kenilworth* and the Trickiness of 'Race' on the Nineteenth-century Stage

Diana E. Henderson

A spectre haunts Sir Walter Scott's historical novel representing the Elizabethan entertainments at Kenilworth castle: the uncanny presence of another fiction, Shakespeare's *Othello*. Published in 1821, *Kenilworth* centres on the domestic tragedy of a couple who elope for love and are thwarted by the supersubtle ways of a rigid court culture. Borrowing *Othello*'s central trio of a jealous husband, his villainous henchman, and a slandered wife, the novel likewise culminates in the wife's murder. The lovers here are Sir Robert Dudley (anachronistically referred to by his later title, the Earl of Leicester) and his first wife, Amy Robsart. Scott's reconstruction of their lives derives in part from scurrilous Elizabethan sources such as *Leicester's Commonwealth*; but the manner and mood reveal the equally powerful influence of Shakespeare's drama in general and *Othello* in particular. Like Desdemona, Amy is framed by the false accusations of infidelity constructed by her husband's trusted follower, Varney (with the aid of his Roderigo-like assistant Lambourne), and the scenes of temptation, inquisition, jealous rage, and manipulated pseudo-'evidence' repeatedly echo and mimic Shakespeare's play.[1] Scott's desire to retell this *Othello* plot is so great that he resurrects the historical Robsart, who had died in suspicious circumstances fifteen years before the 1575 Kenilworth entertainments, so that she can attend them – only to then kill her off once more.

Moreover, Scott's desire to include Shakespeare in his novel results in the equally blatant – and more generally recognisable – anachronism of pretending that the Bankside theatres were thriving before they had in fact been built. Despite the fact that the playwright was just eleven years old when the Kenilworth pageants took place, he appears in Scott's novel at mid-career, petitioning Leicester on behalf of the theatres against the bear-baiters. Like Sir Walter himself, this Shakespeare is both a man of business and an influential, beloved writer. Other characters, including Sir Walter Raleigh and Queen Elizabeth as well as a picaresque ex-performer called Wayland Smith, consciously quote from his plays at key moments. Indeed, Wayland 'swaggered with the bravest of them all, both at the Black Bull, the Globe, the Fortune, and elsewhere' before the audience's apple-throwing led him to renounce his 'half share in the company'. At one point he sings Caliban's song, thus moving *The Tempest* back in time 35 years.[2] In calling attention to Shakespeare's presence and poetry at the expense of historical accuracy, Scott obviously knew what he was doing – but do we?

Some modern critics dismiss *Kenilworth* as a jingoistic attempt to laud 'merrie England' for Britain's post-Union edification, despite its author's complex feelings about the history of Scotland's subsumption; for them, the novel's anachronisms are explicable as part of the 'lusty English romance' genre. John Sutherland claims that '*Kenilworth* was a main source of the cult of Elizabethanism that was to flourish in nineteenth-century Britain and which is still periodically revived by opportunistic politicians and nostalgists.'[3] Certainly such a 'cult' was to gain strength with the ascension of another long-lived queen to the British throne in 1837, and reading *Kenilworth* as a tribute to Good Queen Bess would be understandable if one knew only some of the pageants and dramatisations the work spawned. Yet such a characterisation fails to register the fact that within Scott's novel nearly every episode at or involving Elizabeth's court is tainted by vanity, mercenary corruption or conscious evil. Even the title page of each of *Kenilworth*'s three volumes signals Scott's satiric playfulness: quoting Sheridan's play *The Critic*, the reiterated epigraph reads 'No scandal about Queen Elizabeth, I hope?'[4]

Most of the English courtiers are represented as venal, if not outright dishonest, especially those associated with Leicester – nor is the Earl himself exempted from the charge of corruption, despite his virtues and structural position as the Othello-like figure. The Queen too is wrapped within a larger web of competing interests and policy that extends into the world beyond. The state of England, in short, strips decent men of their ethical accountability and allows the wicked to thrive. Only by ignoring this narrative and tonal context can one transform the book into a mere memento of royalism. Clearly, it is not the representation of politics and court that earns this novel the generic subtitle 'A Romance'. Scott had refused to write what his publisher Constable really wanted, a triumphal Armada novel, and in raising Amy Robsart's ghost he wilfully reminds his readers not only of the glory but the corruption that was England.

It is specifically, and perhaps only, the literary and dramatic legacy of 'merry England' that entitles it to continued veneration. After Leicester addresses Shakespeare within the novel, Scott makes this explicit: 'The Player bowed, and the Earl nodded and passed on – so that age would have told the tale – in ours, perhaps, we might say the immortal had done homage to the mortal' (p. 168). To offset the ugliness barely contained within the main plot, Scott invokes his literary inheritance. And only by altering history, transforming it into romance, can Scott achieve his goal of making Shakespeare the indisputable artistic fountainhead not only for the Elizabethan Renaissance but for Scott's moment as well. Shakespeare becomes the source for an ethical tradition to support Scott's ideal of a British nation, which he emphasises as distinct from the corruption of its political centre. The figure of Shakespeare and the echoing of *Othello* are thus fundamental to the very structure and vision of Scott's novel – just as, I would argue, Scott soon became fundamental to the nineteenth-century's vision of Shakespeare.

Scott's personal investments nevertheless complicate the nationalist agenda that an English Shakespeare supports. Sir Walter draws on the popular potential of Shakespeare – popular in the sense of carnivalesque and of the common people, as well as market-pleasing. This image resonates with Scott's wish to be the 'minstrel of the Scottish borders', preserving the oral ballad tradition in the wake of Britain's legal attempts to obliterate Scottish popular culture after the Jacobite risings. Yet Shakespeare was by Scott's day becoming the Bard of high culture, and was identified with Englishness. In attempting to elevate the status of the novel and be heard within British halls of power, Scott borrows authority along with story-lines and quips, complicating if not compromising his claims of alliance with the people of Scotland. This, along with his dismay at the consequences of the French Revolution, has led Nicola Watson to dismiss his politics as simple 'Tory nationalism', his border position mere bad faith.[5] Though less obviously than do his novels set in Scotland, *Kenilworth* nevertheless attests to Scott's mixed position regarding Englishness and its history, and uses Shakespeare to fortify that border position.

Although Scott's method may have been too muted to encourage traces of dissonance in the stage adaptations of *Kenilworth*, both the novel and those representations informed Victorian ideas about Shakespeare and the Renaissance. For *Kenilworth* was popular in all forms. It received more than fifteen reviews during its first two months in circulation, and ranked

among the most read and respected of the *Waverley* novels for gener-
ations. Scott's biographer Lockhart declared that '*Kenilworth* was one of
the most successful of them all at the time of publication; and it continues, and, I doubt not, will ever continue to be placed in the very
highest rank of prose fiction.'[6] The 1871 *Athenæum* reviewer, writing
on the centenary of Scott's birth, testified that while the popularity of
many of Scott's novels had waxed and waned, '*Waverley* and *Kenilworth*
were always in the front'.[7] And in 1901, an historian indignant at the
novel's 'inexcusable' factual errors conceded that 'It may be said with
safety that the popularity of "Kenilworth", if even equalled, has not
been surpassed by that of any other volume included in the "Waverley"
series.'[8] *Kenilworth's* translation across media was equally remarkable. At
least thirty stage versions were produced within five years after its
publication. Over the course of the century, *Kenilworth* generated
about 120 dramatic productions, twice that many 'derivative dramas'
and burlesques, and at least eleven operas, this last number rivalled
among Scott's novels only by *Ivanhoe*.[9]

Today, to find a reader, much less serious discussion, of *Kenilworth* is not
such an easy task. In 1995 John Sutherland observed 'Canonically, of
course, the novel is an outcast. There cannot be a graduate course in the
Western World where it is taught, and the MLA bibliography confirms
that few modern scholars have wasted their valuable time on the novel.'
Yet after this (excessively harsh) artistic judgement, even Sutherland
conceded *Kenilworth's* sociological importance and mass popularity as
'an achievement [...] worthy of studious examination' (p. 248). Indeed,
to understand how the nineteenth century saw Shakespeare, we need to
look not only at the texts and productions of his plays but also at the
forms in which readers and theatre-goers came to know 'Shakespeare',
the associations they brought with them – and here, no influence was
stronger than the beloved works of Scott. Oversimplifying or forgetting
Kenilworth ignores one highly influential re-vision, and with it recedes
the potential to understand some key changes in the cultural place of
Othello, most notably bearing upon race and gender.

There are clear signals within Scott's text of his consciousness of what
from *Othello* has been repressed – a difference which, whether viewed
predominantly as religious, geographical, or ethnic, is repeatedly in-
dexed by blackness. The troublingly absent presence of *Othello's* story
of blackness and 'race' likewise makes the novel more complicated.[10]
Scott changes his Othello figure from a military Moor into an English
court favourite. There is no 'Turk' without. Unlike Shakespeare's play,
which begins at the centre of the Venetian empire and moves outward,

here the action approaches the courtly centre gradually. It does so in the company of a major character, Tressilian, who also initiates the pattern of verbal echoes from *Othello*. Tressilian is nevertheless 'peripheral' in two senses. Ethnically and geographically, this man of Cornish ancestry comes from the Celtic borders of England rather than its Saxon 'core'; and he is Amy Robsart's rejected suitor who, while trying to protect her, is shackled by a traditional code of honour (associated with the older border culture) and hence is incapacitated at the modern court. Thus even more clearly than in *Othello*, villainy in *Kenilworth* is located at the political centre.[11] Queen Elizabeth, like Shakespeare's Duke of Venice, attempts to render fair judgements, but she is more easily misled (sometimes even duped) by her courtiers, who often work for their own ends rather than those of the nation. And because Amy and Tressilian, the 'good' figures recalling Desdemona and Cassio, both hail from the south-west and are tied with the history and suppression of the Celtic fringe, the sense of the English state's core corruption is more pronounced.

The Celtic Tressilian in fact carries more resonance than a Cassio, and takes on some of the nobler dimensions of Othello himself. Tressilian's rectitude and steadfast, doomed love for Amy neither prevent tragedy nor allow him peace. Whereas the rashly jealous Leicester survives, Tressilian 'seemed to see before him the disfigured corpse of the early and only object of his affection', and embarking for Virginia 'old in griefs, died before his day in that foreign land' (p. 392). Throughout the novel he hovers in the shadows as moral witness, testifying (in typical *Waverley* fashion) to what might have been and has been lost. Tressilian's Cornish ancestry and association with losing sides in history (including his grandfather's Yorkist rebellion against the Tudors) connect him with Scott's more famous Highland Celts – and the author's own vexed relationship to his ancestors and the Jacobite rebellion of '45. [12] Thus *Othello*'s unconventional use of ethnic difference, both as a symbol of transcendent love and as a means by which an 'insider' can unjustly defame and undo a cultural border figure, is not entirely forgotten but rather transmuted in *Kenilworth*. It is resituated, aptly enough for Scott, at the borders of the main narrative, in the treatment of Tressilian. The 'Norman Yoke' theory that regarded Celts as a 'darker' race suggested a pseudo-biological rationale for the association. That theory certainly factored in Scott's thinking, ambivalently: he both felt the cultural appeal and nobility of archaic values associated with the Celts, and believed that lighter races represented more advanced, 'enlightened' civilisations.[13] To the extent that this is allegory, then, its focus shifts to one consistent with Scott's own mix of political resignation and lament for Celtic Scotland, but only by making his more obvious Othello figure (in terms of the plot-line and verbal echoes) an insider, a white Englishman, and a smaller man.

Some might argue that without a difference of ethnicity or cultural origin, Leicester cannot really figure Othello at all, but is simply a jealous husband. Others might find confirmation for the view that one can talk about *Othello* without 'playing the race card', as if the hero's blackness were just one of many traits available to be performed, or not (similar to the recent treatment of Othello's mature age). But the former position must ignore too much of *Kenilworth*'s text to be sustained, whereas the latter view in great part derives from the work of the novel itself, when considered along with related nineteenth-century developments in the theatre and criticism. That is, Scott's choices locate him as a key participant in a phenomenon with wide-ranging consequences not only for how audiences came to think about *Othello* and the genius of Shakespeare but even more generally for literary interpretation itself as a cultural practice. That process was the gradual 'whitening' of Othello.

While the American Mary Preston's ejaculation that 'Othello *was a white man!*' has been cited to show how racism could lead to absurdity in responses to *Othello* after the US Civil War, what remains less recognised is just how pervasive and influential kindred attitudes were earlier in the century in Britain. They testify to the desire of many to extricate Othello from the contemporary associations obvious in retelling the story of a black man once 'taken by the insolent foe / And sold to slavery' (I. 3. 137–8).[14] It is easy to cringe at Preston's version of 'washing the Ethiop white', but it is simply less skilful in expression than, not different in its assumptions from, commentaries by Coleridge, Lamb, and others whose critical legacy remains powerful.[15] Their ideas, in turn, were generated in great part by their responses to what they saw at the theatre. For although many tie the dominance of racialised discourse to the competing renditions of Salvini and Irving late in the century, racialism played an important role in the staging of *Othello* much earlier, during the period of British debate over the abolition throughout the Empire of both slave labour and participation in the slave trade.[16] This was, moreover, the time when other race-based anthropological theories were gaining ascendancy among European intellectuals, elevating Aryans and Normans above 'darker' peoples (including Celts and Jews, to name two 'races' relevant to Scott's novels). At the bottom of these racist hierarchies were Negroes.

Such associations of blackness with baseness appear in English responses to Ira Aldridge, the one famed black actor to play Othello during the 1820s and '30s and again (outside London) at mid-century. Some of the London reviews of his Coburg performance were physically race-based, *The Times* asserting that 'owing to the shape of his lips it is utterly impossible for him to pronounce English' (11 October 1825).[17] When the American Aldridge returned to début at Covent Garden in 1833 – the year Britain finally abolished slavery throughout its empire – *The Times* was slightly less overt: 'His accent was unpleasantly, and we would say vulgarly, foreign.'[18] The charge of vulgarity elides questions of nationality, class, and taste with race, a blurring even more pronounced in the 13 April *Athenæum* review: having claimed to hold 'no ridiculous prejudice [...] because he chances to be of a different colour from ourselves', that reviewer nevertheless concludes: 'In the name of propriety and decency, we protest against an interesting actress and lady-like girl, like Miss Ellen Tree, being subjected [...] to the indignity of being pawed about by Mr. Henry Wallack's black servant.'[19] The actor–producer relationship of Aldridge and Wallack is here transformed into one of servitude. Despite the performances being well received by audiences and the famed British Othello, Edmund Kean, Aldridge's appearance in London was cut short by the pro-slavery lobby and he was effectively exiled from performing in the capital for twenty years.[20] His reception in the provinces and on the continent, especially in Russia, was generally warmer. What is clear is that everywhere Aldridge went, he went as a nineteenth-century black man as well as Othello, evoking among audiences their responses to the contemporary political dilemmas of slavery.

Two decades later, the *Athenæum's* comments on Aldridge's return as Othello (to the Lyceum in 1858 and the Haymarket seven years after) remained mired in the presumption of racial inferiority that the slave system had required. In 1865, an attempt to adapt to new political realities still grotesquely echoes the slurs of Shakespeare's Roderigo: 'We may claim this black, thick lipped player as one proof among many that the negro intellect is human, and demands respect as such'.[21] These responses partially explain why a 'tawny Moor' came to be viewed as more noble and appropriate for *Othello* than a black man (even if the performer 'beneath' was white). Whereas the former might be sexually threatening he remained powerful, even princely, while the latter was at this time indelibly associated with servitude and race-based slavery.

The 'whitening' of Othello in performance had begun during the decades prior to *Kenilworth's* publication. John Philip Kemble to some extent and Edmund Kean, more famously, chose to emphasise the 'tawny Moor', presenting what was considered a more attractive Turkish-influenced figure. Kemble's cuts retain hints of dangerous sexuality consistent with English fantasies of exotic others (particularly Islamic potentates), while diminishing emphasis on Africa or blackness. Kemble was also lauded for emphasising Othello's Moorish garb, a performance choice erroneously thought to be new.[22] Indeed, Kemble went so far in this direction that his devoted biographer James Boaden thought the performance 'grand and awful and pathetic, but he was European: there seemed to be philosophy in his bearing; there was reason in his rage [...] the professional farewell of Othello, came rather coldly from him'.[23] In terms of the ethno-geographic stereotypes then current, Boaden's comments imply that Kemble went too far north in his desire to escape association with putative Negro savagery. Tellingly, it was his decision to retain at least Othello's black complexion that prompted some negative criticism in the press, not the cuts or the costume. Thus the *Public Advertiser* review (29 October 1787) concludes: 'We must approve his dressing Othello in Moorish habit [...] but is it necessary the Moor should be as *black* as a native of Guiney?'[24]

Twenty-five years later, Edmund Kean answered that question in the negative. In 1814 Kean began to perform as a 'tawny Moor' or Arab, becoming the most celebrated Othello of the period. At first, Hazlitt found Kean's 'lofty-minded Moor' wrong because he 'was not fierce', but by 1817 the critic admired him.[25] Loftiness and soulfulness were nevertheless perceived to be at odds with blackness. The Romantic critics' writings repeatedly testify to the impact of Kean's performance choices. Hazlitt stresses Othello's 'eastern magnificence', and Coleridge in his 1822 *Table Talk* similarly avers that 'Othello must not be conceived as a negro, but a high and chivalrous Moorish chief'.[26] Both Coleridge and Lamb discount Othello's blackness, Lamb finding it 'an intolerable obstacle to a true appreciation'. In his 1811 essay 'On the Tragedies of Shakspeare', Lamb deems Desdemona's love admirable when he is reading, but when he sees it onstage it becomes 'revolting' because of Othello's colour:

I appeal to everyone that has seen *Othello* played, whether he did not, on the contrary, sink Othello's mind in his colour; whether he did not find something extremely revolting in the courtship and wedded caresses of Othello and Desdemona; and whether the actual sight of the thing did not overweigh all that beautiful compromise which we make in reading [...] What we see upon the stage is body and bodily action; what we are conscious of in reading is almost exclusively the mind, and its movements [...]²⁷

The point is worth stressing because this was the moment when Coleridge and Lamb helped develop a mode of interpreting Shakespeare which privileged putatively 'transcendent' reading over the vicissitudes of live performance. It is less often recognised how directly this preference for text over performance was involved with – and in great measure may have derived from – their race-based repugnance at seeing a 'black' Othello onstage. Lamb's remarks serve as one salient example for his general principle privileging reading: 'how many dramatic personages are there in Shakspeare [...] improper to be shown to our bodily eye! Othello, for instance' (p. 575). Lamb elaborates that it is far preferable to read about than to see 'a young Venetian lady of the highest extraction [...] wedding with a *coal-black Moor* – (for such is he represented [...]) though the Moors are now well enough known to be by many shades less unworthy of a white woman's fancy)' (italics his; p. 576). 'Less unworthy' – even when embodied by a white man with lighter brown make-up, the ocular proof that Othello was not conceived as white like him proved a sticking point for identification or admiration and hence, Lamb went on to argue, for proper understanding of the transcendent subjectivity he sought in Shakespeare. Without oversimplifying the Romantics' reasoning, one may still observe that the role of *Othello*'s blackness in their theorising remains inadequately acknowledged.²⁸

Scott was well aware of both the performances and the criticisms of *Othello* being generated as he wrote *Kenilworth*. Yet Scott, for all his Tory imperialism, stood in a different relationship to issues of 'race' and nationhood within the British isles. And while the stage shift from blackness to Arabian Moorishness provided impetus for an aesthetic that would almost entirely disconnect the 'essence' of Othello from his ethnicity, it also provided a precedent for a logic of ethnic replacement. Scott thus retains some of Shakespeare's attention to ethnic difference in the form of Celticness, obliquely addressing a 'racial' struggle within Britain that was of direct concern to him.

Scott's ethnic shifts intersect with a change in gendered representation as well, for along with Tressilian the 'beneficiaries' from the Othello-husband's reduction, in terms of novelistic attention, are the women of *Kenilworth*. The shift of focus to a sentimentalised vision of femininity embodied by Amy Robsart gives an even more pointed truth to Mark Twain's satirically overstated claim that Scott was responsible for the American Civil War. Whereas Twain located the 'Sir Walter disease' in Scott's fictions of a chivalric past which the South then adopted and fought to preserve, here one might argue that re-creating *Othello* without a black man abetted the racist alienation of personhood from people of colour – even the tragic, fictitious personhood Shakespeare allowed to Othello. Yet even had Scott not been impelled to recast Othello with an all-white Elizabethan cast, the time was ripe for such a transformation. In an important sense, if Scott had not written *Kenilworth*, someone else would have had to invent a white Othello for the nineteenth century.

The plays based on the novel illustrate that desire. Adapting *Kenilworth* for stage production streamlined its narrative back even closer to its dramatic ur-text. Most of the passages of Shakespearean derivation are transposed verbatim from the novel onto the stage.[29] Yet for all the echoes and generic resemblance, the stage *Kenilworth*s are further removed than the novel from the political and ethnic complexities of *Othello*. In these simpler costume melodramas, the women's roles were the prized ones. Oxberry's 1824 dramatic text regards simplification as a purely formal issue, noting that his play's 'chief display...has been confined to that of the Queen and Amy' (p. iii). He thereby displaces state corruption by focusing on femininity, sentimentalised and heroic: 'The character of Queen Elizabeth will be found more fully displayed than any other – and necessarily so – it stands in history so distinguished that it would be impossible to pass it over slightly' (p. iii). Thus begins the movement that culminates in current scholarly dismissal of *Kenilworth* itself as a jingoistic tribute.[30] Scenes such as the Queen's discovery of Amy in Kenilworth gardens take centre-stage (as in the 1832 frontispiece to Bunn's stageplay). Further, the shift mutes the already veiled allegory of internal colonialism suggested by Tressilian's story. In an all-too-familiar manner, a nuanced narrative built upon multiple social categories is simplified into a single binary opposition – here, that of gender. Like many nineteenth-century and twentieth-century *Othello*s, the stage versions of *Kenilworth* efface 'race' by emphasising gender difference, instead of considering both the kinship and distinction of these two forms of 'otherness'.

Kenilworth staged can be seen as a collective nineteenth-century fantasy solution to the most troubling aspects of *Othello* – going the novel one better. In Scott's version of the *Othello* plot he at least retained the murder of Amy. Moreover, as in *Othello*, the villain Varney shows no remorse, outlives his female victim and seems to control his own fate; others do not kill him. This last point, distinguishing Iago among Shakespeare's tragic villains, has always disturbed audiences, and

Varney's suicidal self-determination seems to have evoked similar distress. As a solution, many stagings simply (and rather astonishingly) changed the ending, allowing Amy to live and altering Varney's cause of death. In the novel, Varney chooses to poison himself, and despite efforts to prevent him succeeds: 'nor did he appear to have suffered much agony, his countenance presenting, even in death, the habitual expression of sneering sarcasm, which was predominant while he lived' (p. 391). James Robinson Planché's version, which débuted at the Adelphi 8 February 1821, reportedly was faithful to the novel's ending, though (perhaps tellingly) no text survives. But on 14 February, Thomas Dibdin's production at the Surrey concluded with Varney – in an uncharacteristically stupid moment – charging onto his own trapdoor in an unsuccessful attempt to prevent Leicester from rescuing Amy. Oxberry's *Kenilworth, A Melo-drama* has an even happier ending which reorders the book's major events: after Varney '*is precipitated down the abyss*' (p. 59), word arrives that Leicester is pardoned and the Kenilworth pageants will go on. And in a *fin de siècle* staging by J. S. Blythe in Glasgow (1899, 1900), the Othello figure finally succeeds in killing the villain.[31] *Kenilworth* so revised could and did become a piece of British propaganda to cheer colonisers as far away as India.[32] Anglophilic alterations likewise help account for the fact that stage productions of *Kenilworth* were far more popular in England than in Scotland.[33]

Although Scott reanimated Amy Robsart and created Tressilian only to record their decline and fall, he served his artistic ancestor, William Shakespeare, more 'kindly'. Others would complete the separation of a transcendent Shakespeare from the politics of his or their day, but Scott kept him, though 'immortal' in retrospect, historically vital within his messy picture of an emergent market economy. In his anachronistic fictional representation locating Shakespeare on the borders between art and business as well as aesthetics and politics, Scott, ironically, was all the truer to history.

Yet in reformulating and diverging from *Othello's* social specificity, *Kenilworth's* legacy is more vexed. On the one hand, Scott's erasure of blackness from the story responds to and promotes the century's 'whitening' of Othello, part of the larger process whereby Shakespeare's texts become a repository of transhistorical aesthetic value removed from the political issues of either time-period. On the other hand, erasing blackness allows the substitution of another ethnic conflict that Scott viewed as current and 'racial': the marginalisation of Celtic culture, which for Scott marked his own border position as a Scot and British citizen. In *Kenilworth*, Scott stands in two places at once: he figures himself as the tragic Celt, Tressilian, in an already lost world, even as he positions himself authorially as a latter-day Bard and Shakespeare's ally in ambivalently chronicling the history of nation-building. But it remains arguable whether the subtler process of refiguring *Othello* was perceived, whereas the romanticised aspects of Scott's Shakespeare surely did endure.[34] And what Scott's novel left undone, the Victorian stage productions of *Kenilworth* completed – in the flesh.

Notes

1. Given frequent passing remarks on particular parallels (especially between Varney and Iago) in later nineteenth-century commentary, the absence of sustained analysis of this topic surprises. Wilmon Brewer, *Shakespeare's Influence on Sir Walter Scott* (Boston: The Cornhill Publishing Company, 1925), pp. 321–8 describes characterological and narrative links, finding them 'remarkable'.
2. Sir Walter Scott, *Kenilworth; a Romance*, ed. by J. H. Alexander (Edinburgh: Edinburgh University Press, 1993), pp. 102–3, 126. All subsequent citations refer to this edition.
3. John Sutherland, *The Life of Walter Scott: a Critical Biography* (Oxford: Blackwell, 1995), p. 247.
4. Scott recalled that, having just written about Mary Stuart in *The Abbot*, he began writing about Elizabeth with 'the prejudices with which a Scottishman is tempted', 'a prejudice almost as natural to him as his native air': see the 1831 Magnum Opus introduction, also cited in Sir Walter Scott, *Kenilworth*, ed. by Andrew Lang (New York: E. B. Hall & Company, 1893), p. xxvii. *Kenilworth* came on the heels of a British production of Schiller's *Maria Stuart* (Covent Garden, December 1819) and was influenced by Sophia Lee's *The Recess* (1785). Scott is in fact comparatively even-handed. A direct connection with Schiller was achieved on the stage, as Mrs Bunn played Queen Elizabeth with great success both in *Maria Stuart* and *Kenilworth*.
5. Nicola J. Watson, 'Kemble, Scott, and the Mantle of the Bard', in *The Appropriation of Shakespeare: Post-Renaissance Reconstructions of the Works and the Myth*, ed. by Jean I. Marsden (London: Harvester Wheatsheaf, 1991), pp. 73–92. Watson's account relies more on evidence from Kemble and Malone than Scott, yet evaluates his 'entire *oeuvre*'. Her claim that Scott's aim in *Kenilworth* was a 'comparable injection of "authentic" historical detail, underwritten by the authority of Shakespeare, into the suspect discourse of fiction' in order to 'instate a vision of an Edenic, post-revolutionary Britain' (pp. 73, 78) cannot account for the text's conscious anachronisms nor its patterns of representation. At the other extreme, Scots Nationalist Paul Henderson Scott tries to

declare Sir Walter's independence from English tradition, asserting that 'none of Scott's ideas or attitudes are derived from Shakespeare' and that his Shakespearean 'allusions, hints, similarities and overtones' are deployed merely as 'surface ornament' (*Walter Scott and Scotland* (Edinburgh: The Saltire Society, 1994), p. 36). He is on firmer ground discussing Scott's pamphlet defence of Scottish financial independence, the Malachi Malagrowther letters, which placed him at odds with the Tory party leadership (pp. 72–83).

6. J. G. Lockhart, *Life of Sir Walter Scott* [abridged] (Edinburgh: Adam and Charles Black, 1853), p. 485.
7. Cited in *Walter Scott: the Critical Heritage*, ed. by John O. Hayden (London: Routledge, 1970), p. 467.
8. Philip Sidney, *Who Killed Amy Robsart? Being Some Account of her Life and Death, With Remarks on Sir Walter Scott's 'Kenilworth'* (London: Elliot Stock, 1901), pp. 1, 9.
9. See H. Philip Bolton, *Scott Dramatized* (London: Mansell, 1992), pp. 394–421 and Jerome Mitchell, 'A List of Walter Scott Operas', in *Scott and his Influence*, ed. by J. H. Alexander and David Hewitt (Aberdeen: Association for Scottish Literary Studies, 1983), p. 511.
10. Scott's oblique reminders include references to 'orient pearl' for Amy's 'neck that is fairer' and repeated allusions to 'Moorish fashion' and decorations (pp. 38, 47, 49).
11. On insider/outsider relations in *Othello*, see especially Edward Berry, 'Othello's Alienation', *SEL 1500–1900* (1990), 315–33; Carol Thomas Neely, 'Circumscriptions and Unhousedness: *Othello* in the Borderlands', in *Shakespeare and Gender: a History*, ed. by Deborah E. Barker and Ivo Kamps (London: Verso, 1995), pp. 302–15; and Michael Neill, 'Unproper Beds: Race, Adultery, and the Hideous in *Othello*', *Shakespeare Quarterly*, 40 (1989), 383–412.
12. See pp. 1, 11, 35–6, 39, 80, 96, 112; on Scott, the '45, and his increasingly resentful portrayal of England, see Sutherland pp. 33 ff., 141, 280, 305–47; *Scott on Himself: a Selection of the Autobiographical Writings of Sir Walter Scott*, ed. by David Hewitt (Edinburgh: Scottish Academic Press, 1981), p. 2; and Henderson Scott, *passim*.
13. On Scott's Celtic/Briton theories, see Sutherland pp. 92, 134, 141; on 'Celtic fringe' resistance to assimilation within British national development, see Michael Hechter, *Internal Colonialism: the Celtic Fringe in British National Development, 1536–1966* (Berkeley: University of California Press, 1975); and on contemporary racial theories, see George W. Stocking, Jr., *Victorian Anthropology* (New York: The Free Press, 1987). Scott's mixed feelings about the Celts as a 'race' resonate with the ambiguous liminal position of Othello as a racially 'other' border figure choosing to serve the more sophisticated empire.
14. Mary Preston, 'Othello' from *Studies in Shakespeare: a Book of Essays* [1869], cited in *Women Reading Shakespeare 1660–1900: an Anthology of Criticism*, ed. by Ann Thompson and Sasha Roberts (Manchester: Manchester University Press, 1997), pp. 126–31; see also Dympna Callaghan, '"Othello was a white man": properties of race on Shakespeare's stage', *Alternative Shakespeares vol. 2*, ed. by Terence Hawkes (London: Routledge, 1996), pp. 192–215.

15. In the Arden 2 introduction to *Othello* (London: Methuen, 1958), pp. li–liii, editor M. R. Ridley cites Preston as 'the reductio ad absurdum' of the 'tawny Moor' line of criticism also invoked by Coleridge – to Ridley's surprise, although he does not explore that connection nor avoid the kind of insidious racial stereotyping found in those he dismisses (see pp. li–liii). Disturbing traces of Ridley's manner persist in the Arden 3; Honigmann, while acknowledging the play's involvement with racism, turns to the 1600–1 portrait of the lighter-skinned, 'aristocratic face' of the Moorish Ambassador in order to stress his nobility, and later concedes that one (presumed white actor) might still manage 'if he wears European clothes and has darkened skin of indeterminate hue' (a make-up artist's quandary; see pp. 2–3, 14–17).
16. Certainly Virginia Mason Vaughan, *Othello: a Contextual History* (Cambridge: Cambridge University Press, 1994) and Adrian Poole, 'Northern Hamlet and Southern Othello? Irving, Salvini, and the Whirlwind of Passion', in *Shakespeare and the Mediterranean: Proceedings of the Seventh World Shakespeare Congress*, ed. by Tom Clayton, Susan Brock and Vicente Forès (Newark: University of Delaware Press, forthcoming), among others, are right to locate a shift in the 1870s, when English audiences identified Othello's 'otherness' with the Italianate passion of Salvini's performance.
17. Cited in William Shakespeare, *Othello* [*Plays in Performance* series], ed. by Julie Hankey (Bristol: Bristol Classical Press, 1987), p. 80. Subsequent references to this volume are to 'Hankey'.
18. Cited by Ruth Cowhig, 'Blacks in English Renaissance drama and the role of Shakespeare's *Othello*', in *The Black Presence in English Literature*, ed. by David Dabydeen (Manchester: Manchester University Press, 1985), p. 18.
19. Cowhig, p. 20.
20. See Cowhig, as well as Herbert Marshall and Mildred Stock, *Ira Aldridge: the Negro Tragedian* (London: Rockliff, 1958). Lois Potter, *Shakespeare in Performance: Othello* (Manchester University Press, 2002), pp. 108–18 supplements their account with additional materials from the Folger's Aldridge scrapbook.
21. Cowhig, p. 21.
22. See Vaughan, pp. 93–134.
23. Cited from Hankey, p. 49. Scott wrote a lengthy review essay of Boaden's biography for the *Quarterly Review* (1826).
24. Cowhig, p. 15. On Kemble's cuts, see Marvin Rosenberg, *The Masks of Othello* (Berkeley: University of California Press, 1961), pp. 47–8.
25. Hankey, p. 57.
26. Samuel Taylor Coleridge, *Table Talk* (London: George Routledge and Sons, 1884), p. 29. See also Coleridge's reiteration of Blumenbach's hierarchy of races, with Caucasian at the top, Negro at the bottom and Malays between (pp. 50–1). Blumenbach posited blackness as a 'degeneration' away from originary Caucasian man; his racial theory 'was the most widely accepted in the pre-Darwinian nineteenth century', although Cuvier's 1817 tripartite division moved towards a polygeneticist challenge (Stocking, pp. 26–7). See also Sudipto Chatterjee and Jyotsna G. Singh, 'Moor or less? The surveillance of Othello, Calcutta 1848', in *Shakespeare and Appropriation*, ed. by Christy Desmet and Robert Sawyer (New York: Routledge, 1999), pp. 65–82; they discuss the racial complexities of performing *Othello* in nineteenth-century

Calcutta, and the racial theories of Petrius Camper (translated in 1784, with a new English edition in 1821)

27. Charles Lamb, *The Portable Charles Lamb*, ed. by John Mason Brown (New York: Viking, 1949), p. 577.

28. Kean rotated *Othello* with Southern's tragedy of *Oroonoko* in his repertory: the choice to impersonate another racially-other tragic hero who kills his beloved hardly seems coincidental. Altering Aphra Behn's novel, Southern made Imoida, the wife of the enslaved African prince, white. Thus parallelism with *Othello* was accentuated at the cost of erasing a woman of colour. Lois Potter notes that Edward Young's 1721 *The Revenge*, with the Moor Zanga as its defiant villain, was also played in repertory with these roles by Kean and Aldridge, among others. Hazlitt found this deceiving slave 'more in conformity to our prejudices, as well as to historical truth' (Potter, pp. 13–14).

29. See W. Oxberry. 'Kenilworth, A Melo-drama'. *The New English Drama, with prefatory remarks, biographical sketches, and notes, critical and exploratory; being the only edition existing which is faithfully marked with the stage business, and stage directions, as performed at the Theatres Royal.* vol. 19th (London: W. Simpkin and R. Marshall, and C. Chapple, 1824), pp. 16, 21–3, 28–9, 49, 50; and Alfred Bunn [and Thomas John Dibdin], *Kenilworth: an Historical Drama, in Two Acts* (London: J. Duncombe [1832]), pp. 8–13, 18–22. The tragedy Leicester also intensified 'the resemblance between the protagonists of this novel and those of Othello', according to Richard Ford, *Dramatizations of Scott's Novels* (Oxford: Oxford Bibliographical Society, 1979), p. 33, who notes that 'Hugh Robsart took on the function of Brabantio and died midway through the play'.

30. Similarly, the version performed on Shakespeare's birthday in 1821 at the Adelphi Theatre was subtitled 'the Days of Queen Bess' (and 'Good Queen Bess' at Drury Lane in January 1824; see Ford, p. 28). In competition, however, was the sub-title at the Surrey Theatre for *Kenilworth or, the Countess of Leicester* – perhaps because the Manager there, in describing another show to be enacted about the daughters of Danaus, asserted that he was 'fully aware that Marriage and Murder are now regarded as the most successful features of modern melodrama' (Playbill, Surrey Theatre 5 and 6 March 1821, from the collection of the Folger Shakespeare Library, Washington, DC). Later in the century, versions of *Kenilworth* were performed as *Amy Robsart*. But the veneration of Queen Elizabeth also sold tickets, especially in English towns such as (ironically) Leicester, where a playbill rhapsodised: '*Queen Elizabeth* will be found to be more fully displayed than any other [character], combining the dignity, yet familiarity – passion, yet gentleness – refinement, yet vulgarity – the acuteness, discernment, quaintness, and general peculiarities that distinguished the mind and manners of that extraordinary woman' (Bolton, p. 403).

31. Dibdin and Bunn feuded over authorship of the version ultimately published under Bunn's name. In J. L. Huie's 1823 adaptation, Varney is tricked onto the trap through Janet's actions. On versions produced at the Olympic and Covent Garden in 1821 and after, see Ford, pp. 27–8; Bolton, p. 394; and Henry Adelbert White, *Sir Walter Scott's Novels on the Stage* (New Haven: Yale University Press, 1927), pp. 124–43. It is worth recalling that Desdemona was often killed behind bed-curtains because the scene was regarded as too

painful to view, and that Schröder's German adaptation allowed Othello and Desdemona to live; Rosenberg describes a similar attempt by Ducis in France, but his Othello Talma, after a few performances, refused the change (p. 32).

32. Noting Scott's popularity among Anglo-Indians from the 1820s onward, Katie Trumpener concludes: 'The Waverley novels both entertain colonial administrators and educate them for their new duties; when Anglo-Indians plan to act out Scott's *Kenilworth*, they do so primarily for amusement – but the novel's elaboration of pageantry and court life will also provide a model for their imperial role in England.' (*Bardic Nationalism: the Romantic Novel and the British Empire* (Princeton: Princeton University Press, 1987), pp. 258–9.)

33. 'Scarcely do the data of theatrical history so distinctly illustrate the regional nature of dramatic taste' (Bolton, p. 395). This pattern accords with what Peter Thomson has remarked about the general relationship between English and Scottish theatre: 'The theatrical taste and repertoire of British regional centres, with only rare exceptions throughout the period [1715–1965], were determined in London...Just occasionally, the traffic was reversed, most notably with John Home's *Douglas* (1756) and with the innumerable adaptations of Scott's Waverley novels, but only on condition that the distinctively Scottish voice was muted.' ('What Scots say', *Times Literary Supplement* (13 December 1996), 20)

34. Mary Elizabeth Braddon's *Aurora Floyd* (1863) may provide oblique testimony to *Kenilworth*'s influence, as well as the wider associations of the *Othello* plot and things Celtic; thanks to the conference participants for suggesting this connection.

2
'To Make the Situation Natural': *Othello* at Mid-Century

John Glavin

'To make the situation natural I must either have made her a bad woman [...] or him a jealous, treacherous, selfish man.'
(G. B. Shaw, 'A Dressing Room Secret' (1910))

In 1907 the Prisko Gallery in Vienna offered for sale an 'Othello and Desdemona' by Veronese. In the painting a blonde woman in Renaissance dress tries to stave off an attacking man, about to stab her with a knife upraised in his right arm – a distinctly white man, with red hair in fact. Othello? A white man who stabs his victim? In fact throughout the nineteenth century Othello did routinely stab Desdemona on the stage. It was a way, discovered in the eighteenth century, to solve the problem of Othello's lines immediately after the stifling: 'What noise is this? Not dead? not yet quite dead? / I that am cruel am yet merciful, / I would not have thee linger in thy pain,' (V. 2. 86–8). The 'So, so' that followed covered the thrust. Julie Hankey, the editor of the brilliant Plays in Performance text of the play, explains that theatrically 'the wound served the double purpose ... being both reviving (as good as a leach) and fatal'.[1] But though he did frequently stab, the nineteenth-century Othello always stabbed in black face – actually, after Edmund Kean, more in tawny face. So it comes as no surprise that the painting now seems to be a 'Tarquin and Lucretia' by Titian. Nevertheless, even allowing for the upraised dagger as clue, we still want to ask: what could both Othello and *Othello* have come to mean in the nineteenth century if by 1900 the hero might be blanched?

We can begin to uncover the answer to that question by looking at G. B. Shaw's 1910 prose piece, 'A Dressing Room Secret', from which this paper takes its title.[2] Shaw has Shakespeare claim he started writing *Othello* with a 'female villain'.

I had a tremendous notion of a supersubtle and utterly corrupt
Venetian lady who was to drive Othello to despair by betraying
him. It's all in the first act. But I weakened on it. She turned amiable
on my hands, in spite of me. [...] I yielded to [...] [the] temptation
[to make her innocent].

His blunder, Shaw's Shakespeare concedes, 'turned the play into a farce',
because 'it was a sin against human nature'.

[B]y making Desdemona a decent poor devil of an honest woman,
and Othello a really superior sort of man, I took away all natural
reason for his jealousy. To make the situation natural I must either
have made her a bad woman [...] or him a jealous, treacherous,
selfish man, like Leontes. [...] But I couldn't belittle Othello in
that way; so, like a fool, I belittled him the other way by making
him the dupe of a farcical trick with a handkerchief that wouldn't
have held water off the stage for five minutes.

But what Shaw's Shakespeare should have done turns out to be very
much like what Trollope did do in *He Knew He Was Right* (1868–69). Of
course, Emily Trevelyan is neither corrupt nor supersubtle. She's not
even just subtle. And though he's jealous, Louis Trevelyan is not treacherous, and more self-punishing than selfish. Yet, despite differences like
these, both Shaw and Trollope are embarked on the same, paradigmatic-
ally Victorian project, 'naturalising' Shakespeare. This process of natur-
alisation recuperates a context for the Prisko gallery's odd attribution.
But much more significantly, it reveals a Trollope who not only blanches
Othello but who also reads *Othello* with extraordinary, indeed exemplary
finesse.

Ornamentalism and Othello

David Cannadine has recently challenged prevailing protocols of imperial and colonial study by proposing a homology-seeking 'Ornamentalism' of class to counter a hegemonic 'Orientalism' of race. 'Orientalism',
in its canonical definition by Edward Said, fashions the subaltern as the
exotic other to the hegemonic, a difference that in every case involves
the repudiation and subduing of the subaltern. *Ornamentalism* constructs instead parallel, even interpenetrating, hierarchies of class across
imperial and colonial borders, aligning exotic upper to metropolitan
upper in a unified global ruling class. Thus, Cannadine can describe

the 'British imperial enterprise' as 'the effort to fashion and tie together the empire abroad in the vernacular image of the domestic, ranked social hierarchy'. Reread in that way, he insists, 'the British Empire was at least as much (perhaps more?) about the replication of sameness and similarities originating from home as it was about the insistence on difference and dissimilarities originating from overseas'.[3]

There seem to me strong reasons for resisting Cannadine's thesis. He has assembled an impressive, extensive and highly readable chronicle of 'ornamental' occasions and organisations. But his evidence feels lopsidedly up-scale. Though a maharajah ranked as a duke at a Buckingham Palace levée, Cannadine offers us no parallel ground for believing a Victorian dragoon, light or heavy, saw himself, or was encouraged to see himself, as mere mirror to a sepoy. The ornamental 'enterprise', therefore, comes across finally as a garnish, or better still in that supreme age of spectacle as window-dressing, disguising and indeed mystifying with public performance the quotidian experience of daily life, and drudgery, below a glittering veneer. However, the very theatricality of the ornamental, though politically unpersuasive, may resonate when we turn it back to theatre itself. Think of all those late-Victorian playhouses calling themselves 'The Empire'. Or consider Nina Auerbach's witty parallel between Henry Irving and Benjamin Disraeli: 'As Disraeli was urging his countrymen to extend England's empire through India and Africa, so Irving, who was said to resemble Disraeli, built a splendid empire in London to show the way.'[4] If theatres called Empire staged imperial fictions, surely *Othello* offered an unequalled opportunity for producing ornamentalist 'sameness', presenting to Victorian audiences a black field-marshal in whom no white paladin should have, would have, or even could have refused to recognise his simulacrum.

In the preceding essay in this volume, Diana Henderson suggested the importance of *Othello* in the first decades of the nineteenth century. Othello was a key role for Edmund Kean, who dominated the Romantic stage. Indeed, he died while playing the part. After his death in 1833, however, the remainder of the nineteenth century records continuous disappointment with performances of the title character, countered by 'a rising interest in Iago'.[5] It's not only that there are no more great Othellos, but that there are rarely Othellos of any kind. Actors either avoided the role, or failed in it. Macready, the outstanding English actor between Kean and Irving, tried the role several times over several decades, but it was one of the two parts – the other was Hamlet – in which he had virtually no success.[6] When he did succeed in the play, he was, predictably, playing Iago. In 1848 Gustavus Vaughan Brooke as the

Moor seemed to many a Kean redivivus, but alcoholism overcame him before he could make more than a glancing impression. And when Charles Fechter 'attempted the part of Othello' in October 1861, 'even his most ardent Hamlet-worshipper was forced to admit that his portrayal was a mistake'.[7] As one reviewer sniffed, his was Shakespeare 'in the most un-English guise', that is, as another scoffed 'not Shakespeare'.[8] Other than Brooke's and Fechter's, there were only occasional revivals during the middle fifty years of the century, generally to disappointing audiences and disappointed reviewers. Of course, the play was too important to the canon to disappear completely from the repertory. But by the mid-century, it had ceased to be – as it had been for the preceding two hundred years – a signature role for a leading man. This paradox becomes particularly strikingly in the 1881 Lyceum season during which Edwin Booth and Henry Irving alternated Othello and Iago. Both failed as Othello: each succeeded as Iago. In those years it seemed that only the distinctly not-English Tommaso Salvini could make the role come alive.

This failure roots, I think, in what is usually represented as the great advance in nineteenth-century acting. Well before Stanislavski, acting had begun to move toward a less conventional, more realistic and empirically based style, parallel to developments in fiction and in psychology. Here Macready can provide a neatly counter-intuitive example. Though we think of him as the last of the major point-seeking, frontal, stylised leading men, his diaries offer an incomparable record of attempts to become one with the role he played, and to estimate success or failure based on that identification. You can open the two volumes of the published diary at almost any point in his long career and quickly find passages that underscore this claim. Toward the beginning, on 20 October 1834, he is unhappy with his Macbeth, because 'I did not surrender my whole mind and heart to the performance', and thus 'though desirous to do well, I did not satisfy myself'.[9] Seventeen years later he is happy with his performance in the title role of Sheridan Knowles's *Virginius*: 'I did indeed "gore my own thoughts" to do it, for my own Katie [his late daughter] was in my mind, as in one part the tears streamed down my cheeks; and in another she who is among the Blest!, beloved one!. Such is a player's mind and heart.'[10] Failure and success both turn on the performer's capacity thoroughly to assume the character's inner life, an inner life drawn directly from his own.

Which returns us to the paradox of Othello. Even an actor like the rigorously bourgeois Macready, obsessed with his status as a gentleman, found no trouble becoming the most toxic of Shakespeare's villains. In

1833 he notes that the villain's is 'a part' he has 'often done before', but before that night 'perhaps I have not played Iago with more entire self-possession, more spirit, and in a more manly unembarrassed tone'.[11] Manly, unembarrassed, the villain is a cinch. It's only the villain's tragic victim Macready cannot convince himself to become. As Diana Henderson, among others, has shown, the line that cannot be crossed here is the colour-line. While the actor can enter and play out the inner life of the moral other, even at its most despicable, he cannot convincingly find in himself the racial other, even at its bravest and most passionate. Nineteenth-century anglophone anxieties about race are simply too powerful to overcome what Joyce Green MacDonald succinctly calls 'the disruptively stubborn sign of blackness'.[12]

The Iago–Othello paradox becomes even more evocative when we contrast the stage history of the play against the power still available to Verdi turning *Othello* into *Otello*. 'When Verdi's opera came to London in 1889, it was as though all the magnificence that had somehow gone out of the stage play, had at last found a home.'[13] The nineteenth century can sing the black male body but cannot speak it. What remains possible to the singer, in the conventionalised hyperbole of grand opera, is no longer feasible on the increasingly realistic, spoken stage. On stage, then, *Othello* could only succeed as burlesque, as Richard W. Schoch has recently shown in his invaluable *Not Shakespeare. Othello, The Moor of Fleet Street. Othello Travestie. The Rival Othellos. Salthello Ovini.* Even Dickens wrote one, *O'Thello, The Irish Moor of Venice*.[14] The only way, the only anglophone way, to make Othello work on the stage is to make it into fun.

And yet, if we turn away from the stage, ornamentalism does enable us to recapture a, if not the, Victorian Othello, though certainly not in ways Cannadine would wish to acknowledge. In *He Knew He Was Right* Anthony Trollope adapts *Othello* not only with extraordinary ingenuity but in a form that seems genuinely 'ornamentalist'. By matching the black hero with a metropolitan mandarin, Louis Trevelyan, a mandarin who not only acknowledges but prizes the parallel, the novel produces exactly the kind of symmetry ornamentalism posits. From the beginning to the end of the 'jealousy' plot Trollope carefully marks this parallel. There is nothing recondite, or even merely implied. Bozzle, the cunning, narcissistic ex-policeman, leads Trevelyan to suspect his innocent wife, fanning his jealousy until Trevelyan loses not his life, but his wits, in the process destroying if not actually taking his wife's life. As the Trevelyans' separation deepens, the narrator comments:

We remember Othello's demand of Iago ['Villain, be sure thou prove my love a whore' (III. 3. 157)]. That was the demand that Bozzle understood that Trevelyan had made of him, and he was minded to obey that order. But Trevelyan, though he had in truth given the order, was like Othello also in this, – that he would have preferred before all the prizes of the world to have had proof brought home to him exactly opposite to that which he demanded. But there was nothing so terrible to him as the grinding suspicion that he was to be kept in the dark. [...] Therefore he gave, in effect, the same order that Othello gave. [15] (II, 347)

Indeed, to underscore the doubling, the next sentence reminds us that Bozzle is writing to Trevelyan in Venice – 'There came many dispatches to Venice.' But there's no reason at this point for Trevelyan to be in Venice, except to underscore the *Othello* connection. And in the final pages, we learn that Trevelyan

would speak of dear Emily, and poor Emily, and shake his head slowly, and talk of the pity of it. 'The pity of it, Iago; oh, the pity of it,' he said once. The allusion to [Emily] was so terrible that she almost burst in anger, as she would have done formerly. She almost told him that he had been as wrong throughout as was the jealous husband in the play whose words he quoted, and that his jealousy, if continued was likely to be as tragical. (II, 358)

Indeed, throughout the novel Trevelyan seems so self-consciously stagey, striking poses and declaiming, that not only his deeds but his manner suggest an echo of that most theatrical of all Shakespeare's protagonists. Hearing that his wife is going to leave Nuncombe Putney, ' "When is she to go?" he asked in a low, sepulchral tone. [...] "Heaven and earth! Where shall I find a roof for her head?" Trevelyan as he said this was walking about the room with his hands stretched up towards the ceiling', at a moment when 'there was no intention on the part of any one to banish Mrs Trevelyan' (I, 205). Later, at Casalunga, 'He put out his thin wasted hands and looked at them, and touched the hollowness of his own cheeks, and coughed that he might hear the hacking sound of his own infirmity,' (II, 267). Without quite making it explicit, passages like these seem to be inviting us to conclude that Trevelyan not only acknowledges the role he's playing but is deliberately aping the source from which his family's plot is borrowed. It may not be that Trevelyan unfortunately finds himself playing Othello, but that

Trevelyan literally finds his self by playing Othello. However, to be fair, it seems also to be the case that, at least by the end of the novel, he has moved from imagining himself as Othello to playing grandly the Lady of Shalott. '"There is a curse upon me, [...] it is written down in the book of my destiny that nothing shall ever love me!"' (II, 268). This role is consonant with the feminising the novel associates with male madness.

Whether or not Trevelyan is consciously making his life into Othello's, it is certainly striking how much of the rest of the play Trollope manages to subsume. We don't find in his pages merely the central triangle of provocateur-jealous husband-maligned wife. Blanching seems also to open ways in which this multi-plotted text can continue virtually all the issues crucial to Shakespeare's text: crossing cultures; colonial government and the imperial experience; travel and the exotic; madness; and even Italy. As a result, *He Knew He Was Right* not only adapts the play's plot to contemporary England but also seems to work much more elaborately as an extended, updated gloss on Shakespeare's play, reclaiming both its subtle psychological analysis and its rich social layering. The only thing missing is race, apparently the price that has to be paid for retrieving the rest. The white actor cannot lose himself within the black role; the black role can only resurface as the white man, not Othello read as an English gentleman but an English gentleman read, and reading himself, as Othello.

But can it be *Othello* or Othello without race? The distinguished actress Janet Suzman insists it cannot be either. In 1987 she bravely staged the play in a South Africa still under apartheid, casting a black actor as Othello with an otherwise all-white cast. Writing with sensitivity and nuance about the play in the light of that production, she claims, 'Othello's jealousy is hardly the bourgeois Victorian version that drives Anthony Trollope's obsessive husband to an early death in *He Knew He Was Right*.' Othello's jealousy can't be transferred to a pillar of the establishment. The jealousies of the master class, driven by offended privilege, are not those of the subaltern. Othello's jealousy for Suzman is, instead, 'compounded by all the insecurities of a black man in a white world, of an older man with a much younger wife, of a warrior unfamiliar with the rules of engagement of the bedroom, and of a foreigner hired to defend a society he has no part in'.[16] That is: of someone who bears no resemblance at all to Louis Trevelyan.

If Janet Suzman is right, then no matter how much of the play Trollope has managed to echo, by cutting out the core he misconstrues his source. White on white may be sad, may be moving, and may even be profound. Nonetheless, it's not important, not important as *Othello* is important. But has Trollope misread the play? Or has he read it in a way close to Suzman's own, and is that in fact the point of his project?

'Not negroes only'

Race does surface in the novel, explicitly, and comically, in a duet-duel between the Hon. Charles Glascock and the American poetess, Wallachia Petrie – that is, in the sideline of a distinctly secondary plot. She is insisting there can be no 'spark of sympathy' between the Americans and the English. Americans stand, she claims, for equality, the English for hierarchy. 'It is the instinct of fallen man to hate equality, to desire ascendancy, to crush, to oppress, to tyrannise, to enslave. Then when the slave is at last free, and in his freedom demands – equality, man is not great enough to take his enfranchised brother to his bosom.' Bored but thinking he gets it, Glascock replies: 'You mean negroes.' But she insists: 'Not negroes only, – not the enslaved blacks, who are now enslaved no more, – but the rising nations of white men wherever they are to be seen. You English have no sympathy with a people who claim to be your equals,' (II, 53).

We are inclined to read this exchange in light of the immediately surrounding romance between Glascock and Caroline Spalding. A few moments earlier Caroline has been wondering if Charles's aunt 'who was a Duchess' and his sister 'who would be a Countess' would be willing to receive Caroline as a bride. 'How grand a thing it is [...] to be equal with those whom you love!' (II, 50). Her word 'equal' gestures toward Wally's word 'equality'. It's not only the apparent disparity of rank that troubles Caroline's romance but the larger cultural difference: can anyone raised in a society that takes equality as a given find and confer happiness in a world based on inherited rank?

But Wally's word carries with it a more haunting, and haunted, echo. By the late 1860s Trollope is unsurpassed in the skill with which he exploits the resonant parallelisms potential to the multi-plotted, multi-parted novel. Throughout *He Knew He Was Right*, episodes, conversations, images in one plot repeatedly call up comparable elements in characters and situations widely severed. So when we read Wally's catalogue of a fallen man's instincts – 'to hate equality, to desire ascendancy, to crush, to oppress, to tyrannise, to enslave' – we can hardly miss the way in which they also point to Trevelyan as an epitome of that fallen man, whose *instinct* toward his wife has followed precisely this catalogue of derogation. And we begin to sense the way in which, like

the Shakespeare who regularly makes the clown a plot's best reader,
Trollope has here deployed the absurd Wally as a kind of keynoter-
manqué. Her defiant 'Not negroes only' reads race as a universal typ-
ology of the oppressed and the disenfranchised. It is almost as though,
now that 'the enslaved blacks [...] are now enslaved no more', they
have been freed to represent not only the history of their own inequality
but the histories of all those inequalities they figure in systems dominated by the white and anglophone master. Race in effect surfaces explicitly in this scene, and implicitly throughout the novel, to supply
Trollope with the narrative and the imagery he requires for talking
most powerfully about gender. 'You English have no sympathy' not
only 'with a people who claim to be your equals' but with any people
who claim to be your equals, most strikingly, of course, with the women
from among whom you select your wives. 'How grand a thing it is,'
Caroline muses, 'to be equal with those whom you love', and how – in
the world of Trevelyan and Glascock, a world managed for them by men
like Sir Marmaduke Rowley at the top and Bozzle at the bottom –
entirely out of the question.

In this world there can be no equality between men and women,
which is why the novel can claim a parity between even the most
ostensibly privileged women and freed but disenfranchised Negroes.
Women are, as Dorothy Stanbury sees with appalling clarity, 'just
nobodies' (II, 14). This is not hyperbole. Men, she argues, can become
somebody through effort or by inherited position. Women can only
have self conferred upon them, by men. The historian of schizophrenia,
R. Walter Heinrichs, helpfully distinguishes three imbricated models of
self circulating through the nineteenth century.[17] The earliest, deriving
from Continental philosophy in a distinguished line from Descartes
through Locke, Leibnitz and Kant, identifies self with consciousness.
A later, more empirically derived strand, associated with David Hume,
reads self as a core or structure of sense perceptions linked by memory.
In the wake of Romanticism, however, a distinctly nineteenth-century
model emerges, in which self registers fundamentally as, and through, a
bundle of relationships. Trollope, like most of his contemporaries, owes
debts to all three. But it is the third, the relational, that seems most
significant for him.

For Trollope, the essential self is the self that others confer upon you.
This is true for men as well as women. Phineas Finn finds it virtually
impossible to recover from the loss of esteem he endures during his
murder trial in *Phineas Redux*. Once London society shows itself willing
to see him as a killer even his acquittal cannot restore the sense of self he

enjoyed before the arrest. But Trollope marks a crucial difference between men and women in this regard. Others confirm or veto the self a
man achieves through effort. Phineas, in *Phineas Finn* (1869) and then
again in *Phineas Redux* (1874), invents a self he then proffers to the world
of Parliament and Society for endorsement. That possibility is denied to
women. Because they may neither work nor own, women can only
claim selves bestowed on them by men. And without a man, there can
be only, as Dorothy insists, nobody. Hence the routine delirium of
Trollope's women when chosen by a man, with their appalling metaphors of ivy and oak, or other sorts of parasitism. However lamentable,
the redemptive ecstasy they express is entirely justified, not merely
erotic but ontological. To be chosen by a man is to become a person.
Every female protagonist in every plot of the novel discovers this for
herself, except for Caroline Spalding, the magically exempt American,
destined for the equally exempt aristocrat, the man with the glass cock.
Even Miss Stanbury is who she is, the formidable Miss Stanbury of
Exeter, because her former fiancé established her with the posthumous
gift of his fortune.

This modelling of self becomes richer and even darker when read
against the genres competing for supremacy within the novel. The
multiple pairs of marriage-seeking sisters set us on the verge of, if
not quite within, Austenland: Emily and Norah Rowley, Dorothy and
Priscilla Stanbury, Arabella and Camilla French, Caroline and Olivia
Spalding. But this is Austen shadowed by difference. At least from *Doctor
Thorne* (1858) onwards, Trollope's novels are shaped, and for many
flawed, by tension between the comic, Austenesque, marriage plot and
a satiric vision of 'the way we live now' pioneered by Trollope's rival
paragon, Thackeray. And we certainly find that tension here in the
manifold satire on colonial, parliamentary and diplomatic enterprise.
But *He Knew He Was Right* strains this tension further by adding a third
element, Shakespeare sieved (I think) through Scott. Diana Henderson's
reading of the *Othello* within *Kenilworth* prompts me to tie Trevelyan to
Tressilian (why else these outlandish names?), and thus to connect this
novel to the 'Scott-project' on which Trollope embarked when he updated *Waverley* as *Phineas Finn* (1867–69). At least from his second novel
The Kellys and the O'Kellys (1848), Trollope had set out to write fiction as
present history, a project supremely realised in the Barsetshire series. By
the late 1860s he seems sufficiently self-confident to rethink this project
as a way of taking on, and transforming, the magisterial legacy of Scott,
and through Scott accessing the tragic heritage of Shakespeare. Certainly, it is a Scott-free Shakespeare that he later boldly reconfigures in

novels like *The Prime Minister* (1876, *The Merchant of Venice*) and *The Duke's Children* (1880, *King Lear*).

It's this Scott–Shakespeare line, I think, that pushes the novel toward its curious and poignant concluding compromise with Austen. In the final chapters of *He Knew He Was Right* there are, in the best Austen manner, multiple marriages. But each bride manages nuptial identity only at the cost of her own sister's permanent isolation. In Austen both Lizzie and Jane Bennet can marry. Happiness is available for both Marianne and Elinor Dashwood. Not so here. The harsh vision that accompanies Scott–Shakespeare seems to demand a sort of maiden tribute before the comic plots can conclude, and so we get only a demi- or semi-Austen. One sister's happiness requires the other's permanent non-entity, even for the otherwise privileged Americans. The lively and perceptive Olivia Spalding unaccountably disappears from the book. An engaged Norah can enjoy Caroline's married glories at Monkhams; Caroline's sister would seem to be too dark a presence to be invited in. For the French sisters this conclusion is bitter, for the Stanburys, bitter-sweet. But with Emily it is horrific. Required to obey, she is moved about as an object at the whim of her husband. She finds her child seized from her arms, and discovers that she has no recourse under the law. All this because she will not accept what Trevelyan, cruelly but correctly, insists upon: that she is a nobody. Emily sees too late to alter her course or his that he can 'become a tyrant because he had the power to tyrannise' (II, 102). The Scott–Shakespeare line claims and refuses to relinquish her. Two hundred and fifty years after Desdemona's tragedy, she repeats Desdemona's discovery: a wife is without recourse against the whims of her master.

That thumping stress on inequality also connects the marriage plots to the novel's satiric, Thackerayan, colonial materials. And in turn the colonial materials reassert the novel's tie to *Othello*. Emily Trevelyan and Norah Rowley, the two principal female characters, are the daughters of a colonial governor, raised entirely outside the metropole. Repeatedly their inability to bend themselves to fit the expectations of conventional English romance and marriage is explained by the alterity of their upbringing. The novel insists on that alterity, even hauling their father over to London, in the midst of his daughters' marital and romantic crises, to testify, clumsily, on colonial mismanagement. The colonial enterprise itself is a joke. And a source for tragedy. Where the colonial daughters have been raised produces how they've been raised produces in turn why they cannot marry well. Norah, it is true, finally marries happily but not well, that is, not into the upper class. She escapes her sister's misfortune because her London season grants her the preview her sister lacked. She sees how unsuited a girl like her is to marry a man like Glascock, and how perfectly matched she is with the radical, déclassé Stanbury.

At first, Trollope seems to be inviting us to read this colonial material in the light of *Jane Eyre*. Early on he insists that Emily 'had picked up such a trick of obstinacy in those tropical regions' (I, 11). Either because the allusion is working in his own imagination, or because he wants to make sure we see the tie, he embeds that remark in a discussion of 'Mrs. Poole', who has behaved so badly her husband has had to move her to Naples. Grace Poole is, of course, the distinctly colonial first Mrs Rochester's 'keeper'. The connection is made even more explicit, and damning, a few pages later. Trevelyan recalls hearing 'that no man should look for a wife from among the tropics, that women educated amidst the languors of those sunny climes rarely come to possess those high ideals of conjugal duty and feminine truth which a man should regard as the first requisites of a good wife' (I, 35). Trevelyan is immediately censured for this line of thinking. And the novel takes it no further. I am therefore inclined to consider it the pentimento of an earlier notion of the novel, one which would have set Brontë against Austen, paralleling Emily and Bertha Rochester, holding Emily responsible for her tragedy, a pentimento for which Trollope paid. Contemporary reviewers were united in belaboring Emily Trevelyan: the *Spectator*, for example, calling her a 'proud, hard, willful woman' (12 June 1869).

Abandoning the Eyre parallel so early suggests Trollope wants to align the colonial motif more closely to Shakespeare's play. It could have been in Brontë's novel that Trevelyan found his attack on the tropical bride. But *Othello* reverses that revelation. The play is driven by a plot about an empire fighting to preserve a colony. That plot exposes not the colony's flaws but those of the metropole it reflects, and of the master who subdues it. As Janet Suzman insists, with Othello and Desdemona 'the sexual and the political' go 'hand in hand'.[18] Their runaway marriage is almost immediately overwhelmed, and then subverted, by the demand that the bridegroom go off to Cyprus to defend it for Venice against the Turks. There's even a plausible argument for reading the time-scheme of the play to prove that the marriage is never consummated, so heavy are the demands of war and colonial administration. The kind of man Othello is, then, the kind of work he does, the kind of society that employs him to do this work, and admires him enthusiastically, it is all of these that come together to determine the kind of death Desdemona suffers at his, and their, hands. Everything we need to know about the price of sustaining empire *Othello* shows us in the way it undermines Othello's marriage.

Desdemona runs away with Othello in large part because his catalogue of significant differences leads her to assume he will not replicate her father. Her suit on behalf of Cassio shows the confidence with which she expects now to be no longer subordinate, sent away when men speak, but Othello's chosen and cherished partner. When she learns to her horror that there is no difference between her father and her husband she understands immediately that she is doomed. Emily Trevelyan makes the parallel error, in the opposite direction. Coming from the colony to the metropole, trained to know herself superior to those her father governs, she assumes she will have a similarly exalted, and of course enriched, status as Trevelyan's wife. But it is precisely because she is a colonial subject, because he has made her what she is in London, that Trevelyan insists on treating her as a cipher, destroying her when she presumes an equality of status he finds literally incredible.

And here I part company with Suzman. Her Othello is marked by a 'vulnerable innocence'. He's got to be played, she insists, as a '*true* foreigner at the Venetian court'.[19] Foreigner, yes, but cynosure, also. Othello is the Venetian generalissimo, the man of the hour, the man of mode. The Venetian ambassadors simply can't believe in the criminal they encounter when they arrive at Cyprus. He had represented everything they and Venice stood for. And we can never forget that, though his colour differs from theirs, the Venetians and Othello share a faith, a faith he is happy to kill for. We diminish the richness of the play if we fail to separate Othello's undoing from the Venetian attempt to map the metropolitan experience over the colonial site. The easy quelling of riot and disturbance in Venice itself, the painless suppression of Iago's malevolence under the assured authority of Doge and Senate, all of that goes missing as soon as the colony is made to stand in for the imperial seat. Cyprus then functions as a site of unmasking: what is hidden or latent in Venice, about Venice and about its hero, Othello, Cyprus makes clear. Which is precisely the dynamic Trollope relocates in Trevelyan's marital misadventure. Like Othello Trevelyan is the epitome of the imperial order, and like Othello he is undone by the colonial encounter, an encounter which forces him to reveal his deepest 'instinct', the drive to subordinate. We are being invited, then, to read Emily as the prototypical subaltern victim, a position made bitterly ironic by her former status as a lady and the daughter of a governor, and to read Trevelyan as the equally prototypical colonial master – and therefore mad: 'the hallucination in her husband's mind did not really consist of a belief in her infidelity but arose from an obstinate determination to yield nothing' (II, 379).

Victorians would have recognised Trevelyan's madness as paranoia. Emil Kraeplin, in his canonical *Manic Depressive Insanity and Paranoia* (1896), argues that the term paranoia 'in a special sense', that is naming a particular mental illness, first appeared in 1863, five years before the novel.[20] The paranoiac was understood to suffer from 'a form of insanity essentially affecting intellectual activity', distinguished from mania on the one hand and melancholia on the other, the principal diagnostic categories prior to the 1860s. Read this way paranoia becomes 'a disorder of meaning [...] that transforms the commonplace into the supernatural [...] construct[ing] meaning where there is none',[21] driving the paranoiac to 'empty speech acts, whose informational content refers to neither world nor self'.[22] (It's for this reason, I think, that the novel's sympathetic hero is a writer for a radical newspaper, a crusading figure against disordered meanings.) Shortly after paranoia's 'discovery', it became the most frequent diagnosis in the spectrum of mental illness: 'the number of paranoiacs in our mental hospitals had grown from 70 to 80 percent of all cases'.[23] But paranoiacs are not merely deluded. It was widely held that 'delusions pre-exist in all normal brains'.[24] Hence everyone's capacity to dream. And hence the constantly iterated parallel between Trevelyan and Miss Stanbury. Both repeatedly insist they are persecuted. Each holds comparably prejudiced, erroneous views of other characters and of their situations. Miss Stanbury's banishment of her nephew, destroying his finances and his prospects, obviously parallels Trevelyan's ruin of his wife. In the paranoiac, however, delusions 'cause a break in normal associations',[25] those associations which, as we saw, underpin and frame the Trollopian self. Miss Stanbury for all her tyrannical eccentricities is in that sense, finally, normal. She misjudges, and lashes out, but (as a woman?) she cannot stand solitude, and is therefore forced repeatedly to acknowledge the possibility of her own error rather than embracing, as Trevelyan does, self-righteous isolation.

With Trevelyan, then, the colonial and the paranoiac become one. In his delusion of mastery the paradigmatic politics and the typical madness of the mid-century coalesce. The colonial frame of mind – for Wallachia Petrie, *the* anglophone male frame of mind – with its 'instinctive' recoiling at difference, its repudiation of any claim that the other can be the equal, mirrors the paranoid demand to be removed from a shared realm of interaction and meaning. Kraeplin claimed that the preeminent characteristic of the close to a thousand paranoiacs he had observed was their loss of the faculty of 'integration'.[26] And that is also Trevelyan's final boast, self-immured at Casalunga: 'It has been my study to untie all the ties; and, by Jove, I have succeeded,' (II, 334). It's a curious echo of Othello, who also at the end feels still the need to boast, who cannot, even as he confronts the shame of what he has done, surrender a narrative of mastery.

And that is surely, at least in part, why the novel, as it moves toward its climax, moves to Italy. In one sense all the Italian journeys confirm the homage: see, my *Othello* is Italian also. But there is something else besides, something that roots in the novel's subversive, and (as we now might claim) meta-ornamentalist critique. Florence, where the characters spend so much of the novel's second half, had quite recently been appropriated as the capital of the new Italian state. The Kingdom of the Two Sicilies, governed by the House of Savoy, had conquered the north of Italy, driving out of Tuscany the family of Lorraine. (Shortly thereafter, when they were able to conquer the middle of the peninsula, the Piedmontese would move the capital further south to Rome, from which they forced the withdrawal of its rule, the Pope.) Though the Savoy had installed themselves in the former residence of the Tuscan Grand Dukes, the Pitti palace, Tuscany was ruled by its conquerors as a kind of colony. Florence is, thus, at the moment of the novel, a kind of colonial capital. And as we watch the elaborate and empty pantomime of ministers interacting, we feel how entirely bogus this new state is, how contaminated it already has become by prior and contemporary narratives of mastery that bound and abet it. Whatever new thing Florence may be claimed to mean, that claim surely is jeopardised by what we see and know of decaying Siena a brief ride away, and by ruinous Casalunga, just beyond Siena, with its outcast cynosure. The territory into which the mad and ruined master withdraws mimics horrifically the desiccated, depleted mastery he has sought to impose.

G. B. Shaw insisted that a naturalised Othello must dwindle into a meaningless, violent, middle-class melodrama. *He Knew He Was Right* shows how wrong Shaw could (often) be. Trollope's adaptation relocates the tragedy of the original by reclaiming the source of that tragedy, its world's colonial enterprise. He becomes thereby, for the nineteenth century, the play's most capable reader, and at the same time an extraordinary reader of that century. In his blanched *Othello* mastery and madness surface intertwined as they did for Shakespeare: the meaning of the time.

Notes

1. *Othello: Plays In Performance*, ed. by Julie Hankey (Bristol: Bristol Classical Press, 1987), p. 319 (hereafter cited as Hankey).
2. *Shaw on Shakespeare*, ed. with intro. by Edwin Wilson (London: Penguin, 1969), p. 252.
3. David Cannadine, *Ornamentalism: How the British Saw Their Empire* (New York: Oxford University Press, 2001), p. xix.
4. Nina Auerbach, *Ellen Terry: Player in Her Time* (New York: Norton, 1987), p. 189.
5. Hankey, p. 61.
6. George C. D. Odell, *Shakespeare from Betterton to Irving* (New York: Benjamin Blom, 1966), II, 217.
7. Odell, II, 253.
8. Richard W. Schoch, *Not Shakespeare: Bardolatry and Burlesque in the Nineteenth Century* (Cambridge: Cambridge University Press, 2002), p. 90. Born to a German father and English mother, Fechter was educated in France and began his stage career there.
9. *The Diaries of William Charles Macready*, ed. by William Toynbee (New York: Putnams, 1912), I, 190.
10. *Diaries of Macready*, II, 485.
11. *Diaries of Macready*, I, 10.
12. Joyce Green MacDonald, 'Acting Black: *Othello, Othello* Burlesques, and the Performance of Blackness', *Theatre Journal*, 46.2 (1994), 231–50.
13. Hankey, p. 95.
14. Charles Haywood, 'Charles Dickens and Shakespeare: or, The Irish Moor of Venice, *O'Thello*, with Music', *The Dickensian*, 73 (1977), 67–88.
15. This and all subsequent citations of Trollope's novel refer to the volume and page numbers of the Unabridged Dover republication of the first book edition, published by Strahan and Company, London, 1869 (two vols bound as one, but paginated as two).
16. Janet Suzman, 'South Africa in *Othello*', in *Shakespeare and the Twentieth Century*, ed. by Jonathan Bate, Jill L. Levenson, Dieter Mehl (Newark: University of Delaware Press, 1998), p. 24.
17. R. Walter Heinrichs, *In Search of Madness: Schizophrenia and Neuroscience* (Oxford: Oxford University Press, 2001), p. 421.
18. Suzman, p. 27.
19. Suzman, p. 26.
20. Emil Kraeplin, *Manic-Depressive Insanity and Paranoia* (1896; repr. New York: Arno, 1976), p. 206.
21. Heinrichs, p. 119.
22. German E. Berrios, *The History of Mental Symptoms: Descriptive Psychopathology since the Nineteenth Century* (Cambridge: Cambridge University Press, 1996), p. 126.
23. Kraeplin, p. 202.
24. Berrios, p. 116.
25. Berrios, p. 116.
26. Kraeplin cited by Heinrichs, p. 24.

3
Dickens and Hamlet

Juliet John

'If any one of Shakespeare's plays was known by an individual during the Victorian era that play was *Hamlet*.'[1] Valerie L. Gager's claim about the popularity of *Hamlet* is perhaps difficult to substantiate, but there is no doubt that, of all Shakespeare's plays, *Hamlet* was the play to which Dickens most often alluded.[2] At first sight Dickens's interest in *Hamlet* may seem surprising. Dickens, or Mr Popular Sentiment as Trollope infamously called him, was accused of vulgarity and intellectual deficiency from his own day onwards. G. H. Lewes perhaps put the charges most bluntly, maintaining that there was not 'a single thoughtful remark' in the whole Dickens canon, and that Dickens 'never was and never would have been a student'.[3] *Hamlet*, on the other hand, became synonymous with the tortured, alienated intellectual at the play's centre – a man superbly endowed with intelligent thoughts, but a little short on action. During the nineteenth century, when so many artists and thinkers felt themselves to be, in Isobel Armstrong's term, 'secondary', Hamlet metamorphosed from a flawed Prince to the archetypal hero as artist and thinker.[4] Dickens's fascination with Hamlet, however, was not born of this hero-worship. It was fuelled rather by anxieties that the nineteenth-century valorisation of Shakespeare's Hamlet promoted a model of intellectual and aristocratic disengagement from the public sphere unhelpful in an age of burgeoning democracy and mass culture.

The glamorisation of Hamlet which disturbed Dickens had its roots in the Romantic period. As Jonathan Bate argues, 'the presence of Hamlet in Romantic discourse usually indicates that the artist is examining his own face'.[5] While Dr Johnson admired Shakespeare's characters as universal types of a 'species', Coleridge famously identified with Hamlet as an individual, announcing: 'I have a smack of Hamlet about myself, if I may say so.'[6] It is perhaps unsurprising to find that 'the common

46

nineteenth-century view' of *Hamlet* was, according to Gager, 'as Shakespeare's autobiographical drama'.[7] John Keats argued, for example, that Prince Hamlet was 'more like Shakespeare himself in his common every day Life than any other of his Characters'.[8] The Romantic identification of the artist and intellectual with Hamlet has become naturalised in subsequent accounts. Thomas Carlyle asked rhetorically, 'how could a man delineate a Hamlet [...] if his own heart had never suffered?'[9] T. S. Eliot observed more generally that creative 'minds often find in Hamlet a vicarious existence for their own realization'. His examples are Romantic: 'Such a mind had Goethe, who made of Hamlet a Werther; and such had Coleridge, who made of Hamlet a Coleridge.'[10] Indeed, the Romantic model of the artist has been so seductive to intellectuals in the post-Romantic era, or age of mass culture, that it is not unusual to find Hamlet reinvented not simply as a model of the artistic or intellectual life but as a normative model of identity. Hamlet thus becomes not so much the archetypal intellectual but simply archetypal – Hamlet as Everyman. The Romanticist Harold Bloom, for example, has claimed Hamlet as 'the paradigm for all introspection since the Renaissance period'. In the context of a discussion of Hamlet, he goes further, claiming:

> The tragic hero in Shakespeare [...] is a representation so original that conceptually *he contains us*, and fashions our psychology of motives permanently. Our map or general theory of motives may be Freud's, but Freud, like all the rest of us, inherits the representation of the mind, at its most subtle and excellent, from Shakespeare.[11]

In a cruder formulation of the same idea, Martin Scofield describes *Hamlet* as 'a mirror in which every man has seen his own face'.[12]

New Historicist critics have argued (like Bloom) that the Renaissance, and particularly Shakespeare, inaugurated 'a recognizably modern literature of individuated, motivated character'.[13] Jonathan Arac has countered convincingly that this view is undermined by its failure to recognise that this 'modern' Shakespeare, and indeed this 'modern' model of character, are Romantic constructs.[14] It is no accident that Coleridge was arguably the most influential Shakespearean critic of the Romantic period as well as an enthusiast of the emergent science of 'psychology'; indeed, he was one of the first to use the terms 'psychological' and 'psychologist'. The *OED*'s example of Coleridge's use of the term 'psychological' is interestingly with reference to Shakespeare: 'Shakespeare was pursuing two Methods at once; and besides the

Psychological Method, he had also to attend to the Poetical. [*Note*] We beg pardon for the use of this insolens verbum: but It Is one of which our Language stands in great need.'[15] *Hamlet* was of course crucial to Coleridge's thinking about both Shakespeare and himself and it is a text central to the growth of character criticism, psychology and psychoanalysis in the nineteenth century.[16] In Arac's words, 'In the literary development of character in the nineteenth century the depths, recesses, and intricacy made possible by [...] self-alienation, [...] became the model for what it was to be a character.'[17]

What Arac does not stress, however, is that the Romantic model of self, epitomised by its construction of Hamlet, was clearly shaped by a deep fear of the 'mass'. Valorisation of interiority, individuality and intellect is a response to, arguably a retreat from, external dangers. The Romantic 'turn inwards' can be interpreted in many ways, most obviously perhaps as a response to the barbarism of the French Revolution, and to industrialisation and the mechanisation attending it. Fear of mass culture, however, or of shifting patterns of cultural ownership, is at least as visible in Romantic literary criticism. This is particularly true of criticism of the theatre, perhaps, because the Romantic period saw the emergence and dominance not of a second Shakespeare, but of melodrama. Melodrama was a genre specifically designed for, and hugely popular with, the illiterate and artisans. Guilbert de Pixérécourt, the self-styled 'father of le mélodrame', declared openly: 'I am writing for those who cannot read.'[18] He developed 'a melodramatic artistry aimed entirely at an unlettered populace', which proved so successful on its importation to Britain that it became the most popular kind of theatrical entertainment for much of the nineteenth century.[19] Moreover, 'more people went to the theatre during the nineteenth century than at any time in history'.[20] Melodrama is an anti-intellectual genre which employs externalised aesthetics – music, gesture, the body, heightened, simple, emotional language – to communicate an often simple moral message to its audience. The melodramatic aesthetic system proved so successful that even the plays of Shakespeare were frequently subjected to melodramatic treatment. The opinion of a London costermonger, for example, that '*Macbeth* would be better liked if it was only the witches and the fighting' conveys a sense that the acting of Mr Wopsle, or indeed the players in *Hamlet*, would not have been out of place on the nineteenth-century stage.[21]

There is no doubt that Romantic essayists perceived the mass appeal of melodrama as a cultural and intellectual threat. Leigh Hunt was explicitly dismissive of melodrama: 'As to melodrama, nobody looks for expression in the whiskered cheeks and Tamerlane gestures of a bandit: an elephant can dispense with delicacy of inspection.'[22] When an after-piece of his was rejected by 'the public', Lamb sought solace in a club of like-minded people who subscribed to the idea that theatre audiences (the 'public, or mob') were 'senseless, illiterate savages', 'capricious ungrateful rabble' – the opposite, in fact, of the 'man of genius'.[23] Coleridge regarded melodrama as a 'modern Jacobinical drama', while other contemporaries attacked its 'monstrous aesthetic configuration' and criminal audiences.[24] It is arguable, in fact, that discussions of Shakespeare by Coleridge and Lamb are responses to the growing popularity of melodrama and its tendency to popularise figures like Hamlet, Macbeth and Richard III (as Coleridge and Lamb see it). Most telling of all is the fact that it is only in the 1810s that they begin to write about drama in this way – as melodrama rises to prominence. Charles Lamb's famous elevation of the experience of reading Shakespeare over that of seeing Shakespeare performed, for example, renders explicit the cultural élitism which regularly informs high Romantic denunciation of the theatre and the mass culture it could appear to represent; visible 'signs' of emotion are more vulgar than its invisible workings, emotional experience unmediated by the mind is 'low', action is less interesting than motive:

> To know the internal workings and movements of a great mind, of an Othello or a Hamlet [...] seems to demand a reach of intellect of a vastly different extent from that which is employed upon the bare imitation of the signs of these passions in the countenance or gesture, which signs are usually observed to be most lively and emphatic in the weaker sorts of minds, and which signs can after all but indicate some passion, [...] anger, or grief, generally; but of the motives and grounds of the passion, wherein it differs from the same passion in low and vulgar natures, of these the actor can give no more idea by his face or gesture than the eye [...] can speak, or the muscles utter intelligible sounds.[25]

Intelligent people, Lamb argues, experience the same passions as 'low and vulgar natures'; what makes intelligent people more valuable than 'weaker sorts of minds' (not people) is 'the internal workings and movements' of their minds. The claim that Othello, like Hamlet, has a 'great mind' is not only difficult to credit; it shows how intellectual acumen was in danger of becoming the universal yardstick by which to approve literary character in Romantic criticism. Hamlet, of course, had become the epitome of just such a character.

Throughout Dickens's many references to *Hamlet*, there are few if any that are complimentary about the play's central character as an archetype or role model. Perhaps the most explicit reference comes in *A Christmas Carol*, where Dickens refers to Hamlet's 'weak mind'. Interestingly, in this quotation and many others, what most seems to preoccupy Dickens is Hamlet's difficult relations with others, particularly his family. He writes:

> If we were not perfectly convinced that Hamlet's Father died before the play began, there would be nothing more remarkable in his taking a stroll at night, in an easterly wind, upon his own ramparts, than there would be in any other middle-aged gentleman rashly turning out after dark in a breezy spot – say Saint Paul's churchyard for instance – literally to astonish his son's weak mind. (*A Christmas Carol* (1843), Stave One)

In the original manuscript of *Carol*, the following digression was included after the preceding quotation, only to be deleted subsequently:

> Perhaps you think that Hamlet's intellects were strong. I doubt it. If you could have such a son tomorrow, depend upon it, you would find him a poser. He would be a most impracticable fellow to deal with, and however creditable he might be to his family, after his decease, he would prove a special incumbrance in his lifetime, trust me.[26]

In 'Gone Astray', Dickens's narrator writes: 'I considered him the glass of fashion and the mould of form: a very Hamlet without the burden of his difficult family affairs,' (*Household Words*, 13 August 1853). Indeed, the ghost of Hamlet's father seems to gain more overt sympathy from Dickens than his analytical son. Joe Gargery's comment in *Great Expectations* seems to capture the tone of several of Dickens's remarks nicely: 'Which I meantersay, if the ghost of a man's own father cannot be allowed to claim his attention, what can, Sir?' (vol. II, ch. 8). Though 'derisive laughter', as Michael Slater terms it, is not always the keynote of Dickens's references to Hamlet, his point seems to be that Hamlet's self-absorption causes great difficulties for others and is not primarily the product of difficulties that others force upon him.[27] In other words, the Romantic model of the 'egotistical sublime' is anti-social and regressive rather than modern and progressive. The lack of real understanding that must characterise Hamlet's intellect is comically reinforced in a letter to C. C. Felton (21 May 1842): 'I would give something [...] if you could only stumble into that very dark and dusty Theatre [...] and see me, with my coat off, the Stage Manager and Universal Director [...] endeavouring to goad Hamlet into some dim and faint understanding of a prompter's duties.'[28] Gager's interpretation of this reference as 'a role-reversal joke on Hamlet's advice to the players'[29] is supported not only by Dickens's non-fictional remarks on Hamlet but by his fictional treatment of the Prince of Denmark.

In his most extended inter-textual treatment of *Hamlet* in *Great Expectations*, for example, Dickens's technique involves looking at Hamlet from the perspective of an audience who refuse to engage with or understand abstract speculation. In Shakespeare's *Midsummer Night's Dream*, the literalness of Bottom's players is the butt of the joke, but in the *Hamlet* of *Great Expectations*, literalness exacts its revenge. Juxtaposition of the hyperbolic with the bathetic, the extraordinary with the familiar, is the key to Dickens's humour in his description of Wopsle's Hamlet, and indeed in many of his other descriptions of the minor theatre. (We think most obviously, for example, of the Crummleses centring their theatricals around a 'pump-and-tub scene' (ch. 24), for example, in *Nicholas Nickleby*.) Furthermore, as John Carey observes, Dickensian comedy often 'consists of seeing what is actually there instead of what convention has agreed to pretend is there'.[30] Thus, the chapter devoted to Wopsle's Hamlet (*Great Expectations*, vol. II, ch. 12) begins by describing 'the king and queen of that country [Denmark] elevated in two arm-chairs on a kitchen-table'. They are attended by 'a venerable Peer with a dirty face who seemed to have risen from the people late in life', among others. The ghost has a cough and has his lines – 'a ghostly manuscript' – attached to a truncheon, 'to which it had the appearance of occasionally referring, and that, too, with an air of anxiety and a tendency to lose the place of reference which were suggestive of a state of mortality'.

Thus far, Dickens's comic technique does not seem that dissimilar to that of Shakespeare in *A Midsummer Night's Dream*, but the key difference between the play-within-a-text scenes resides in the composition and demands of the respective audiences. Whereas the play-within-a-play scenes in both *Dream* and *Hamlet* consist of an aristocratic audience humouring players who are less cultured and educated than themselves, nineteenth-century theatre history would strongly suggest that Wopsle – who has probably paid to perform – is playing to a predominantly artisan audience. The audience does not, then, as in *Dream*, demand more imagination from the players; they demand more pragmatism and common sense from the characters represented. In *Nicholas Nickleby*, the players and their props are the butt of the joke. But in *Great Expectations*, the play and its central character become as much an object of derision as the players and their homely props. The audience's ready answers to Hamlet's philosophical (and rhetorical) questions indicate more than their frustration with the quality of the production; they demonstrate quite clearly the gap between Hamlet's 'archetypal' sensibility and the sensibility of the average working man in the nineteenth century. Perspective is of course all in both tragedy and comedy; it takes only a turn of the screw to make any tragedy comic. In Shakespearean tragedy, if the audience views the protagonist from the outside rather than empathetically, the effect is frequently comic.[31] The majority of Dickens's references to *Hamlet* seem to be comic, but his master-stroke in *Great Expectations* is to make the audience answer back:

> Whenever that undecided Prince had to ask whether 'twas nobler in the mind to suffer, some roared yes, and some no, and some inclining to both opinions said 'toss up for it'; and quite a Debating Society arose. When he asked what should such fellows as he do crawling between earth and heaven, he was encouraged by loud cries of 'Hear! Hear!' (vol. II, ch. 12)

In some of Dickens's writings on the illegitimate theatre, the treatment of the audience is arguably patronising (the treatment of the archetypal artisan Joe Whelks in 'The Amusements of the People' and subsequent journalistic writings by Dickens is an obvious example).[32] But what is interesting in this chapter is that the audience's sentiments are endorsed rather than mocked by Pip the narrator. Furthermore, Pip's perspective in this scene is not undermined by the double perspective which runs through the novel. Perhaps the most interesting incident is Dickens's rendering of Wopsle's play-within-a-play scene from *Hamlet*: 'When he recommended the player not to saw the air thus, the sulky man [from the gallery] said, "And don't *you* do it, neither; you're a deal worse than *him!*" ' (*Great Expectations*, vol. II, ch. 12). It is easy to assume that Wopsle's acting is the only joke here. It is equally plausible, however, that Dickens is mocking Hamlet's performance of authenticity and intellect, as stylised in its way as the formulaic over-acting of the players. Certainly, self-importance founded on superiority of class, money and/ or education is remorselessly mocked (as well as subtly analysed) throughout the novel. Wopsle, in the same chapter, for example, sustains his absurdity by maintaining, as if still in character as Hamlet: 'My view is a little classic and thoughtful for them here; but they will improve, they will improve.' The performance underlying Pip's assumed social superiority is rendered most comically obvious in the novel by Trabb the tailor's boy's pantomimic shadowing and imitation of the dandyish Pip.

It would clearly be a falsification of the text, however, to argue that Dickens unambiguously disapproves of Pip's aspirations. The double time-scheme of the narrative enables the interweaving of sympathy and critique in response to Pip's expectations in *Great Expectations*. Pip's sense of guilt, alienation, secrecy and (misplaced) duty reminds us of the similar feelings experienced by Shakespeare's Prince of Denmark – though it is important to note that Pip's self-analysis is for the most part conveyed implicitly through outwardly focused story-telling rather than through explicit, inwardly focused self-*analysis*. It is a cliché of Dickens criticism that he dramatises rather than analyses character, and this is no less true of a late novel like *Great Expectations* than it is of the early works. Less commented upon is Dickens's use of intertextual references for implicit character analysis, and it will come as no surprise that the *Hamlet* references in *Great Expectations* are not confined to the performance of Wopsle. At the end of the chapter including Wopsle's performance as Hamlet, for example, Pip turns in for the night with the gloomy grandeur of the great Dane, explicitly comparing himself to his Shakespearean predecessor:

> Miserably I went to bed after all, and miserably thought of Estella, and miserably dreamed that my expectations were all cancelled, and that I had to give my hand in marriage to Herbert's Clara, or play Hamlet to Miss Havisham's Ghost, before twenty thousand people, without knowing twenty words of it. (vol. II, ch. 12)

Pip does of course play Hamlet to Miss Havisham's ghost for much of the novel, before the revelation that Magwitch is his benefactor jolts him from actor as role-player to actor as man of action. Pip's anxious dream, in which he is to act a part he does not know, crystallises the sense of imposture which attends him throughout the novel, the sense that his outward seeming is a cloak for the criminal self that exists within.

Interestingly, Pip's identification with Hamlet is less obvious to the casual reader than his identification with George Barnwell, the artisan protagonist of George Lillo's domestic tragedy, *The London Merchant; or, The History of George Barnwell* (1731), which was hugely popular with Victorian theatre audiences. William Axton has argued convincingly that the intertextual references to *The London Merchant* in *Great*

Expectations act as a commentary on Pip's situation.[33] It is not difficult to see how they do so: the play shows how a good young man's passion for a bad woman who is his social superior (Millwood) leads him to murder his uncle for money, an act which leads to the death by hanging of himself and his accomplice. In *Great Expectations*, it is again Mr Wopsle who plays the tragic protagonist, in this case Barnwell: considering that 'a special Providence had put a 'prentice in his way to be read at' (vol. I, ch. 15), he reads the play at Pip.[34] Interestingly, there is no sense of comedy in (an admittedly younger) Pip's response to the reading:

> What stung me, was the identification of the whole affair with my unoffending self. When Barnwell began to go wrong, I declare that I felt positively apologetic [...] At once ferocious and maudlin, I was made to murder my uncle with no extenuating circumstances whatever; [...] all I can say for my grasping and procrastinating conduct on the fatal morning is, that it was worthy of the general feebleness of my character. Even after I was happily hanged and Wopsle had closed the book, Pumblechook sat staring at me, and shaking his head, and saying, 'Take warning, boy, take warning!' as if it were a well known fact that I contemplated murdering a near relation, provided I could only induce one to have the weakness to become my benefactor. (vol. I, ch. 15)

Dickens's language in the passage lends weight to Gager's view that 'Although ostensibly referring to Lillo's work, the strong Hamlet–Claudius–Ophelia parallels are unmistakable' in this passage.[35] What Gager does not explain, however, is why Dickens chose Barnwell and not Hamlet as the most prominent symbol of Pip's guilt and anxiety, while 'Wopsle is identified with Hamlet throughout the novel'.[36] When Pip hears of the attack on his sister, for example, we read that 'With my head full of George Barnwell, I was at first disposed to believe that *I* must have had some hand in the attack upon my sister' (vol. I, ch. 16). It is noteworthy that Pip relates to the character of George Barnwell as if he is a real person, whereas after seeing Wopsle's Hamlet, Pip worries that he might have to act the role of Hamlet. While Wopsle and Hamlet have in common a lack of perspective on their own self-importance, Pip and George Barnwell share a similar class background and a taste for deviant, socially superior women.

Pip's sense of alienation, rootlessness and uncertainty in the text, all qualities he shares with Hamlet, are identified in the novel as products of his class background and mobility rather than of a trans-historical artistic sensibility. Indeed, whenever men – and it is always men – suffer from Romantic *weltschmertz* or world-weariness in the novels, Dickens is at greater pains to historicise the state of mind than he is to invoke Hamlet as the first father of the 'modern' sensibility. Eugene Wrayburn, in *Our Mutual Friend*, for example, is a displaced aristocrat trying to negotiate the Victorian middle-class work ethic and his desire for a lower-class woman.[37] Arthur Clennam – with his Hamlet-like instruction, 'Do Not Forget' – is the personification of the insecurity of the middle classes in the Victorian age. The historical conditions which contribute to the masculine, internalised angst which pervades Dickens's late novels in particular – class mobility, industrialisation, urbanisation, secularisation, individualism – are all very much of the nineteenth century. Whilst it may be 'modern' for writers to describe this condition, Dickens refuses to either accept or glamorise it. He is particularly alert to the choices available to the artist in an increasingly fragmented society. Thus, while he despises a character like Henry Gowan who believes in nothing, particularly his art and its consumers, David Copperfield is a model of the artist who can lead a good and useful 1life.

David Copperfield writes, but like Dickens, he does not write or even talk much about writing. He is an author who is an observer rather than the centre of attention. He is outwardly focused rather than self-reflexive. He represents an alternative to the narcissistic, alienated model of the artist which proved so seductive to the Romantics of the nineteenth century. *David Copperfield* is a novel laced with references to *Hamlet*. But it would be a mistake to assume, as Gager does, that Hamlet is a model for David. Her claims that '*Hamlet* may be viewed as a first-person narrative with its protagonist as author' and '*Hamlet* may be considered the most "novelistic" of Shakespeare's dramas'[38] demonstrate the extent to which certain myths have become naturalised: first, the idea of Hamlet as archetypal artist, second, the idea that *Hamlet* the play is synonymous with its protagonist, and third, the idea that investigations of subjectivity must always be 'novelistic'. As has already been suggested, Dickens was acutely aware that *Hamlet* offered its audience far more than its central character, and indeed, that *Hamlet* was a play and not a novel or first-person narrative of any kind. *David Copperfield* deliberately forges a model of the artist to counter that of the Romantic Hamlet. *Hamlet* references in *David Copperfield* are designed to demonstrate the gulf which exists between David, who makes practical use of his intellect through writing, and Hamlet, who uses words to evade action. Gager's interpretation of the following quotations from *David Copperfield* and

Hamlet respectively as similar in import, for example, shows the extent to which she is intent on discerning synonymity rather than dissonance.[39] Where David announces his identity straightforwardly, 'I am David Copperfield, of Blunderstone' (ch. 13), Hamlet's self-description draws attention to his fractured sense of identity with a strategically placed line break – 'This is I, / Hamlet the Dane!' (*Hamlet*, V. 1. 257–8). Again, where Hamlet consciously vacillates between an inwardly focused sense of self and paranoid speculation about how others perceive him and his self-projections, David is often as innocent as a 'daisy' about the perceptions of others and, arguably, about his own personality. His naivety about role-playing of all sorts, as well as perhaps about himself, is most memorably demonstrated in the scene in which he becomes reacquainted with Steerforth after a trip to the theatre to see *Julius Caesar* and a pantomime. David is so absorbed by 'the mingled reality and mystery of the whole show' that afterwards he feels as if he has 'come from the clouds' to a 'muddy, miserable world' (ch. 19). When David tells Steerforth that he thought the play 'a delightful and magnificent entertainment', the more worldly Steerforth laughs: 'you are a very Daisy. The daisy of the field, at sunrise, is not fresher than you are. [...] there never was a more miserable business' (ch. 19). Throughout the novel, it is Steerforth who possesses the self-conscious, theatrical sophistication and angst of Hamlet, while David remains an onlooker rather than a performer, a remarkably unobtrusive narrator and artist.

The remarkable ordinariness of David is of course deliberate. Dickens's desire to professionalise the reputation of novel-writing is well known. While he wanted to establish novel-writing as a worthy occupation, however, he rejected the Romantic mystification of the artist. Artists were not, in Shelley's terms, 'the unacknowledged legislators of the world', but they were respectable, productive citizens engaged in regular work.[40] The startling disjunction between the amount of fiction that Dickens produced and the little he talked or wrote about it is testimony to his belief in the desirable invisibility of artistry. This is nowhere better demonstrated than in a letter to G. H. Lewes of [?9 June] 1838. In answer to Lewes's enquiry about how he came to describe the mental state between sleeping and waking in chapter 34 of *Oliver Twist*, Dickens replied:

> How it came I can't tell. It came like all my ideas, such as they are, ready made to the point of the pen – and down it went. Draw your own conclusion and hug the theory closely. [...] The truth is [...] that if readers cannot detect the point of a passage without having

their attention called to it by the writer, I would much rather they lost it and looked for something else.[41]

Dickens and David have in common the way in which they view novel-writing as work to be done (rather than 'performed') and not analysed. David, moreover, is an even better role model than Dickens of the artist as worker because he lacks the dominating personality and celebrity of his creator. It is notable how many of the early chapter titles in *David Copperfield* begin with the first person 'I': 'I am Born', 'I Observe', 'I have a Change', to give just a few examples. But it is equally striking that each title seems to denote an event or an action rather than indicating a subject-centred process of self-analysis or a stage of self-discovery. David as subject is rendered conspicuously inconspicuous. Indeed, when self-discovery or self-analysis does occur, it is ruthlessly repressed. Perhaps the best example comes at the end of chapter 14 before the chapter entitled 'I Make Another Beginning':

Thus I began my new life, in a new name, and with everything new about me. Now that the state of doubt was over, I felt, for many days, like one in a dream. [...] The clearest things in my mind were, that a remoteness had come upon the old Blunderstone life – which seemed to lie in the haze of an immeasurable distance; and that a curtain had fallen over my life at Murdstone and Grinby's. No one has ever raised that curtain since. I have lifted it for a moment, even in this narrative, with a reluctant hand, and dropped it gladly. The remembrance of that life is fraught with so much pain to me, with so much mental suffering and want of hope, that I have never had the courage to examine how long I was doomed to lead it. Whether it lasted for a year, or more, or less, I do not know. I only know that it was, and ceased to be; and that I have written, and there I leave it. (ch. 14)

Significantly, the next chapter begins with Mr Dick, an author who cannot write or progress because he is unable to escape from the suffering of his part. Self-development, in David's case, is an act of self-creation or self-determination enabled only because he refuses to think of his life as an organic, linear narrative or 'bildungsroman'. The idea that abrupt transformation is as faithful a model of self-development as the Romantic idea of organic growth is one that Dickens found vividly embodied in the nineteenth-century theatre. Transformation was the essence of the kind of nineteenth-century pantomime which David and Steerforth observe in the novel, and pantomime references are indeed as important in the novel as Shakespearean allusions.[42] In melodrama too, abrupt transitions of emotion rather than identity are the norm, as is transparency of selfhood. In chapter 17 of *Oliver Twist* Dickens memorably likens life to melodrama, 'the tragic and comic scenes, in as regular alternation, as the layers of red and white in a side of streaky, well-cured bacon'.[43] Success as an artist and psychological health depend on *not* growing in the sense that we post-Freudians have come to understand growth. Unlike Hamlet, David can progress because he strives to escape rather than interrogate the self.

Dickens's novelistic allusions to *Hamlet* invariably violate the illusion that Hamlet is Everyman by framing them with people with a more obvious claim, in a nineteenth-century context, to represent every man. Humour often frames Hamlet allusions – Micawber, for example, is implicitly compared to Hamlet throughout *David Copperfield* – but even when it does not, as in the case of Clennam and Wrayburn, Dickens's message is the same. Excessive introspection is no substitute for socially constructive action. In an academic environment, it is very easy to accept the notion that the Romantic Hamlet is archetypally 'modern' but Dickens reminds us that outside academia, the Prince of Denmark would appear anything but typical. This technique, moreover, goes further than subverting the notion that Hamlet's sensibility is universal; it reveals this particular kind of sensibility to be no natural characteristic of the artist or intellectual. The Romantic Hamlet naturalised during the nineteenth century was a particular kind of intellectual, one who, to Dickens, suggested a reactionary othering of the masses and their culture by an intelligentsia refusing to engage with the challenges of modernity.

Notes

This essay is indebted to the scholarship of Valerie L. Gager's *Shakespeare and Dickens: the Dynamics of Influence* (Cambridge: Cambridge University Press, 1996), which has proved an invaluable source of reference. I would also like to thank Calum Forsyth and Alice Jenkins for helping me to write it. I have used the Clarendon edition of Dickens's novels where available and the Oxford Illustrated where the Clarendon is unavailable, unless otherwise stated. Given the wide range of editions in which these novels are available, however, I normally cite only chapter numbers (or where appropriate, volume, book, and chapter).

1. Valerie L. Gager, *Shakespeare and Dickens: the Dynamics of Influence* (Cambridge: Cambridge University Press, 1996), p. 58.

2. *The Dickens Index* by Nicolas Bentley, Michael Slater and Nina Burgis (Oxford: Oxford University Press, 1988) lists more references to *Hamlet* than to any other Shakespeare play.
3. 'Dickens in Relation to Criticism', *Fortnightly Review*, 11 (Feb. 1872), 141–54 (pp. 151–4).
4. *Victorian Poetry: Poetry, Poetics, Politics* (London: Routledge, 1993), p. 3.
5. *Shakespeare and the English Romantic Imagination* (Oxford: Clarendon Press, 1989), p. 19. I was reminded of several of the quotations in this paragraph by Gager's *Shakespeare and Dickens*.
6. In his Preface to *The Plays of William Shakespeare*, Johnson wrote: 'In the writings of other poets a character is too often an individual; in those of Shakespeare it is commonly a species' – *Samuel Johnson*, The Oxford Authors, ed. by Donald Greene (Oxford: Oxford University Press, 1984), pp. 419–56 (p. 421); *Coleridge's Shakespearean Criticism*, ed. by Thomas Middleton Raysor, 2 vols (London: Constable, 1930), II, 352.
7. Gager, p. 242.
8. *The Letters of John Keats*, ed. by Maurice Buxton Forman, 3rd edn (London: Oxford University Press, 1947), p. 347 (to Miss Jeffrey, 9 June 1819).
9. 'The Hero as Poet' (Lecture III), in *On Heroes and Hero-Worship and the Heroic in History*, from *Past and Present and Heroes and Hero-Worship* (London: Chapman and Hall, 1893), pp. 1–232 (p. 101).
10. 'Hamlet', *Selected Essays* (1932; London: Faber & Faber, 1959), p. 141.
11. Introduction, *William Shakespeare: the Tragedies*, Modern Critical Views (New York: Chelsea House, 1985), p. 3.
12. *The Ghosts of Hamlet: the Play and Modern Writers* (Cambridge: Cambridge University Press, 1980), p. 3.
13. Joel Fineman, 'The Turn of the Shrew', in *Shakespeare and the Question of Theory*, ed. by Patricia Parker and Geoffrey Hartman (London: Methuen, 1985), p. 157.
14. 'Hamlet, *Little Dorrit*, and the History of Character', in *Critical Conditions: Regarding the Historical Moment*, ed. by Michael Hays (Minneapolis: University of Minnesota Press, 1992), pp. 82–96.
15. *Diss. Sc. Method*, ii. 40.
16. See, for example, his lecture on *Hamlet* (2 January 1812).
17. Arac, p. 89.
18. Maurice Willson Disher, *Blood and Thunder: Mid-Victorian Melodrama and its Origins* (London: Muller, 1949), p. 62.
19. Michael R. Booth, *English Melodrama* (London: Jenkins, 1965), pp. 44–5.
20. Gabrielle Hyslop, 'Researching the Acting of French Melodrama, 1800–1830', *Nineteenth Century Theatre*, 15 (1987), 85–114 (p. 85).
21. Quoted by Henry Mayhew, *London Labour and the London Poor: a Cyclopaedia of the Condition and Earnings of Those That Will Work, Those That Cannot Work, and Those That Will Not Work*, 3 vols (London: Morning Chronicle, 1851), I, 15.
22. Hunt, 'Patent Theatres and Mr Arnold (27 January 1831), in *Dramatic Criticism*, ed. by Lawrence Huston Houtchens and Carolyn Washburn Houtchens (New York: Columbia University Press, 1949), pp. 256–60 (pp. 257–8); quoted in Rodney Stenning Edgecombe, 'Dickens, Hunt and the "Dramatic Criticism" in *Great Expectations*: A Note', *Dickensian*, 88 (1992), 82–90 (p. 85). Much of the material in this paragraph is taken from my book, *Dickens's*

Villains: Melodrama, Character, Popular Culture (Oxford: Oxford University Press, 2001), ch. 2.

23. Charles Lamb, 'On the Custom of Hissing at the Theatres, with Some Accounts of a Club of Damned Authors' (1811), in *The Works of Charles and Mary Lamb*, ed. by E. V. Lucas, 6 vols (London: Methuen, 1912), I, 101–7 (p. 105). Hays and Nikolopoulou suggest that Lamb's opposition had general currency (*Melodrama: the Cultural Emergence of a Genre*, p. viii).

24. Coleridge, 'Critique of [Maturin's] *Bertram*' (repr. from *Courier*, Aug. and Sept. 1816), in *Biographia Literaria*, ch. 23, in *The Collected Works of Samuel Taylor Coleridge*, ed. by James Engell and W. Jackson Bate, 16 vols, Bollingen Series, XXV (London: Routledge & Kegan Paul, 1983), VII, 207–33 (p. 221); Hays and Nikolopoulou, introduction to *Melodrama: the Cultural Emergence of a Genre*, p. viii.

25. Lamb, 'On the Tragedies of Shakespeare, Considered with Reference to their Fitness for Stage Representation' (1811), in *Romantic Critical Essays*, ed. by David Bromwich, Cambridge English Prose Texts (Cambridge: Cambridge University Press, 1987), pp. 56–70 (p. 57).

26. Quoted by Michael Slater in his notes to *A Christmas Carol* in *The Christmas Books*, 2 vols (Harmondsworth: Penguin, 1971), I, 257.

27. 'Some Remarks on Dickens's Use of Shakespearean Allusions', *Studies in English and American Literature in Honour of Witold Ostrowski* (Warsaw: Polish Scientific Publishers, 1984), p. 142; cited by Gager, p. 10.

28. *The Letters of Charles Dickens*, ed. by Madeline House, Graham Storey and Kathleen Tillotson, Pilgrim Edition (Oxford: Clarendon Press), III, 243–4.

29. Gager, p. 272.

30. John Carey, *The Violent Effigy: a Study of Dickens' Imagination* (London: Faber & Faber, 1973), p. 55.

31. In ch. 17 of *Oliver Twist*, Dickens himself comments on the effect of perspective in the theatre: 'Such changes appear absurd; but they are not so unnatural as they would seem at first sight. [...] The actors in the mimic life of the theatre, are blind to violent transitions and abrupt impulses of passion or feeling, which, presented before the eyes of mere spectators, are at once condemned as outrageous and preposterous.'

32. See *Household Words*, I (30 March 1850), 13–15, and (13 April 1850), 57–60.

33. See Axton's *Circle of Fire: Dickens' Vision and Style and the Popular Victorian Theatre* (Lexington: University of Kentucky Press, 1966).

34. 'A special providence' is of course an echo of *Hamlet*, V. 2. 219–20.

35. Gager, p. 274.

36. Gager, p. 294.

37. Wrayburn consciously compares himself with Hamlet. See John, *Dickens's Villains*, pp. 195–6, for an analysis of Eugene and Hamlet.

38. Gager, pp. 237, 241.

39. Gager, p. 238.

40. *A Defence of Poetry; or, Remarks Suggested by an Essay Entitled 'The Four Ages of Poetry'* (wr. 1821), in *Romanticism: an Anthology*, ed. by Duncan Wu (Oxford: Blackwell, 1994), pp. 956–69 (p. 969).

41. *Letters of Dickens*, Pilgrim Edition, I, 403–4.

42. See Edwin M. Eigner, *The Dickens Pantomime* (Berkeley and Los Angeles: University of California Press, 1989).

43. See also n. 31 above.

4
Shakespeare at the Great Exhibition of 1851

Clare Pettitt

In the British Nave of the Crystal Palace, sandwiched between an 'Improved open fire pedestal stove, with candelabrum for gas' by W. Bailey & Sons and an 'Ornamental rustic dome of cast-iron, bronzed, 20 feet in diameter by 30 feet high'; and some 'Garden-seats, [and] chairs' by the Coalbrook Dale Company, visitors to the Great Exhibition of 1851 would have found exhibit number 83, listed in the *Official Catalogue* as 'Unfinished statue of Shakspeare, from the Stratford bust' by John Bell (Figure 4.1).[1] According to the *Athenæum*, this was 'one of the noblest works in the Exhibition', and it was noteworthy enough for the official map of the Great Exhibition of the Works of Industry of All Nations to mark 'Shakspere' as one of its principal landmarks.[2]

Bell's full-length statue was among the most prominent of the many representations of Shakespeare at the exhibition. We are told that '[p]articularly admired was a round table of rosewood, finely inlaid with mother-of-pearl, metal and ivory, having in its centre a portrait of Shakespeare surrounded by scenes from [his plays]', and, in addition to the Shakespeare table, there was a Shakespeare salver, and a Shakespeare shield (Figure 4.2).[3] Titania and Ariel appeared often. J. G. Lough exhibited sculptures of Titania, Puck, and Ariel, for example, (Figures 4.3 4.4, 4.5), and the Coalbrook Dale Company offered a model of 'Puck throned on a Mushroom', by a Mr Pitts (Figure 4.6).[4] There was also a 'Model of Shakespeare's house as it now exists'; a sculpture of the Shakespeare Jubilee of 1769; an enamelled plate showing a scene from Shakespeare's *Richard II*; and a 'Profile bust of Shakspeare, in plaster of Paris, being made to imitate ivory, and being equal to it in hardness'.[5]

Elkington's of Birmingham, the firm at the forefront of the new electroplating technologies, exhibited an electroplate vase decorated on its four sides with statuettes representing Newton, Bacon,

Figure 4.1 'Unfinished statue of Shakspeare, from the Stratford bust', by John Bell

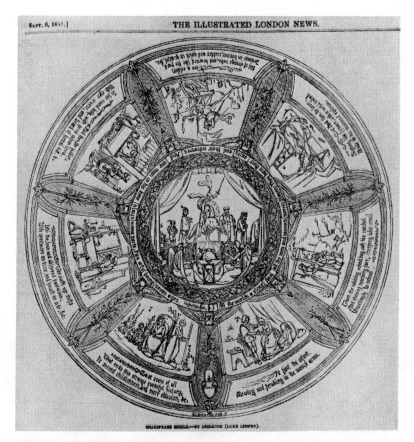

Figure 4.2   'The Shakespeare Shield', by Leighton (Luke Limner)

Shakespeare and Watt, with a model of Prince Albert 'surmounting the composition' (Figure 4.7).[6] The whole was 'intended to represent the triumph of science and the industrial Arts in the Great Exhibition'.[7] That Shakespeare and Watt appeared shoulder to shoulder on Elkington's vase demonstrates how slippery the boundaries between cultural production and commercial manufacturing seemed to have become at the Great Exhibition – an event which powerfully dramatised what Walter Benjamin was to identify as 'the forcefield between art and technology' in the nineteenth century.[8] Shakespeare is pressed into service alongside scientists and industrialists, as one of the 'authors' of modern Britain. The vase also offers material proof of how important it

Figure 4.3   Sculpture of Titania, by J. G. Lough

Lough's "Puck."

Figure 4.4 Sculpture of Puck, by J. G. Lough

Lough's " Ariel."

Figure 4.5   Sculpture of Ariel, by J. G. Lough

had become in 1851 to find an ancestry and provenance for modern inventive practices in order to defuse their threat to traditional notions of 'art'. Henry Ellison confronted just such a threat in a sonnet originally published in the year of the Exhibition, entitled, 'To Artists who Look with Jealous Eyes on Artistical Processes, Such as Chromalithography [*sic*], etc. etc'.

> Fear not – the great, creative mind of Man
> Takes a far wider scope than sense can span;
> And all these rare inventions have but worth
> As means and instruments, whereby he can
> Mould more completely to his will this earth,
> And give his own divine conceptions birth![9]

Industrial production processes put pressure on traditional eighteenth-century ideas of the creative individual, and the consequent anxiety about authorship surfaces in much of the literature surrounding the Exhibition.

Thomas Richards has pointed to the way that the exhibits in the Crystal Palace 'promised, in a way which it is very hard to pin down, that each and every one of them would one day be democratically available to anyone and everyone'.[10] The patriotic rhetoric which surrounded the Exhibition encouraged British visitors to feel a complacent sense of ownership and identity in what they saw there, celebrating, with the *Edinburgh Review*, 'the inventive genius of [England's] sons'.[11] Furthermore, the relentless emphasis on reproductive technologies in the Crystal Palace suggested a new 'democratic availability' for cultural artefacts, which it was now possible to copy and disseminate in larger numbers and more cheaply than ever before. The entire north-western corner of the building vibrated all day with 'Machinery in Motion', and some of the machines were manufacturing cultural artefacts on the premises, such as the vertical printing press 'invented by Mr Applegath' which was working at the Exhibition 'the whole time printing the "Illustrated News"'.[12] No Raphaels were on display, but a 'Photographic copy of Holloway's print of Raphael's Elymas' was.[13]

Indeed, visitors to the Exhibition could order copies of the Bell statue of Shakespeare from Henry Cole, the Chair of the Society of Arts, and one of the driving forces behind the 1851 event. His trading name was Felix Summerley, and his catalogue listed a 'Shakespeare Clock' also modelled by John Bell. Both the statue and the clock were manufactured in a new material, Parian, by Minton & Co. There was also listed 'The Shakespeare Salver or Card Dish', featuring designs by Daniel Maclise of 'The Seven Ages of Man'. Prospective buyers were assured that the electroplate dish 'will aim to be worthy of the best days of Benvenuto Cellini'.[14] Bell's statue, which was itself copied from the Janssen bust in the Holy Trinity Church, Stratford, spawned a new generation of copies in Felix Summerley's workshops.

John Ruskin, Henry Cole's adversary on many fronts, was horrified by the Crystal Palace, which he described as a 'colossal receptacle for casts and copies of the art of other nations'.[15] And indeed there was so much on display at the Exhibition of 1851 that was copied, imitated, die-cast, lithographed, electroplated, stereotyped, daguerrotyped, 'Talbotyped', 'galvano-plastic' and so on, that the event itself begged questions about the relationship of commercial to aesthetic value and the status of the 'authentic' and 'original' in an emerging economy of reproduction and imitation.[16] Much that was displayed as 'art' at the Exhibition was machine-made, even if hand-finished. Even the much-discussed statue, 'The Amazon' by Kiss, was a zinc and bronze copy of the original in Berlin, although most visitors seem to have been unaware of this, and approached it as if it were the original. Ruskin saw copying as the destruction of the original, and as tantamount to the destruction of history. When *he* gazed into the Crystal Palace to read the future, Ruskin saw only a sad travesty of the past, and history lying in ruins:

> We shall wander through our palaces of crystal, gazing sadly on copies of pictures torn by cannon-shot, and on casts of sculptures dashed to pieces long ago. We shall gradually learn to distinguish originality and sincerity from the decrepitudes of imitation and palsies of repetition; but it will be only in hopelessness.[17]

But the novelists, Charles Dickens and Wilkie Collins, took a more sanguine view. Dickens welcomed both new copyright legislation and the technological advances which he saw as leading to a wider dissemination of culture than had been possible in the eighteenth century. In a speech in 1853 he declared, 'I believe there are in Birmingham at this moment many working men infinitely better versed in Shakespeare and in Milton than the average of fine gentleman in the days of bought-and-sold dedications and dear books.'[18] For Dickens, the new cultural availability was a valuable solvent of a class hierarchy which he himself, 'not high bred but excellent company', had good reason to oppose.[19]

Figure 4.6 'Puck throned on a Mushroom', by Mr Pitts

So the surroundings in the Crystal Palace lent new, complex and contradictory significances to the images of Shakespeare for visitors to the 1851 Exhibition. At first glance, Shakespeare at the Exhibition was represented in the same way as the young Elizabeth Barrett Browning's 'Beloved Shakespeare! England's dearest fame!'[20] This Shakespeare stood seemingly unambiguously as an emblem and reminder of the Crystal Palace's central message, which Jeffrey Auerbach suggests was that 'Britain's greatness rested on the ideas and successes of its heroes'.[21] Yet images of the playwright also resonated in all kinds of contradictory ways with major debates and anxieties at mid-century about originality, authorship, and intellectual property: debates which the Exhibition also unwittingly put on display in the summer of 1851. For, while it presented a seeming cornucopia of democratically available products and knowledge, the Crystal Palace offered, at the same time, an energetic celebration of private property and ownership. Speaking about the forthcoming Exhibition, Prince Albert had claimed in 1849 that, 'knowledge acquired becomes at once the property of the community at large'.[22] Yet the Catalogue tells a different story, excusing the vagueness of some of its descriptions of exhibits as due to the inventor's desire 'to reveal as little as possible of the specific character of his articles', and the *Athenæum* had reported on the eve of the Exhibition, that '[a] fear of piracy was the shadow here and there infesting the general cordiality with which the [Exhibition] was hailed'.[23] Indeed, the Patent Amendment Act of 1852 was one of the most direct consequences of the Exhibition. Images of Shakespeare were perhaps so popular at the Exhibition because the Stratford playwright offered a symbolic resolution to this contradiction between public and private property – a contradiction enshrined in the patent and copyright laws themselves, which attempt a compromise between the work as the natural property of original and unique genius, and of the work as the property of the nation.

Mark Rose has suggested that in the copyright debates of the eighteenth and nineteenth centuries:

> The attempt to anchor the notion of literary property in personality suggests the need to find a transcendent signifier, a category beyond the economic to warrant and ground the circulation of literary commodities. Thus the mystification of original genius, pressed to its logical extreme in the limiting case of Shakespeare, became bardolatry.[24]

Indeed, Shakespeare was repeatedly cited in support of extending the copyright term for authors, although in the nineteenth-century debates,

Figure 4.7 Electroplate vase with statues of Newton, Bacon, Shakespeare and Watt, surmounted by Prince Albert

he comes to be used to underpin several different, and often opposed, points of view. Invoking the original 'genius' of Shakespeare in a bid to extend the copyright term to protect exceptional creative work, Wordsworth quoted approvingly from one of Thomas Talfourd's parliamentary speeches in a letter of 1838, 'but who will suggest that if Shakspeare [*sic*] had not written "Lear", or Richardson "Clarissa", other poets and novelists would have invented them? [...] Who can improve [...] these masterpieces of genius? They stand perfect, apart from all things else, self-sustained, the models for imitation, the source whence rules of art take their origin.'[25] Yet contrary to Talfourd and Wordsworth's view of Shakespeare as an exceptional and original talent, 'peerless and alone', Mr Fitzjames Stephen, arguing against proposals for copyright reform as obstructive to literary development in a Parliamentary Commission on Copyright later in the century, suggested that rather than creating original work, 'Shakespeare is supposed to have taken considerably from Hall and other works of that kind'.[26] Anthony Trollope, in his *Autobiography*, also punctured the image of Shakespeare as a disinterested 'genius' by insisting on the economic importance of copyright protection, '[a]s far as we know Shakespeare worked always for money, giving the best of his intellect to support his trade as an actor. [...] Take away from English authors their copyrights, and you would very soon take away from England her authors.'[27] Rose's portrayal of Shakespeare in the copyright debate as 'a category beyond the economic' is not, then, quite the whole picture. In the nineteenth century, 'Shakespeare' is also requisitioned by those who, like Trollope, portray the author as 'a man devoting himself to literature with industry, perseverance, [and] certain necessary aptitudes'.[28]

Others viewed Shakespeare less from the point of view of production than from that of consumption. *Macmillan's Magazine*, for example, in 1878, declared that 'no other [dramatist] ever so pleased every class of audience, from the roughs of California to the most cultivated gatherings of artists, poets, critics'.[29] Trevor Ross has argued that after the landmark copyright case of *Donaldson v. Becket* in 1774, 'the Works of *Shakespeare*, [were] declared to be the Property of any Person', adding that '[n]ever before in English history had it been possible to think that the nation's canonical literature might belong to the people'.[30] Leah Price has shown how late eighteenth-century compilers and scholars such as Knox and Enfield 'established Shakespeare's uniqueness by placing him in a generic vacuum', and Shakespeare's cross-class appeal was much celebrated in the Victorian period.[31] His anomalous status meant that he emerged from the copyright debates of the nineteenth century as a protean and fungible quantity. The image of Shakespeare, in fact, was able to perform complex ideological work: standing for both autonomous authorship (despite the fact that much of his work was collaborative and fundamentally 'unreproducible' as performance), and for the common patrimony of English culture, as distinct from the nobility of inherited class.[32]

In the years leading up to and just following the Great Exhibition, the provenance of Shakespeare's own texts fell under serious scrutiny. In 1853 John Payne Collier, founder of the Shakespeare Society, published his monumental edition of Shakespeare, incorporating much of his own re-writing, while Delia Bacon was busily researching her thesis that Bacon, in fact, was the author of Shakespeare's plays.[33] The ground was already being prepared for Frederick Furnivall and his quasi-scientific verse analysis techniques in the 1870s. This anxious quest for the authentic 'author' also made for acrimonious scuffles over representations of Shakespeare himself. At mid-century hundreds of fake portraits were circulating. In 1849, the *Athenæum* reported a controversy over the authenticity of the 'Chandos Portrait', which Collier's dealer claimed to be by Cornelius Janssen taken 'from the life' with only 'a few slight touches of re-paint'.[34] The *Athenæum* itself was sceptical, suggesting that the painting was instead, 'a copy made for Sir William Davenant from a portrait for which Shakespeare sat'.[35] In the late 1840s, efforts to locate and identify 'Shakespeare' were energetic: there was a move, for example, to renovate Shakespeare's house at Stratford. In 1848 Dickens and his amateur theatrical company put on a benefit performance of *The Merry Wives of Windsor* for the house, and the following year the *Athenæum* appealed for funds to save what it describes significantly as 'a relic so essentially *national*'.[36]

Shakespeare was perhaps even more appropriate as a dominant image at the Exhibition than at first appeared. Mechanised technologies of reproduction and the principle of division of labour had attenuated traditional ideas of authorship so that '[t]he most striking and serious difficulty felt by the committee, is that of determining to whom the merit of perfection in various branches of manufacture is to be attributed. [...] Who is to decide whether to the designer or to the manufacturer the palm of merit is due?'[37] The problem of distinguishing one originary source for much of what was on display at the exhibition was eloquently paralleled by the difficulty of knowing 'Shakespeare', which troubled nineteenth-century commentators in much the same way. He was the ultimate disappearing artist – the paucity of known facts or authentic records meant that, despite the mid-nineteenth century anxiety to locate the man, he was reachable only through copies, fair and otherwise, and unreliable reproductions. 'Shakespeare' was as much a fragile and embattled category to nineteenth-century readers, as he was totemic of a newly democratised and triumphalist culture.

Charles Dickens was involved in the administration of the Exhibition, and was lobbying for Henry Cole's suggested reforms to the patent laws, at the same time that he was setting up his own Guild of Literature and Art which was to offer aid 'to those who have made their order illustrious, [and] maintained the renown of their country in Literature and Art'.[38] In the summer of 1851, the Guild's fund-raising production of Edward Bulwer Lytton's play, *Not So Bad As We Seem*, was running in London alongside the Exhibition. In the play, the character of Wilmot, played by Dickens, disguises himself as the publisher Curll and refuses the poor poet, David Fallen's masterpiece saying that he '[c]an't expect such prices for poetry now-a-days, my dear Mr. Fallen. Nothing takes that is not sharp and spicy.'[39] Such a fear echoes Wordsworth's warning in the 1800 Preface to the *Lyrical Ballads* that '[t]he invaluable works of our elder writers, I had almost said the works of Shakespeare and Milton, are driven into neglect by frantic novels, sickly and stupid German Tragedies, and deluges of idle and extravagant stories in verse'.[40] The play energetically supports protection through copyright and public grants for the arts, while upholding a Romantic view of original and solitary genius.

A young Wilkie Collins was busy performing in Dickens's Guild play throughout most of 1851 and into 1852, while he was writing a 'Christmas Book' that he planned to call 'The Mask of Shakespeare'. The themes of Collins's Christmas book seem to have been suggested by the Guild's campaign for the protection of needy writers, and by the Great Exhibition's display of 'incessant copying without discrimination', as Matthew Digby Wyatt had put it.[41] Indeed, Collins seems to draw particularly upon Henry Cole's 'Felix Summerley' manufactory which was selling copies of Bell's version of the Janssen bust throughout the Exhibition. The relentless emphasis on reproductive technologies in the Crystal Palace suggested a new 'democratic availability' for cultural artefacts, which it was now possible to copy and disseminate in larger numbers and more cheaply than ever before, and this potential for the democratisation of culture lies at the heart of Collins's story.

'*King Public* is a good king for Literature and Art!' Collins declared at
the beginning of 1852 and in this story he seems less concerned with the
protection of intellectual property than with its dissemination.[42] The
'curious *fact*' that had suggested the story to Collins was that of a stone-
mason working in the Stratford-upon-Avon church, who had surrepti-
tiously taken 'a mould from the Shakespeare bust. What he had done
was found out, however; and he was forthwith threatened by the au-
thorities having care of the bust, with the severest pains and penalties of
the law – though for what special offence was not specified.'[43] But later
he is exonerated and assured 'that he need fear no penalty whatever, and
that if he thought he could dispose of them, he might make as many
casts as he pleased, and offer them for sale anywhere'. So he sold
'great numbers' of them in England and North America.[44] Collins
takes Shakespeare, seen in the early nineteenth century as the property
of the literate elite, and shows him as standing instead for a common
and accessible culture, just as the Bard had done at the Exhibition.
'What is Shakespeare' asks the narrator, 'but a great sun that shines
upon humanity – the large heads and the little, alike? Have not the
rays of that mighty light penetrated into many poor and lowly places for
good?' (p. 86).

Reuban Wray is an actor 'of the lower degree' (p. 83) and is 'a remnant
of a bygone age, [trying] to keep up with a new age which has already
got past him' (pp. 87–8). Wray, despite taking only 'spear-bearer' parts
on stage, knows every line of Shakespeare. On the night that he hides in
the church and secretly takes the cast he says, 'I felt as if I had robbed the
bank, or the King's jewels, or had set fire to a train of gunpowder to blow
up all London; it seemed such a thing to have done!' (p. 99).[45] Terrified
he may be arrested for his 'theft', he flees with his granddaughter and a
loyal artisan friend, known as Julius Caesar, and with the Shakespeare
cast packed in the 'cash-box' of the title. When he is later robbed, and
the cast smashed, Wray's own identity begins to fracture, and his sanity
is only saved because his granddaughter and Julius Caesar make the
journey back to Stratford to re-cast the bust. The family is adopted by
a wealthy benefactor, significantly named Mr Colebatch, who suggests
that Wray starts to produce the casts commercially, and the story ends
with the success of the new business. Thus, with the help of Colebatch's
benign patronage, Wray is able, after all, to 'keep up with the new age'.
Wray's poverty and low class status allow the story to establish a crucial
distinction between cultural and economic value: Wray is a poor man,
but his bust of the Bard is 'the treasure which the greatest lord in this
land doesn't possess' (p. 102). When he is persuaded to share this

treasure with 'other lovers of Shakspeare' (p. 137), surely Henry Cole (Colebatch) himself would have applauded the dissemination of cheap culture in 'batches'.

Wray insists that the Stratford bust is 'the only true likeness of Shakspeare! It's been done from a mask, taken from his own face after death – I know it, I don't care what people say, I know it,' (p. 96). Yet what Wray is happy to take as 'proof' (p. 102) in fact begs questions about the closeness of his copy to the 'original'. Wray's precious cast is, in fact, at a considerable remove from Shakespeare's living face if it is a cast of the bust which was 'done from' another cast of Shakespeare's face after death. Indeed, on his visit to Stratford in 1840, Tennyson had felt rather differently about the bust, 'I should not think it can be a very good likeness.[46] And Collins's story itself later demonstrates how copies can deceive by their very perfection. Wray's first cast, 'a beautiful cast! A perfect cast!' (p. 100) is later substituted by another, taken by his grand-daughter, and Wray's easy acceptance of the new cast as the old one stands as proof of the ability of copies to mask their true provenance. 'Shakespeare' is reproduced many times, and in various ways in the story, both on the stage and in plaster-of-Paris, but never so eloquently for the story's real theme, as when his image is smashed to smithereens by robbers. Wray's pathetic attempts to restore the cast starkly reveal the fragility of the icon, and the nullity behind it. Rather than leading back to Shakespeare, the text moves away, replacing one copy with another until the original is entirely effaced. Although the narrative does not seem fully aware of the modernity of its themes, it offers a vertiginous sense of the loss of the original, such as has fascinated writers on modernity from Benjamin to Baudrillard ever since. Jean Baudrillard, for example, makes the phenomenon central to his theory of modernity: 'the original no longer even exists, since things are conceived from the beginning as a function of their unlimited reproduction'.[47] No such pessimism is available in Collins's story, though – to a young writer in 1851 the prospect of easier and easier facilities of reproduction seemed liberating rather than threatening.

Yet, despite the rhetoric of democratic availability, 'Shakspeare' is not freely available to all at the end of the story, only to those who are able and prepared to pay the substantial price of a guinea for him. Rhetorically, the story seems to claim that 'culture' both has and does not have a price. The Exhibition dramatised a similar paradox, presenting itself as neither a museum nor a department store. While the Commission had decided that the objects displayed at the Exhibition should not carry price tags, they all had prices.[48] Charles Babbage felt that this decision was a grave mistake, '[t]he price in money is the *most important element* in every bargain; to omit it, is not less absurd than to represent a tragedy without a hero, or to paint a portrait without a nose'.[49] Collins, with Babbage, seems to celebrate a free-trade consumerism which transports culture into private, domestic spaces, thus, paradoxically, enabling the construction of a 'public' culture. As Dickens also saw, it was only by allowing and encouraging the private ownership of culture, through 'the increase of commerce and the exchange of commodities' that 'culture' could construct itself as a public phenomenon.[50] It is the image of Shakespeare that wakes Tidbury-on-the-Marsh from the economic paralysis of the story's opening scene, in which the branch banker vainly awaits a customer from behind 'the brass rails of his commercial prison-house' (p. 77). At the end of *Mr Wray's Cash-box*, Shakespeare has been transmogrified into a 'pretty round sum of money' – cultural capital has been converted into commercial capital, and Shakespeare is newly 'owned' by the 'loads' of people who desire a stake in the national heritage, and are able to afford one (p. 136).

Mr Wray's Cash-box clearly bears the imprint of the year in which it was written. The muddle of the narrative, which seems to end undecided as to whether culture is 'priceless', or costs a guinea, eloquently bespeaks the bewilderment of this period, which, as Dickens had told his Birmingham audience, saw more readers of Shakespeare than ever before. Howard Felperin and Marianne Novy, among others, have written about the 'the constitutional right of everyone [...] to read and comment on Shakespeare', in the nineteenth century, and such universality, in itself, raised anxieties.[51] *Punch* published a cartoon on 5 July 1851, entitled 'Dinner-Time at the Crystal Palace' (Figure 4.8). The cartoon shows Bell's statue of Shakespeare presiding over a crowd of proletarian visitors who perch around its base to eat their packed lunches and breast-feed their babies.[52] An inscription has been added, 'One touch of nature makes the whole world kin.' Initially, this seems to be a simple comment on Shakespeare as, in some ill-defined way, common property, 'the poetic bond that unites all men, however professional distance may separate them' (p. 84), as Collins puts it in *Mr Wray's Cash-box*, but if we trace the inscription back to *Troilus and Cressida*, we are guided to a less anodyne interpretation. In the play, Ulysses is trying to persuade Achilles to fight:

> One touch of nature makes the whole world kin,
> That all with one consent praise new-born gawds,
> Though they are made and moulded of things past,

Figure 4.8   'Dinner time at the Crystal Palace'

> And [give] to dust, that is a little gilt,
> More laud than gilt o'er-dusted.
> The present eye praises the present object.
> . . .
> Since things in motion sooner catch the eye
> [Than] what stirs not.
>
> (*Troilus and Cressida*, III. 3. 175–84)

Punch was initially critical of the Exhibition – Thackeray withdrew as a contributor partly because of the journal's unpatriotic attitude – but there is a fitting irony in the use of the 'unstirring' statue of the great Shakespeare to condemn the public's fascination with 'new-born gawds and things in motion'. Shakespeare may have been on show at the Exhibition to represent a glorious national heritage which both underpinned and transcended the new, but his image in the nineteenth century was as much a reminder of how that very past was necessarily 'made and moulded' over and again by the ever ongoing present.

Notes

1. *By Authority of the Royal Commission: Official Catalogue of the Great Exhibition of the Works of Industry of All Nations, 1851*, Third Corrected and Improved Edition, 1 August 1851 (London: Spicer Brothers, 1851), p. 10. Hereafter referred to as *Official Catalogue*.
2. Quoted from the *Athenæum* in Henry Cole, *Fifty Years of Public Work of Sir Henry Cole, K. C. B.* (London: George Bell and Sons, 1884), II, 183. Map in *Official Catalogue*, pp. 12–13.
3. Yvonne ffrench, *The Great Exhibition: 1851* (London: The Harvill Press, n.d. [?1951]), p. 246. 'Shakespeare Shield', *Official Catalogue*, p. 148.
4. For Lough's sculptures, see *Official Catalogue*, p. 8; W. Davis's Titania and Oberon, 'Come, trip we under the night-shade', p. 149; Miller's Bas-reliefs of Titania and Ariel, p. 155.
5. *Official Catalogue*, pp. 150, 152, 152 and 153.
6. *Art Journal Illustrated Catalogue* (London: Bradbury and Evans, 1851; repr. in facsimile: New York: Dover Publications Inc., 1970), p. 195.
7. *Art Journal*, p. 195.
8. Susan Buck-Morss, *The Dialectics of Seeing: Walter Benjamin and the Arcades Project* (Cambridge, MA and London: MIT Press, 1989), p. 124.
9. Henry Ellison, 'To Artists Who Look with Jealous Eyes on Artistical Processes, Such as Chromalithography, Etc. Etc.' in *The Poetry of Real Life. Sonnets.* (London: John Lee, 1854), p. 66.
10. Thomas Richards, *The Commodity Culture of Victorian England: Advertising and Spectacle* (London, NY: Verso, 1990), p. 19.
11. [Anon.], 'Art. II–1. *The Patent Journal*. Nos. 1.–100. London: 1846–7–8. 2. *The Mechanic's Magazine*. Vols XLVII. And XLVIII. London: 1846–7–8', *Edinburgh Review*, 89 (January 1849), 47–83, (p. 81).
12. Henry Hensman, 'On Civil Engineering and Machinery Generally', *Lectures on the Results of the Great Exhibition of 1851, Delivered Before the Society of Arts, Manufactures, and Commerce, at the Suggestion of H.R.H. Prince Albert, President of the Society* (London: David Bogue, 1852), v.i, 403–40 (p. 431).
13. *Official Catalogue*, p. 152.

14. Henry Cole, *Fifty Years*, v.ii, pp. 182, 183, 188. The dish, if not original, is an early example of the limited edition, 'a limited number of copies will be made [...] when the models will be destroyed' (p. 188).

15. John Ruskin, 'The Opening of the Crystal Palace Considered in Some of its Relations to the Prospects of Art', (London: Smith, Elder, and Co., 1854), p. 7. This pamphlet was published upon the re-opening of the Crystal Palace at its new site at Sydenham in 1854.

16. See Nikolaus Pevsner, *High Victorian Design: a Study of the Exhibits of 1851* (London: Architectural Press, 1951).

17. Ruskin, 'Opening of the Crystal Palace', p. 18.

18. Presentation to Dickens, and Banquet to Literature and Art, Birmingham, 6 January 1853. Toast to the 'Literature of England.' *The Speeches of Charles Dickens*, ed. by K. J. Fielding, (Oxford: Clarendon Press, 1960), p. 157.

19. Charles Kingsley to his wife, April 1855 (Unpublished Letters to Fanny No. 225), quoted in Susan Chitty, *The Beast and the Monk: a Life of Charles Kingsley*, (London: Hodder & Stoughton, 1974), p. 174.

20. Elizabeth Barrett Browning, *Essay on Mind* (1826), Book II, line 964.

21. Jeffrey A. Auerbach, *The Great Exhibition of 1851: a Nation on Display*, (New Haven and London: Yale University Press, 1999), p. 113.

22. Prince Albert's 1849 speech at the Mansion House, quoted in Henry Cole, *Fifty Years*, II, 213.

23. Henry Cole, 'Introduction', *Volume One: Index and Introductory. Official Descriptive and Illustrated Catalogue by Authority of the Royal Commission of the Great Exhibition 1851* (London: Spicer Brothers, 1851), I, 25. *Athenæum* (22 December 1849), 1305.

24. Mark Rose, *Authors and Owners: the Invention of Copyright* (Cambridge, MA, London: 1993), p. 128.

25. Sergeant Talfourd, Speech on Second Reading of Copyright Bill, 1838, *Hansard* xlii 1838 (Third Series), column 565–6. Wordsworth quotes Talfourd's speech at some length in a letter to Sir Robert Peel, in an attempt to persuade him to support Talfourd's Copyright Bill. William Wordsworth to Sir Robert Peel, 3 May 1838, Letter No. 1260. *The Letters of William and Dorothy Wordsworth: the Later Years*, Volume II (1831–40) ed. by Ernest de Selincourt (Oxford: Clarendon Press, 1939), pp. 934–6 (p. 935).

26. William Cox Bennett, 'Our Glory Roll' in *Our Glory Roll and Other National Poems* (London: Routledge & Sons, n.d. [?1868]), 'One then, O mother-land, was thine, still peerless and alone, / Thy Shakespeare, greatest gift that God has given His earth to own,' p. 5. 'Minutes of the Evidence taken Before the Royal Commission on Copyright together with an Appendix preceded by Tables of the Witnesses and of the Contents of the Appendix', in *Reports from Commissioners, Inspectors, and Others* Vol. 6 Session 17 January–16 August 1878 (London: George Edward Eye and William Spottiswoode, 1878) v. xxiv, (p. 157 (415)) This discussion centred around the dramatisation of novels.

27. Anthony Trollope, *An Autobiography* (London: Williams & Norgate Ltd., 1946), pp. 106–7. Originally published posthumously in 1883.

28. Trollope, *Autobiography*, p. 107.

29. Edward Rose, 'Shakespeare as an Adapter', *Macmillan's Magazine*, 39 (November 1878–April 1879), 69–77, (p. 69).

30. 'Preface', *The Cases of the Appellants and Respondents in the Cause of Literary Property, Before the House of Lords* (London, 1774), repr. in *The Literary Property Debate: Six Tracts, 1764–1774*, ed. by Stephen Parks (New York: Garland, 1975). See Trevor Ross, 'Copyright and the Invention of Tradition', *Eighteenth-Century Studies*, 26:1 (Fall 1992), 1–27, (p. 3 and p. 2).

31. Leah Price, *The Anthology and the Rise of the Novel from Richardson to George Eliot*, (Cambridge: Cambridge University Press, 2000), p. 110.

32. Paulina Kewes has argued against any contemporary view of Shakespeare as a heroic genius, and she takes issue with Michael Dobson, arguing that 'bardolatry' was a post-1700 phenomenon: 'In Shakespeare's time, the identity of the author was generally unknown to his audience and often to his readership, and he had little control over, and only a limited reward from, the performance or publication of his work.' Paulina Kewes, *Authorship and Appropriation: Writing for the Stage in England 1660–1710* (Oxford: Clarendon Press, 1998), p. 1; Michael Dobson, *The Making of the National Poet: Shakespeare, Adaptation and Authorship, 1660–1769* (Oxford: Clarendon Press, 1992).

33. See Howard Felperin, 'Bardolatry Then and Now', in *The Appropriation of Shakespeare: Post-Renaissance Reconstructions of the Works and the Myth*, ed. by Jean I. Marsden (Hertfordshire: Harvester Wheatsheaf, 1991), pp. 129–44.

34. *Athenæum* (10 February 1849), 146–7, (p. 146).

35. *Athenæum* (10 February 1849), 147.

36. See Nigel Cross, *The Common Writer: Life in Nineteenth-Century Grub Street* (Cambridge: Cambridge University Press, 1985), p. 70. Mary Cowden Clarke, whose *Complete Concordance to Shakespeare* was published in 1845, played Dame Quickly in Dickens's production. However, the proceeds never seem to have been received by the administrators of the house fund. *Athenæum* (5 May 1849), 463. Emphasis added.

37. *Journal of the Great Exhibition of 1851 its Origin, History and Progress*, published by the *Critic*, London Literary Journal Office (London: John Crockford), No. 2 (23 November 1850), p. 33.

38. 'Prospectus for the Guild of Literature and Art, April 1851,' Appendix D, *The Letters of Charles Dickens, Volume Six 1850–1852* ed. by Graham Storey, Kathleen Tillotson and Nina Burgis (Oxford: Clarendon Press: 1988), p. 855. Charlotte Brontë's attendance is recorded in George Smith, 'Recollections of a long and busy life' (Typescript, The National Library of Scotland MSS 23191-2), i, 115. 'Charles Dickens, Mr. Forster and other men of letters gave a performance [of the play]. I took Charlotte Brontë and one of my sisters', quoted in *The Letters of Charlotte Brontë, with a Selection of Letters by Family and Friends*, v.2 (1848–1851) ed. by Margaret Smith (Oxford: Clarendon Press, 2000), p. 642. From 1850 to 1851 Dickens was a Vice-President of the Royal Society of Arts, but his letters over this period reveal him as far more interested in the success of the Guild than of the Great Exhibition.

39. Sir Edward Bulwer Lytton, *Not So Bad as We Seem; or, Many Sides to a Character: a Comedy in Five Acts, As First Performed at Devonshire House, in the Presence of Her Majesty and His Royal Highness The Prince Albert*, 2nd edn (London: Published for the Guild of Literature and Art, by Chapman and Hall, 1851), p. 84.

40. William Wordsworth, Preface to Two-Volume Edition of *Lyrical Ballads*, 1800. See Martha Woodmansee, *The Author, Art, and the Market: Re-reading the History of Aesthetics* (New York: Columbia University Press, 1994), pp. 113–14.
41. Matthew Digby Wyatt, 'An Attempt to Define the Principles which should Determine Form in the Decorative Arts', *Lectures on the Results of the Great Exhibition*, v.i, pp. 215–51, (p. 239). Wyatt visited the Collins family in Rome, when Collins was a boy of thirteen. See Catherine Peters, *The King of Inventors: a Life of Wilkie Collins*, (London: Secker & Warburg, 1991), p. 42.
42. Wilkie Collins to Edward Piggott, (16 February 1852) – Collins is speaking of his dramatic tour with Dickens in *Not So Bad as We Seem*. In *The Letters of Wilkie Collins* Volume 1 (1838–1865) ed. by William Baker and William M. Clarke, (London: Macmillan, 1999), p. 82.
43. Wilkie Collins to Richard Bentley (23 October 1851), *Letters*, I, 73. The bust by Gerard Johnson (or Geraert Janssen) in the parish church at Stratford was originally coloured, but had been whitewashed by Edmond Malone in 1793. Its colour was restored in the late 1860s. Information from *The Letters of Alfred Lord Tennyson 1821–1850*, ed. by Cecil Y. Lang and Edgar F. Shannon, Jr. (Oxford: Clarendon Press, 1982), I, 182, n.1.
44. Preface to *Mr Wray's Cash-box* in Wilkie Collins, *The Frozen Deep and Mr Wray's Cash-box* (Stroud, Gloucestershire: Alan Sutton Publishing, 1996), pp. 75–141, (p. 75). All subsequent references are to this edition and appear in parentheses in the text.
45. Collins wrote to his friend Edward Piggott [Autumn 1852], 'I am nothing like so well acquainted with the process of [...] [taking a cast], as I ought to be. I want to know all about *moulds, plaster of Paris*, and so forth – and I must apply to some sculptor.' (*Letters*, I, 74)
46. Alfred Tennyson to Emily Sellwood (*c.*8 June 1840), *Letters of Alfred Lord Tennyson*, I, 182.
47. Jean Baudrillard, *Simulacra and Simulation* trans. by Sheila Faria Glaser (Ann Arbor: University of Michigan Press, 1994), p. 99. Originally published in French in 1981.
48. Henry Cole wrote that '[a]fter much examination and inquiry, the Commissioners resolved that prices were not to be affixed to the articles exhibited' ('Introduction', *Official Descriptive and Illustrated Catalogue*, I, 15).
49. Charles Babbage Esq., *The Exposition of 1851; or, Views of the Industry, the Science, and the Government of England* (London: John Murray 1851), p. 81. Emphasis original.
50. Babbage went on to argue that '[t]he essential principle of the Exposition being the increase of commerce and the exchange of commodities, it might even be contended that sales should be permitted on the premises' (*Exposition*, p. 88).
51. Felperin, 'Bardolatry Then and Now', p. 130.
52. As the Exhibition neared its close, the number of working-class visitors increased and the proletarianisation of the formerly middle-class preserve of the British Nave was noticed by commentators. One diarist, Gideon Mantell, wrote 'many dirty women with their infants were sitting on the seats giving suck with their breasts uncovered, beneath the lovely female figures of the sculptor', and that others ate their packed lunches sitting around the base of Osler's glass fountain (*The Journal of Gideon Mantell*,

ed. by E. Cecil Curwen (London: Oxford University Press, 1940), p. 273; quoted in Auerbach, *Great Exhibition*, p. 155). It is, then, significant that *Punch's* artist chose to use Bell's statue of Shakespeare in his cartoon, despite its absence from these accounts.

5
Implicit and Explicit Reason: George Eliot and Shakespeare

Philip Davis

In November 1877 the publisher Alexander Macmillan was trying to persuade George Eliot to write the life of Shakespeare for John Morley's new English Men of Letters series. Although she finally declined the invitation, I want to argue that, imaginatively, George Eliot was *the* absolutely inspired choice for the task – even though Morley himself had earlier approached Matthew Arnold and John Seeley, who both declined. Herbert Spencer had called George Eliot the female Shakespeare. Alexander Main said that she had done for the Novel what Shakespeare did for the Drama. The very breadth of her sympathy was frequently described as Shakespearean.[1]

It is true that, when we consider the status of such compliments, there is always the danger of a conventional and pious gesturalism in the contemporary linking of a Victorian author with the name of Shakespeare. But it is an unambitious historicism that sees the Victorian view of Shakespeare as largely to do with the Victorians alone and very little to do with Shakespeare himself. The riskier and more interesting question is: in what sense could it have been true to say that George Eliot was – to use the title of this volume – 'Victorian Shakespeare'?

The best contemporary attempt at answering the question lies in an article which caught the eye of Thomas Hardy: Peter Bayne's 'Shakespeare and George Eliot' in *Blackwood's Magazine* (April 1883).[2] Bayne starts with a generic distinction, to do with time and its effect upon space in play and novel: 'The dramatist must put into an hour what the novelist spreads out into a volume,' (p. 524). What in drama is compressed and implicit, in the novel is more explicit and expansive. For the novel seems to be the nineteenth century's translation of a lost age of drama. To turn play into novel, says Bayne, the dramatist's 'suggestions [. . .] must admit of being expanded into chapters':

Only the noblest dramas are of gold fine enough to be beaten out; but Shakespeare's bide the test. Some of them, however, would require a supremely gifted hand to effect the transmutation, – a hand about as gifted as his own; and in one or two instances we are tempted to wish that he had written them out as novels. (p. 525)

'No modern hand would have been quite equal to the task', Bayne claims. But one modern hand, he goes on, would have felt as much interest as Shakespeare himself felt

> in the question started in 'All's Well that Ends Well', respecting the unprincipled Parolles,
> 'Is it possible he should know what he is, and he be that he is?'
> Such a question, it is obvious, must be, comparatively speaking, thrown away on the stage. There is not time in the onward movement of an acted play for the reflection through which alone the significance of such a remark can be appreciated. Take another illustration from the same drama.
> 'The web of our life is of a mingled yarn, good and ill together: our virtues would be proud, if our faults whipped them not; and our crimes would despair, if they were not cherished by our virtues.' (p. 525)

In comparison with its Victorian equivalent, what makes Shakespeare's rhetorically balanced prose still close to poetry is the intricate force released by its barely leaving time for consciousness to catch up and register all its depth. Bayne concludes:

> Among moderns, no writers except Goethe and George Eliot approach Shakespeare in their fondness for such deep sayings; and it was partly, no doubt, on account of his profound appreciation of the reflective element in Shakespeare, that Goethe decisively pronounced his drama things to be understood better in the study than in the theatre. 'Shakespeare's works,' he exclaims, 'are not for the eyes of the body.' (pp. 525–6)

This emphasis on 'the writing out' of Shakespearean drama into a novel is characteristic of an age obsessed with the necessity for translation and transmutation – from past into present, from magical to secular, from instinct to knowledge, from theatre to study. It is also characteristic of an age preoccupied with evolutionary changes, as from the physical – 'the eyes of the body' – to the conscious – the eyes of the mind

Bayne is right. 'The web of our life is of a mingled yarn' – a web inextricably holding together faults and virtues, good and ill in one syntactic matrix – this was always likely to be a thought central to the structure of *Middlemarch* (1871–72): 'I at least have so much to do in unravelling certain human lots, and seeing how they were woven and interwoven, that all the light I can command must be concentrated on this particular web,' (ch. 15). Similarly, the thought – 'how could he know what he was and still be it?' – is precisely what lies at the heart of *Middlemarch*, and it is not difficult to think of George Eliot's unravelled versions of it. Thus with Lydgate – the doctor constantly advising the poor to adjust their diet to their means, while himself neglecting the necessities of his own domestic economy –

> has it not by this time ceased to be remarkable – is it not rather what we expect in men, that they should have numerous strands of experience lying side by side and never compare them with each other? (ch. 58)

Or there is Casaubon, confronted by Dorothea innocently asking him when he finally intends to write up his copious notes into the long-delayed book: he must listen to her spell out as in 'hard distinct syllables from the lips of a near observer, those confused murmurs [...] those muffled suggestions of consciousness', which he had long tried to keep indistinct and unconscious (ch. 20). If Casaubon knew what he was, he could not bear to be it: so he must not know it. Or, again, there is Bulstrode suddenly feeling 'the scenes of his earlier life coming between him and everything else':

> as obstinately as when we look through the window from a lighted room, the objects we turn our backs on are still before us, instead of the grass and the trees. The successive events inward and outward were there in one view: though each might be dwelt on in turn, the rest still kept their hold in the consciousness. (ch. 61)

In such moments under the threat of self-reflection, it would be difficult, says Peter Bayne, to find 'a more practically useful or philosophically profound commentary' upon Shakespeare's Claudius or Macbeth or Angelo than in George Eliot's 'delineation of corresponding characters'

(p. 527) – that is, 'mixed characters', caught in conflict 'between light and darkness', in a world 'compounded of good and evil' (p. 526).

'By this time', as George Eliot puts it, it is the novelist who picks up and explicitly articulates the thoughts which the characters can hardly bear to think and barely manage to avoid. In the tradition of Victorian reading that culminates in A. C. Bradley's *Shakespearean Tragedy* (1904), the play shadows forth the psychological novel that lies behind it, just as the poetry latently contains the deep thoughts that prose feels summoned to spell out.

To many distinguished mid-Victorian readers it was as though the very speed, the paradoxically resonant transience, of drama and verse in Shakespeare had penetrated beyond the present of its own utterance and momentarily summoned a future which the nineteenth century was only just beginning consciously to realise. As Carlyle romantically put it in *On Heroes and Hero Worship* (1840), Shakespeare was as the voice of 'Nature' itself:

> There is more in Shakspeare's intellect than we have yet seen. It is what I call an unconscious intellect; there is more virtue in it than he himself is aware of. [...] The latest generations of men will find new meanings in Shakspeare; new elucidations of their own human being; new harmonies with the infinite structure of the Universe; concurrences with later ideas. [...] How much in Shakspeare lies hid [...] much that was not known at all, not speakable at all: like roots, like sap and forces working underground! Speech is great; but Silence is greater. (Lecture 3, 'The Hero as Poet')

By making each effort at formulation a fresh act, by avoiding the mere re-use of set names and formulae, Shakespeare's language constantly reached down, below fixed consciousness, to those very root-sources of human mentality out of which comes all subsequent growth. Through the creation of an unspoken subtext behind soliloquy and between dialogue, Shakespeare had created a tacit reservoir of meaning, a language, said Carlyle, resonant with the silence of sheer anterior being around it. As Bayne might have put it, it is George Eliot above all who finds in the novel, in the sub-vocal voice of the narrator, a new language of silence, shared within the inner act of individual private reading, rather than exploding in public theatre: a language that was like the reader's hearing 'the grass grow, and the squirrel's heart beat' or the 'roar which lies on the other side of silence' (*Middlemarch*, ch. 20).

Shakespeare was, as Carlyle's American equivalent, Ralph Waldo Emerson put it in *Representative Men* (1850), the Poet of the race. A 'full man', he 'wrote the text of modern life' (ch. 5, 'Shakespeare; Or the Poet') – a life of complex intermixtures held together in solution, like the very gene-pool (as we might say) of later development. And as it was with Carlyle and with Emerson, so too with Ruskin, in speaking of Shakespeare's 'penetrative imagination':

> Hence there is in every word set down by the imaginative mind an awful under-current of meaning, and evidence and shadow upon it of the deep places out of which it has come. It is often obscure, half-told; for he who wrote it, in his clear seeing of the things beneath, may have been impatient of detailed interpretation: but, if we choose to dwell upon it and trace it, it will lead us always securely back [. . .].

He goes on to cite as a fine instance of what he means Macduff's 'He has no children' (*Macbeth*, IV. 3. 216).[3] 'Who', said Peter Bayne, 'could have tracked so well as George Eliot such a suggestive clue as Shakespeare gives us in relation to the experiences of Macbeth, when he makes him shrink from prayer with Duncan's blood upon his hands? [. . .]

> 'I had most need of blessing, and "Amen"
> Stuck in my throat.' [. . .]

'–she who traced, step by step, the career of Bulstrode' (p. 526). 'George Eliot,' concluded Bayne, 'is an evolutionist in her treatment of character,' (p. 536).

Tracing, tracking, dwelling upon and unravelling: these are the attributes of the Victorian realist novelist finding and taking more time than Shakespeare. In a densely-worded syntax that more minutely filled in the links between thoughts, the novelist spelt out the gradual evolution of a life: 'for character too is a process and an unfolding' (*Middlemarch*, ch. 15).

Yet all this might seem merely consonant with the prediction made in 1825 by Macaulay in his essay on 'Milton': that what was in store was an age of prose and of explanation. 'As civilisation advances,' he wrote, 'poetry almost necessarily declines.' In science, argued Macaulay, progress means that the first speculators get left behind. But in poetry the first practitioners are never surpassed – rather, it is poetry itself that gets left behind. If Shakespeare had been asked to write a book about the complex motives of human action, he could not have done it – what he could do was bring into being the motives themselves, in the creation of his plays. Now, says Macaulay, we know more and create less. Thinking has become more general, more consciously explicatory and philosophical, more secondary. Carlyle himself restates the case from his own point of view in his great essay 'Characteristics' (1831), which is virtually an account of the loss of 'dynamical', unconscious Shakespearean thinking in the face of modern 'mechanical' over-consciousness. I have written elsewhere on how a generation of Victorian critics, such as Anna Jameson, equivalently slackened the dynamic of Shakespearean creativity by taking his characters out of the word-bursting pressure of time and space in the plays, and treating them to the alternative spaciousness of the language of quasi-novelistic commentary.[4]

Nowhere is this sense of a lost dynamic of creative thinking more powerfully registered than when banished to the realm of a private correspondence, written in dismay at the state of Victorian poetry. It was in a letter written to A. W. M. Baillie (10 September 1864) that Gerard Manley Hopkins offered his diagnosis of Victorian poetry as 'Parnassian' – the conventionally established Poetry (with a capital P, perched on top of Mount Parnassus) offering loftily coloured diction and heavy lamenting monotones. 'In Parnassian pieces,' wrote Hopkins, 'you feel that if you were the poet you could have gone on as he has done.' But in the original creative poetry of a Shakespeare, says Hopkins, 'every fresh beauty could not in any way be predicted or accounted for by what one has already read'.[5] Even in short-hand, this is the most crucial, poetic account of Victorian Shakespeare – of what Shakespeare and his live thinking meant to the greatest Victorians. In its swift progress the o'erleaping imagination of Shakespeare – like a supremely developed model of human mentality at its maximum – left behind it hidden transitions and rich gaps which later ages struggled to fill in. Such a mind

> makes progress not unlike a clamberer on a steep cliff, who, by quick eye, prompt hand, and firm foot, ascends how he knows not himself, by personal endowments and by practice, rather than by rule, leaving no track behind him, and unable to teach another. It is not too much to say that the stepping by which great geniuses scale the mountains of truth is as unsafe and precarious to men in general, as the ascent of a skilful mountaineer up a literal crag. It is a way which they alone can take; and its justification lies in their success.

Yet these are the words not of Hopkins but of one of his mentors, John Henry Newman, from a sermon on 'Implicit and Explicit Reason' delivered in Oxford in 1840.[6] They fit very well with Browning's rejoinder to Ruskin, in a letter of 10 December 1855, concerning Ruskin's criticism of *Men and Women* as obscure and abrupt in its speedy mountain-leaps: 'You ought, I think, to keep pace with the thought tripping from ledge to ledge of my "glaciers" as you call them; not stand poking your alpenstock into the holes, and demonstrating that no foot could have stood there; – suppose it sprang over there?' But then Ruskin had already admitted that he had found 'truths & depths' in the work 'far beyond anything I have read except Shakespeare – and – truly, if You had just written Hamlet, I believe I should have written to you, precisely this kind of letter'.[7]

But in the complex shifts, displacements and cross-purposes of mid-Victorian England, it is finally to Newman – and the world of religion rather than poetry – that one must turn for the most rigorous formal defence of prose as something still potentially more than a language of mere secondary explication.

For Newman the whole Christian 'world of thought' is 'the expansion of a few words, uttered, as if casually, by the fishermen of *Galilee*' *(University Sermons*, p. 317, Sermon 15 'The Theory of Developments in Christian Doctrine'). 'The gaps, if the word may be used,' which occur around the short, simple and yet mysteriously incarnate utterances of the Gospel, 'make it probable', says Newman, that they were intended such that later developments of their meaning, later explicitness 'should fill them up' – like bequeathed memory, locating the resonance of the unspoken in the implicit spaces left around and within the speech.[8] There is always something implicit, a spirit, in between the sentences. History is the gradually emergent development, amidst many minds, of that implicit fullness:

> The Apostles had the fullness of revealed knowledge, a fullness which they could as little realize to themselves, as the human mind, as such, can have all its thoughts present before it at once. They are elicited according to the occasion. A man of genius cannot go about with his genius in his hand: in an Apostle's mind great part of his knowledge is from the nature of the case latent or implicit.[9]

This is the Christian alternative to Darwin's theory of evolution.

What is more, religion is not for Newman an added extra: what is true of the Apostles and the Gospels remains true all the way down in the world. Thus his *University Sermons* make clear that there always has to be something implicit that comes before thinking, which the language of thinking itself then comes out of. Human beings are never reasoned into their beliefs, that is not the order of things. Right or wrong, the beliefs and intuitions must come first, before we even know we have them; only secondarily can we try to find and test the reasons implicit within our holding them.

That is why in the section of his *Idea of a University* (1852, 1873) devoted to 'Literature' Newman quotes both Macbeth and Hamlet to show how 'their thinking out into language' is like 'the very shadow' of all that still lies deep and implicit within themselves.[10] Thinking in Newman is always closer to literature and to the literary sense of meaning and mentality than it is to the mere literalness of impersonal science or formal logic. And that was because, to him, literature itself was a way of thinking closer than was often supposed to finally religious sources of creativity in human beings.

This may help us to see why George Eliot, writing to Sara Hennell (13 July 1864), said that Newman's recently published autobiography, *Apologia Pro Vita Sua*, was like seeing her own life through the looking-glass, in another form: 'how different in form from one's own, yet with how close a fellowship in its needs and burthens – I mean spiritual needs and burthens' (*Letters*, IV, 159). For where Newman ever increasingly took the religious road, even to the Church of Rome, George Eliot took the literary way, for what she, if not Newman, recognised to be equivalent spiritual purposes. It is in the work of George Eliot, I shall argue, that the relation between what Newman called 'implicit' and 'explicit' thinking is most fully investigated, as central to the development of meaning in the modern world.

To the great Victorian critics, Shakespeare seemed an implicit, almost pre-conscious thinker. Ruskin shows how in Shakespeare's penetrative imagination the implicit and explicit come so speedily into being, that the two seem almost co-existent for the moment. In Shakespearean drama there always seems time for just one shot at immediate unexplained actualisation. As in *Macbeth*, it must be 'done' quickly.

But with George Eliot at her most powerful it is as though everything still has to be done twice, once as in *inner* drama, and then again in prosaic realism. So, for example, within Mrs Bulstrode, at the moment when her husband's past is first shockingly revealed to her, there was 'that concentrated experience which in great crises of emotion reveals the bias of a nature, and is prophetic of the ultimate act which will end an intermediate struggle' (ch. 74). Thus, in a 'mere flash' of a second she knows, as by a kind of pre-vision, that she will indeed still stand by him. But it then takes two long pages of preparation – 'she needed time' says George Eliot twice – actually to embody that resolve in reality, to put the thought incarnate into ordinary testing practice and to become that loyal person again for the rest of her life. 'Even strictly measuring science,' says George Eliot in chapter 41 of *Daniel Deronda* (1876), 'could hardly have got on without that forecasting ardour which feels the agitations of discovery beforehand, and has a faith in its preconception that surmounts many failures of experiment'. With George Eliot, that is to say, it is as though genius sees the solution in a flash but has then to go back into ordinary life to prove her intuition the second time around and show all its realistic working-out.

This means that, contrary to Macaulay's forecast, George Eliot's is not simply a language of mere secondary explanation. Her so-called didacticism still has that creative dynamic which Carlyle, in 'Characteristics', declared vital to the thinking of his age. It was Edward Dowden who first argued, in the *Contemporary Review* (August 1872), that the language of George Eliot is not didactically imposed from above: rather, it comes emergently into being, 'in the midst' of the characters it has also created – as thoughts of themselves which they themselves dare not think, as a mediation called for in the painful space left by all that is lost, unadmitted or missing in their lives. 'The author is present in the midst of them,' writes Dowden, 'indicating, interpreting' as 'that "second self" who writes her books, and lives and speaks through them.'[11] This is the same Dowden who three years later in 1875 wrote *Shakespeare, his Mind and Art*, seeking just that: to infer the mind of Shakespeare from within his art. With the existence of George Eliot, however, the mind of the work is made more explicit within it, the sub-vocal language on the 'other side' of silence more sustained as a mediating presence in the spaces – the 'gaps' to use Newman's word – between the very characters. As George Eliot herself wrote (in a letter to John Blackwood, 4 April 1861) concerning the relation between Tom and Maggie Tulliver in *The Mill on the Floss* and the criticism that she had been unfair to the brother: 'as if it were not *my* respect for Tom which infused itself into my reader – as if he could have respected Tom if I had not painted him with respect; the exhibition of the right on both sides being the very soul of my intention in the story' (*Letters*, III, 397). This isn't simply even-handed liberalism. In the space between the characters

– the space that in *Daniel Deronda* George Eliot was to call a third presence (ch. 36) – life-forces are created. There, as in Shakespeare, the characters unknowingly help to create each other, as it were, through dialogue. Silas Marner would not have known just how much he simply and unidealistically wanted to keep the child who had come to him, if Dolly in her very kindness had not offered to help out with her: 'But I want to do things for it myself, else it may get fond o' somebody else, and not fond o' me' (*Silas Marner*, 1861, ch. 14). Dorothea would never have quite realised the religion implicit within her, had not Will Ladislaw begun to praise it as 'a beautiful mysticism': 'Please not to call it by any name. [. . .] It is my life. I have found it out, and cannot part with it. I have always been finding out my religion since I was a little girl,' (*Middlemarch*, ch. 39). Without these challenges of inadvertent misunderstanding, such people would not know what they had deep within them as their 'life'. It comes to them in a flash, back-to-front, out of oppositions and negatives. So, painfully, Tom and Maggie help to define each other, even through their opposition.

Indeed, as so many members of the George Eliot circle variously testify, that almost impossibly sympathetic and impartial sense of both sides possessing simultaneously co-existent claims is a Shakespearean process of contrast – and none the less so for being bequeathed to George Eliot via the influential novels of Sir Walter Scott.

Thus, for example, in his essay on *Scott* in the English Men of Letters series (1878), R. H. Hutton argued that the author of *Waverley*, caught between tensions inherited from the clash between the ancient and the modern worlds, characteristically works by large dramatic contrasts and great public conflicts – 'affording an opportunity for the delineation of the pros and cons of the case, so that the characters on both sides of the struggle would be properly understood' (p. 105). Needing 'a machinery for displaying his insights into both sides of a public quarrel' (p. 105), Scott's imagination in a novel such as *Old Mortality* seized upon the moderate wavering figure of Morton as 'the imaginative neutral ground', the great dramatic space in-between, 'on which opposing influences [of the Cavalier Claverhouse and the puritan Burley] are brought to play' (p. 106). In the more private and understated world of George Eliot, conflicts of course are not so dramatic, public history is making no obvious demands for an outcome. Thus where meaning too often gets missed for being ordinary, that space in between is occupied not by one of Scott's hesitant heroes but by George Eliot herself, as the world's missing mediator – precisely at the point where the Shakespearean dynamic of dialogue breaks down.

Then it is that sentences get made in George Eliot such that the syntax, moving between different people in a way that the people themselves barely can, itself seems a creative achievement: 'she had felt the waking of a presentiment that there might be a sad consciousness in his life which made as great a need on his side as on her own' (*Middlemarch*, ch. 21). As the sentences interweave themselves from within the web of considerations, the very moment of formulation is as George Henry Lewes describes, using a different metaphor: 'The words float suspended, soulless, mere sounds. No sooner are these floating sounds grasped by the copula, than in that grasp they are grouped into significance: they start into life, as a saturated saline solution crystallizes on being touched by a needle-point.'[12] So it is with Gwendolen in crisis in *Daniel Deronda* (ch. 28):

> she who had been used to feel sure of herself, and ready to manage others, had just taken a decisive step which she had beforehand thought that she would not take. [...] she was appalled by the idea that she was going to do what she had once started away from with repugnance.

In both these formulations, the needle-point is those ostensibly simple mid-sentence connectives 'which' and 'what', respectively, now used to link different times ('beforehand', 'once') not according to chronology but in new and painful moral connection. Bayne is right to point to something crucial for George Eliot in Shakespeare's Claudius or Angelo, and here it is also revealed as something syntactic, within the web's intermixture: ' "Forgive me my foul murther"? / That cannot be, since I am still possess'd / Of those effects for which I did the murther' (*Hamlet*, III. 3. 52–4); 'What dost thou? or what art thou, Angelo? / Dost thou desire her foully for those things / That make her good?' (*Measure for Measure*, II. 2. 172–4). Indeed, it is another of George Eliot's circle, Herbert Spencer, who, in 'Progress, its Law and Cause' (first published in the *Westminster Review*, April 1857), points to all that is at stake in the evolution of the human mind through the generation of a complex syntax.[13]

As Spencer indicates, what is involved is a search for the very syntax of the world, its generated structures and evolved relations. Ruskin said that unlike Dante or Milton, Shakespeare was the figure of immanence, rather than religious transcendence.[14] For that reason the Victorian period is full of commentators anxiously concerned about the work of Shakespeare being no more than (as it were) the world all over again, lacking an extrapolatable morality or an external philosophy that could give extra meaning to the universe. But George Eliot's realism was a recommitment to such immanence, content as she was to do her work (as Dowden put it) 'in the midst' of things.

To the Victorians, in following the Romantic proclamation of Shakespeare's genius, it was as though the human mind took what was increasingly seen as an evolutionary leap in Shakespeare. Perhaps the best Victorian account of those sudden, full utterances of genius is that given by another of George Eliot's admirers, F. W. H. Myers in *Human Personality* (posthumously published in 1903). It is there that he speaks of the inspiration of poetic Genius as 'a subliminal uprush' (p. 56), which, arising in the midst of the particular, appears on the very verge of the general. It is 'the sudden creation of new cerebral connections or pathways' (p. 82). Myers's argument is that during our long evolutionary adaptation to new environments there has been a continual displacement of the 'threshold' of consciousness (p. 14). There are certain faculties that 'natural selection had lifted above' that threshold, for the working purposes of everyday existence (p. 77); other powers, which were not called into consciousness as immediately useful, were stored 'subliminally' below consciousness, in a kind of dynamic memory (p. 14). It was these latter unseen powers that genius brought from the subliminal level upwards into conscious mind.

Hazlitt had already used the language of mental chemistry when in *Lectures on the English Poets* (1818) he spoke of Shakespeare working not from 'a preconcerted theory of character' but 'in a continual composition and decomposition' of life's elements (Lecture 3, 'On Shakspeare and Milton'). Each time he wrote, this great Maker seemed to re-create the world as for the first time again – yet another new compound made out of different combinations of life's basic elements. For each of Shakespeare's plays forms, says Hazlitt, a 'magic circle' within which – resorting to the language of magnetism – each character 'must be a kind of centre of repulsion to the rest'. Thus crowdingly, 'their hostile interests brought into collision, must call forth every faculty of thought, of speech, and action'.[15] As Alexander Koyré has helped to show, Shakespeare's work bursts out of the pressure of a closed world-view opening up even from within itself.[16] There are unpublished notes in George Eliot's notebook in the Huntingdon Library (Ms. HM 12993) on vacuum versus plenum and its relation to the nineteenth-century law of the conservation of force: these indicate her abiding interest in a fully immanent universe, Shakespearean or Darwinian. For they refer to a crowded world-system in which a dangerously creative struggle for life and space and motion goes on even at atomic level, the parts jostling, shifting and changing precisely because the whole must remain quantitatively immutable.

George Eliot continues that art of creative life-experiment described by Hazlitt as Shakespeare's own. 'Dynamic' was a word that George Eliot's publisher John Blackwood queried when reading the proof-copy of *Daniel Deronda*, but as Gordon Haight reports, it was already used by both the visionaries Carlyle and Emerson and the scientists Tyndall and Spencer (*Letters*, VI, 183, 10 November 1875). But George Eliot *was* Victorian Shakespeare to the extent that, as in Shakespeare, her art was seen as that of a mind dynamically keying into elements and processes of the plan of life. To George Eliot, famously, the novel's equivalent of Shakespeare's magic circle was the web, the scientific force-field of intervolved energies, of life and character and story all still 'in the making' within the melting-pot of the novel (*Middlemarch*, ch. 15). Equally famously, Lydgate 'wanted to pierce the obscurity of those minute processes which prepare human misery and joy, those invisible thoroughfares which are the first lurking-places of anguish, mania and crime, that delicate poise and transition which determine the growth of happy or unhappy consciousness' (*Middlemarch*, ch. 16). Conscious of being no longer close to the origin of things but immersed in the midst of a complex evolved universe, already long established socially and historically, George Eliot needed to make through prose a microscopic attempt to find, deep down within the niches of the minutely Particular, intimations of the Universal, of Life's hidden infrastructure – as she works from below upwards in the search for an overall framework of generalisation sufficiently stable to give significance to the smallest detail within it. So, equivalently says George Eliot, Dorothea in search of a framework might have compared her experience in trying to come to terms with the meaning of her marriage to Casaubon 'to the vague alarmed consciousness that her life was taking on a new form, that she was undergoing a metamorphosis in which memory would not adjust itself to the stirring of new organs' (ch. 50). As Myers put it, it was with consciousness as it was with light – there are invisible ultra-violet rays beyond the end of the spectrum: 'The "X rays" of the psychical spectrum remain for a later age to discover,' (*Human Personality*, p. 19). George Eliot's prose begins that later age.

Thus, the greatest evolutionary development that emerges from these experiments upon life was the creation of the mind of 'George Eliot' herself, that 'second self' that Dowden described as arising in the midst of its own creation. For why did he say 'second self'? It was because a primary self could only exist as the characters themselves do in *Middlemarch*, egoistically 'encumbered with the accidents of flesh and blood and daily living' (Haight, p. 64). But a second self, created precisely by reflection upon such primary selves, was an enormous evolutionary leap. Emerson had said of Shakespeare, 'He was the farthest reach of subtlety compatible with an individual self, – the subtlest of authors, and only just within the possibility of authorship,' ('Shakespeare; Or, the Poet'). As Marian Evans's second self, able to reflect upon human beings while still being in and of them, George Eliot was the result of an equivalent, almost superhuman, authorial effort. As novelist, George Eliot could employ within her work all that otherwise she could barely have endured, as a woman outside her books: namely, an extraordinary susceptibility, to create, and an extraordinary moral stamina, to judge.

If as Hazlitt puts it in writing on *Hamlet* in his *Characters of Shakspeare's Plays* (1817), Shakespeare always gives us 'the original text' of life, then this second self of George Eliot does not exist in the first place but mitigates, spells out and re-writes, in order to offer a sustained but dynamic second-order language, below the level of speech, that locates life's real dramas not now on the outside but hidden within. The super-evolved brain at the centre of *Middlemarch* sees the relation not only between the thoughts in the mind of each character but also between the characters themselves in the mind of George Eliot: '– but why always Dorothea? Was her point of view the only possible one?' 'Suppose we turn from outside estimates of a man to wonder, with keener interest, what is the report of his own consciousness [...]' (*Middlemarch*, chs 29, 10). Thus raised, her mind thus differs from the minds of her characters not in kind but only in degree.

And that is an evolutionary achievement, pushed on by art and artificial selection. My argument is not that the mind called 'George Eliot' had evolved beyond that of Shakespeare, but that it consolidated the creative mind, of which Shakespeare's was the supreme example, into a kind of person. By mapping itself onto the processes of art, George Eliot's is a mind that exists in order to create, from within art, a level of consciousness that might remain permanent outside art, in the blueprint of the human race, for the future.

That possible future is part of the purpose, finally, of *Daniel Deronda*. Significantly, it was, once again, Edward Dowden who was the great champion of *Daniel Deronda*, pointing out how late works, in George Eliot as in Shakespeare or Turner or Beethoven, are most powerful when struggling to go beyond all previous resolutions (Haight, p. 119). In *Problems of Life and Mind*, volume I (1874), George Henry Lewes had written on how in the human brain 'one neural process tends to re-excite those processes which formerly were excited in conjunction with it'. These 'pathways of discharge' form the lines of 'least resistance', reducing and rigidifying the mind to its own habitual connections. A new connection, the very formation of a metaphor in the spirit of Shakespeare, may change those pathways – though as old age advances in an individual or in a society, the usual tendency is 'to prevent new acquisitions, and resist new combinations' (pp. 144–5). What *Daniel Deronda* stands for in an England of decay is something other than the 'rote-learned language of a system, that gives you the spelling of all things, sure of its alphabet covering them all':

> Man finds his pathways: at first they were foot-tracks, as those of the beast in the wilderness; now they are swift and invisible: his thought dives through the ocean, and his wishes thread the air: has he found all the pathways yet? What reaches him, stays with him, rules him: he must accept it, not knowing its pathway. (ch. 40)

To turn *thought*, at the micro level, into *way*, at the macro level – that is the aim of George Eliot.[17] 'What reaches him, stays with him.' But to turn reaching into staying, the novel needs time.

Notes

1. See *The George Eliot Letters*, ed. by G. S. Haight, 9 vols (New Haven: Yale University Press, 1954–78), VI, 207, 465; hereafter cited as '*Letters*'.
2. *Blackwood's Magazine*, 133 (April 1883), 524–38. See *The Literary Notebooks of Thomas Hardy*, ed. by L. A. Björk, 2 vols (London: Macmillan, 1985), I, entry 1297 (and annotation p. 381). Page references hereafter in the body of the text.
3. *Modern Painters*, vol. II, in *The Library Edition of the Works of John Ruskin*, ed. by E. T. Cook and Alexander Wedderburn, 39 vols (London: Allen, 1903–12), IV, 252.
4. 'Nineteenth-Century Juliet', *Shakespeare Survey*, 49 (1996), pp. 131–40.
5. *Gerard Manley Hopkins: Selected Letters*, ed. by Catherine Phillips (Oxford: Oxford University Press, 1990), pp. 23–6.

Philip Davis 99

6. J. H. Newman, *University Sermons*, ed. by D. M. MacKinnon and J. D. Holmes (London: SPCK, 1970), p. 257; hereafter cited as *'University Sermons'*.
7. David De Laura, *Ruskin and the Brownings: Twenty-five Unpublished Letters* (Manchester: John Rylands Library, 1972), pp. 324–6.
8. *An Essay on the Development of Christian Doctrine*, 1878 edn, p. 63.
9. See J. H. Newman, *An Essay on the Development of Christian Doctrine*, ed. by Ian Ker (Notre Dame, Indiana: University of Notre Dame Press, 1989), p. xxiv.
10. See Part II 'University Subjects', lecture 2 ('Literature') sections 3–5.
11. See *A Century of George Eliot Criticism*, ed. by G. S. Haight (London: Methuen, 1966), pp. 64–5; hereafter cited as 'Haight'. Also repr. in *George Eliot: the Critical Heritage*, ed. by David Carroll (London: Routledge, 1971).
12. *Problems of Life and Mind*, (1875), II, 145.
13. But it is Emerson's disciple, William James who gives the idea its sharpest articulation: 'There is not a conjunction or a preposition, and hardly an adverbial phrase, a syntactic form or inflection of voice, in human speech, that does not express some shading or other of relation which we at some moment actually feel to exist between the larger objects of our thought. [...] We ought to say a feeling of and, a feeling of if, a feeling of but, and a feeling of by, quite as readily as a feeling of blue or a feeling of cold.' (*Selected Writings*, ed. by G. H. Bird (London: Everyman, 1995), p. 189)
14. *Modern Painters*, vol. I, in *Works*, ed. by Cook and Wedderburn, VI, 452–3 (footnote).
15. *Complete Works*, ed. by P. P. Howe, 21 vols (London and Toronto: J. M. Dent & Sons, 1932), XVIII, 305–6.
16. Alexandre Koyré, *From the Closed World to the Infinite Universe* (Baltimore: Johns Hopkins University Press, 1957); see also my *Sudden Shakespeare* (London: Athlone Press, 1996).
17. Compare Herman Melville in 'Hawthorne and his Mosses' (1850) on 'those deep far-away things in [Shakespeare], those occasional flashing-forths of the intuitive Truth in him [...] that undeveloped, (and sometimes undevelopable) yet dimly-discernible greatness'. Melville goes on to argue that in 'this world of lies', the truth can only be told thus 'covertly, and by snatches' (*After Shakespeare*, ed. by John Gross (Oxford: Oxford University Press, 2002), p. 45.

6
'Where Did She Get Hold of That?' Shakespeare in Henry James's *The Tragic Muse*

Philip Horne

I

Where did who get hold of what? And who wants to know? Henry James's novel of 1890, *The Tragic Muse*, which may be his wittiest, is a novel about artistic vocation, about the mostly undramatic struggle to live for art, and the mystery of genius. One of the two main protagonists is an actress, so a good deal of it directly addresses the conditions of the late-Victorian theatre, and the relation between British, French and (a little) Italian culture. One reason for James's growing interest in this topic at this time was his own imminent attempt to make his name, and more money than in a fiction market that was becoming difficult for him, through writing plays *for* the late-Victorian theatre. It is a novel in which Shakespeare plays a large part, and one which consciously recapitulates the history of the nineteenth-century theatre in England and France.

First of all, then, once again, who wants to know, who asks 'Where did she get hold of that?' We must go back a little, both in the novel's plot and in James's critical, or spectatorial, involvement with the theatre, to see how and why it matters. The person asking the question is an ambitious young English diplomat in Paris named Peter Sherringham, a man who when not pursuing his career has a developed taste for the theatre, and in particular for the French theatre, the Théâtre Français. In this he mirrors James himself, and many among the British audiences of the Comédie Française and other French companies who visited London from 1871 onwards. In her essay on 'Immigrant Shakespeares' in the companion volume to this (*Victorian Shakespeare:*

Theatre, Drama and Performance, ch. 4), Jane Moody notes what a transformation had been wrought in the attitude of English audiences to such foreign visitors between 1848 when the exiled Théâtre Historique caused a violent disturbance at Drury Lane, and 1879 when the Comédie Française were unanimously fêted at the Gaiety Theatre. James himself described this latter visit as 'incomparably the most noteworthy event that has occurred in many a long year in the theatrical annals of London'.[1]

Early in *The Tragic Muse*, which opens in Paris, Sherringham takes up, as patron to protégée, a striking, cosmopolitan young English actress called Miriam Rooth, of at least half-Jewish parentage, encouraged by her offputtingly pretentious widowed mother. Miriam, in the book's nineteenth chapter, will be the 'she' who, in her acting, will have got hold of the 'that'. Sherringham plays with the idea that Miriam may become the figurehead of the revival of British theatre he feels is urgently needed. He finds himself sententiously declaring that 'There's something to be done for [the theatre in our country], and perhaps mademoiselle's the person to do it'; and half-jokes later to Miriam, 'I consider that you and I are really required to save our theatre.'[2] His formula for effecting this salvation is, 'Study here and then go to London to appear' (*TM*, p. 92) – that is, absorb the traditions and disciplines of the high French theatrical approach, acquire a mastery, and *then* enter the world of the London stage, and act in the language of Shakespeare with a technique not inferior to that of the Comédie Française. This trail *had* been blazed. As John Stokes kindly reminds me, the woman James called in 1880 'the most interesting actress in London', the American-born Geneviève Ward (1838–1922), possessed of 'a finish, an intelligence, a style, an understanding of what she is about, which are as agreeable as they are rare', had studied at the Théâtre Français before coming to England (*SA*, p. 154).

Peter goes to hear Miriam 'recite' (*TM*, p. 50) for his old friend Madame Carré, recently retired *from* the Comédie Française, whom he describes as 'the Balzac, as one may say, of actresses' (p. 55). 'The venerable artist will pass judgement' (p. 50) – that is, she will judge the amateur English efforts by high French standards. The aesthete Gabriel Nash has arranged for this audition in a spirit of ironic mischief and scorn for the theatre. Nash, unlike Sherringham, thinks the modern theatre a poor form – 'What can you do with an idea, with a feeling, between dinner and the suburban trains?' (p. 55) – and he has fixed up this apparent favour for Miriam, whom he thinks 'splendidly stupid' (p. 49),

'Precisely to stop her short. The great model will find her very bad. Her judgements, as you probably know, are rhadamanthine.' (p. 51)

At the private trial, we see Miriam 'huddled there, silent and rigid, frightened to death, staring, expressionless' (p. 84). Her exaggeratedly respectable mother eagerly tells Madame Carré that as well as Molière 'she knows Juliet, she knows Lady Macbeth and Cleopatra' (p. 87). Miriam announces however that 'I can say "L'Aventurière"', Emile Augier's verse-play of 1848, whose heroine is a mercenary sexual adventuress. Her recital exposes 'a long strong colourless voice', and she delivers her lines of French verse 'with a rude monotony' and then 'with an effort at modulation which was not altogether successful and which evidently she felt not to be so'. 'The scene, [...] when it was over, had not precisely been a triumph for Miriam Rooth,' (p. 91). More attempts reveal her tone for everything:

a solemn droning dragging measure suggestive of an exhortation from the pulpit and adopted evidently with the 'affecting' intention and from a crude idea of 'style'. It was all funereal, yet was artlessly rough. (p. 92)

So this first audition is a failure. And yet there is something about Miriam: 'something surmounted and survived her failure [...] the element of outline and attitude, the way she stood, the way she turned her eyes, her head, and moved her limbs,' (p. 93). Peter has already said to his cousin Nick Dormer, the novel's other hero, struggling to believe in his vocation as a painter, that 'You must paint her just like that [...]As the Tragic Muse,' (p. 91). The 'something' is pictorial, one might say – but it is also something humanly expressive.

Madame Carré insists that the polyglot Miriam can't act in all her languages, that she 'must have a particular form of speech, like me' (p. 86). Faced with the necessity of choosing, Miriam declares 'In English I can play Shakespeare. I want to play Shakespeare,' (p. 95). Soon afterwards, though mainly from politeness, Peter Sherringham allows Miriam to recite again for him and some guests. The girl has been coached in Rome by an Italian tragedian called Signor Ruggieri, 'in the proper manner of pronouncing his language and also in the art of declaiming and gesticulating' (p. 91); and this appears when she first tackles Shakespeare.

Miss Rooth gave a representation of Juliet drinking the potion, according to the system, as her mother explained, of the famous Signor Ruggieri – a scene of high fierce sound, of many cries and contortions: she shook her hair (which proved magnificent) half-down before the performance was over. (p. 99)

II

James's extraordinarily allusive novel draws here and elsewhere on contemporary debates about the drama and the art of the actor.[3] The 'system [...] of the famous Signor Ruggieri' seems to lean more on James's sense of Ernesto Rossi (1827–1896) than of Salvini (1829–1915), whom he preferred. (Jane Moody makes the point that James can reasonably be described as 'the first international theatre critic'.) In January 1876 James wrote of Rossi's *Romeo and Juliet* in Paris (cut, and in Italian) as a successful piece of physical theatre, with special reference to the later scenes, into which Rossi introduced some non-Shakespearean business: 'Rossi's speeches are often weak, but when he attempts an acutely studied piece of pantomime, he never misses it,' (*SA*, p. 54). The word 'pantomime' evidently involves a fairly serious limiting judgement, but this *is* praise. Thinking about what Miriam's display of force – of what Sherringham thinks of in the revised edition as 'blundering energy' (*TM*, p. 100)[4] – means in the novel, one might recall an earlier remark about Rossi, from Rome in 1873, on his Othello: 'Rossi is both very bad and very fine; bad where anything like taste and discretion is required, but "all there," and much more than there, in violent passion,' (*SA*, p. 55). James even manages to find profit in Rossi's mutilated Italian version of *Romeo and Juliet*:

One never sees Shakespeare played without being reminded at some new point of his greatness; the other night what struck me was the success with which, for the occasion, he had Italianized his fancy. The things that trouble us nowadays in *Romeo and Juliet* – the redundancy of protestation, the importunate conceits, the embarrassing frankness – all these fall into their place in the rolling Italian diction, and what one seems to see is not a translation, but a restitution. (*SA*, p. 53)

So Miriam's Italian experience, and lessons with the fictitious Ruggieri, may constitute one element in a combination that might produce a satisfactory, 'Italianised', modern production of the play.

Perhaps the most important aspect of James's seeming reference here
to Rossi's *Romeo and Juliet* is the implicit contrast with versions of the
play originating closer to home. One would have been Henry Irving's of
1882 with Irving, 44, as Romeo and Ellen Terry, 35, as Juliet. It was not
one of Irving's great successes; the *Theatre*'s critic referred to 'so much
depressed action and uneventful luxury'.[5] Given that James was an
admirer of cultivated intelligence and a connoisseur of the visual arts,
one might expect him to coincide with Irving in his sense of *Romeo and
Juliet*. Irving told Ellen Terry, as she recalled later:

> *Hamlet* could be played anywhere on its acting merits. It marches
> from situation to situation. But *Romeo and Juliet* proceeds from pic-
> ture to picture. Every line suggests a picture. It is a dramatic poem
> rather than a drama, and I mean to treat it from that point of view.[6]

James's response to Irving's production, however, was markedly unen-
thusiastic:

> I had never thought of *Romeo and Juliet* as a dull drama; but Mr. Irving
> has succeeded in making it so. It is obstructed, interrupted; its pas-
> sionate rapidity is chopped up into little tableaus. In a word, it is slow
> [...] To make this enchanting poem tame, – it was reserved for the
> present management of the Lyceum to accomplish that miracle.
> ('London Plays' (1882), *SA*, p. 164)

While James and Irving both use the word 'poem' for the play, they
obviously have different notions of poetry. Irving says that it 'proceeds
from picture to picture'; this is witheringly rewritten by James as
'chopped up into little tableaus'. As a 'point' to 'point', so to speak, it
lacks 'passionate rapidity', is excruciatingly obstructed. And the moral
James draws with regard to the state of the English theatre is directly
connected with his theme in *The Tragic Muse*:

> Scenery and decorations have been brought to their highest perfec-
> tion, while elocution and action, the interpretation of meanings,
> have not been made the objects of serious study. (*SA*, p. 165)

Another London production of the play hovering in the margin here
(even if James didn't see it, which he probably did) would have been
that which put on show in 1884 the Juliet of Mary Anderson
(1859–1940), an untrained but beautiful American actress whom James

had met socially at the Mrs Humphry Wards on 30 January 1884 a few months after her London début at the Lyceum in September 1883. Mary Anderson, who became a lifelong friend of James's, was very much of the didactic and respectable Anglo-Saxon persuasion (unlike the polyglot, semi-Bohemian, half-Jewish Miriam). She married and retired from acting in 1890, the year James's novel appeared in book form. Audiences liked her looks even as reviewers tended to deplore her delivery of the lines. Her *Romeo and Juliet*, with the handsome but unintelligent William Terriss as Romeo, in Lewis Wingfield's striking pseudo-medieval costumes patched together from 'genuine relics of Renaissance brocade and damask',[7] opened on 1 November 1884 at the Lyceum during Irving's American tour of 1884. It was a considerable commercial, if not critical success. Mary Anderson inspired Mrs Humphry Ward's first novel, *Miss Bretherton* (1885), on which James was a close adviser, and she can thus be said to have inspired *The Tragic Muse* itself, this being a reworking of the same theme. Miriam is James's fulfilment of the wish James had told Mrs Ward that her novel, which ends in the heroine's marriage and retirement from the stage, had provoked in him:

> I am capable of wishing that the actress might have been carried away from Kendal [the prototype for James's Peter Sherringham] altogether, carried away by the current of her artistic life, the sudden growth of her power, and the excitement, the ferocity and egotism...which the effort to create, to 'arrive' [...] would have brought with it. (*TM*, p. xvi)

As often with James's fiction, *The Tragic Muse* seems partly driven by a critical divergence of view from another work. James's Miriam faces the same choice as Mrs Ward's Isabel Bretherton, between conventional marriage and the dedicated life of the stage, but she is not saved from the necessity of deciding by the good luck of a medical condition that demands, and excuses, her retirement and marriage. *The Tragic Muse* refuses to cough up the usual happy ending, what James called in 'The Art of Fiction' 'a distribution at the last of prizes, pensions, husbands, wives, babies, millions, appended paragraphs, and cheerful remarks',[8] but it also refuses the novelist's conventional hierarchy of values, with romantic love perched always unquestionably at the top. The passions of James's characters are not always for each other. They are frequently for ideas, or for kinds of life, including the life of art, and may be mutually incompatible, may force quiet, unspectacular sacrifices many readers don't want to face in their novels.

III

Let us turn back to our question. Where did who get hold of what? We know the question is asked by Peter Sherringham, about the middle of the novel, about the acting of Miriam Rooth. What exactly prompts it? The scene it refers to is a deliberate contrast with the earlier audition at Madame Carré's.

About a third of the way through the novel, Sherringham has been in England for his regular diplomat's leave of absence of two months – an absence which has brought home that he is in love with Miriam. On his return to Paris Peter learns Miriam has just set off to see Madame Carré again, with a young actor called Basil Dashwood. Peter rushes to Madame Carré's – and as he comes in behind a heavy curtain, finds that 'Miriam was already launched in a recitation' (*TM*, p. 213).

Miriam was in the act of rolling out some speech from the English poetic drama –

For I am sick and capable of fears,
Oppressed with wrongs and therefore full of fears.

He recognized one of the great tirades of Shakespeare's Constance and saw she had just begun the magnificent scene at the beginning of the third act of *King John*, in which the passionate injured mother and widow sweeps in wild organ-tones the entire scale of her irony and wrath. (p. 213)

The scene is II. 2., where poor Salisbury has to bring Constance the news that her champion the French king has made a deal with John in another victory for what the Bastard in the previous scene has called 'That smooth-fac'd gentleman, tickling commodity, / Commodity, the bias of the world' (II. 1. 573–4). Miriam's lessons in the 'rolling Italian diction' may now be paying off in this 'rolling out' of her speech.

Sherringham listens from behind the curtain, recognising her virtuosity, 'the long stride she had taken in his absence'. He remains where he is till she arrives at the words, 'Then speak again, not all thy former tale, / But this one word, whether thy tale be true,' (II. 2. 25–6). He slips in as someone – Basil Dashwood – reads Salisbury's short reply, saying 'Go on, go on!'

Miriam [...] fixed him with her illumined eyes, that is with those of the raving Constance [...]. Miriam's colour rose, yet he as quickly felt that she had no personal emotion in seeing him again; the cold passion of art had perched on her banner and she listened to herself with an ear as vigilant as if she had been a Paganini drawing a fiddle-bow. This effect deepened as she went on, rising and rising to the great occasion, moving with extraordinary ease and in the largest clearest style at the dizzy height of her idea. That she had an idea was visible enough, and that the whole thing was very different from all Sherringham had hitherto heard her attempt. (p. 214)

He sees that Miriam knows that 'the sun of her talent had risen above the hills':

This conviction was the one artless thing that glimmered like a young joy through the tragic mask of Constance, and Sherringham's heart beat faster as he caught it in her face. It only showed her as more intelligent, and yet there had been a time when he thought her stupid! (p. 214)

As Miriam continues, Peter, James's engaged spectator, keeps on absorbing the significance of her reading, especially 'the variety of expression that she threw into a torrent of objurgation'. Her performance

was a real composition, studded with passages that called a suppressed tribute to the lips and seeming to show that a talent capable of such an exhibition was capable of anything.

> But thou art fair, and at thy birth, dear boy,
> Nature and Fortune join'd to make thee great:
> Of Nature's gifts thou mayst with lilies boast,
> And with the half-blown rose.

As the girl turned to her imagined child with this exquisite apostrophe [...] she opened at a stroke to Sherringham's vision a prospect that they would yet see her express tenderness better even than anything else. Her voice was enchanting in these lines, and the beauty of her performance was that though she uttered the full fury of the part she missed nothing of its poetry.

'Where did she get hold of that – where did she get hold of that?'
Peter wondered while his whole sense vibrated. 'She hadn't got hold
of it when I went away.' (pp. 215–16)

Here, then, is the question in its context, referring to Miriam's performance in its combination of 'art' and 'composition' with 'raving' and
'tenderness'. The question clearly doesn't refer to the text of *King John*
itself, nor even to the idea of its richness (Miriam says to Sherringham a
little later: 'You know you read *King John* with me before you went away.
I thought over immensely what you said. I didn't understand it much at
the time – I was so stupid. But it all came to me later,' (p. 218).)
Witnessing Miriam's great leap forward – so clear it even causes Madame
Carré to admit having made a mistake – gives Sherringham a vivid
perception, one that bears directly on the debate about acting freshly
stirred in the England of the 1880s by the 1883 publication of Diderot's
Paradoxe du comédien with a Preface by Irving. Peter perceives

the perfect presence of mind, unconfused, unhurried by emotion,
that any artistic performance requires and that all, whatever the
instrument, require in exactly the same degree: the application, in
other words, clear and calculated, crystal-firm, as it were, of the idea
conceived in the glow of experience, of suffering, of joy. (p. 216)

Miriam agrees, saying 'that at the moment of production the artist can't
too much have his wits about him' (p. 216).
Why has Sherringham chosen *King John*, and why has Miriam picked
this scene? After all, Dashwood remarks of the English audience, 'I'm
afraid they don't want *King John*' (*TM*, p. 219). Constance was one of the
great roles of Sarah Siddons, who was painted by Reynolds as 'The Tragic
Muse', and had even written a treatise on the character of Constance.
These scenes thus connect Miriam to the heart of the English theatrical
tradition. Yet in her Jewishness and her French initiations Miriam is of
course more conspicuously associated with the great Rachel, whose
posthumous portrait by Gerôme as 'La Tragédie' in the Comédie Française she confronts in Chapter XXI (p. 229). So Miriam is in fact a blend
of influences, and we could recall Dickens's comment on Fechter (also
cited by Jane Moody): 'The fusion of two races is in it, and one cannot
confidently say that it belongs to either.'[9]
Why does James pick the particular lines he does to quote? They
become in a sense *his* 'points', a test of his imagination of successful
acting. The first pair of lines, as Christopher Ricks once pointed out (in a

lecture), comes from four lines which all end in 'fears' and thus do something that is horribly, obsessively not rhyming. The two lines cited by James imply the second pair, giving the sense of Miriam's being launched. There is a paradox here that maybe the lines apply directly to Miriam: we don't yet know of Miriam's transformation, and maybe she *is* 'full of fears' as before, and as Constance claims to be, rather than full of confidence.

The second moment – 'Then speak again' – could be read as Miriam telling herself to speak again, in a test of whether her speech is true, that is aesthetically true. It may also refer to Madame Carré's previous negative judgement of her, inviting her seriously to revise it. The third moment quoted, where Constance softens and turns to the young Arthur – 'But thou art fair, and at thy birth, dear boy' – illustrates a talent 'capable of anything' (p. 215) rather than 'capable of fears'. (The moment comes *earlier* in the Shakespeare scene than 'the huge firm earth' speech James has already evoked; Sherringham is reviewing what he has seen, going back over it in his mind.) Miriam's celebration of Nature here is of course, like Shakespeare's lines themselves, in itself a triumph of art. We may also be struck by the way Miriam retorts *after* her performance to Mme Carré's indulgent grumbling about Shakespeare's language, complaining of Constance that unlike Camille in Corneille's *Horace* 'She rails like a fish-wife', and that 'Camille doesn't squat down on the floor in the middle of them,' (p. 217). Miriam's reply is a burst of further performance:

> ' "For grief is proud and makes his owner stoop.
> To me and to the state of my great grief
> Let kings assemble," '

Miriam quickly declaimed. 'Ah if you don't feel the way she makes a throne of it!' (p. 217)[10]

Miriam sees how Constance is, in the phrase James so liked, 'making a scene', and sees the theatrical potency of the way the poetic and the gestural come together here. Overall, the brilliance of this choice of Shakespearian scene – Miriam's, and James's – lies in its exemplification of a strong female role commanding the stage – and a bare stage at that. Miriam says 'Oh I hate scenery!' (p. 219), and in terms of the debate about pictorialism it is surely significant that Constance's imaginative power to impose an illusion on others – like an actress – is part of what Miriam singles out: 'Ah if you don't feel the way she makes a throne of it!' (p. 217).

IV

We should end with a brief return to the other Shakespeare play James conjures with. Miriam says to Mme Carré after her *tour de force* as Constance: 'I'll do Juliet – I'll do Cleopatra' (p. 219).[11] James leaves himself too little space at the end for what would in any case have been the extremely hard job of describing Miriam's eventual triumph as Juliet (the novel has a 'makeshift middle',[12] a 'centre [...] *not* [...] in the middle' (p. 5)). In any case Miriam's apotheosis may, unlike her Constance, be best left to the reader's imagination. To adapt James on his approach in 'The Turn of the Screw': 'Make him *think* the triumph, make him think it for himself, and you are released from weak specifications.'[13] To make real to ourselves the non-existent Miriam is our task as readers in the novel, the challenge, or the education, it offers us. In the *Aspern Papers* Preface he gives an account of the criticism of a friend who attacked as implausible his evocation of great public figures with special qualities not seen in the real world, and Miriam is an example.

> It was all very well for instance to have put one's self at such pains for Miriam Rooth in 'The Tragic Muse'; but *there* was misapplied zeal, there a case of pitiful waste, crying aloud to be denounced. Miriam is offered not as a young person passing unnoticed by her age – like the Biddy Dormers and Julia Dallows, say, of the same book, but as a high rarity, a time-figure of the scope inevitably attended by other commemorations. Where on earth would be then Miriam's inscribed 'counterfoil,' and in what conditions of the contemporary English theatre, in what conditions of criticism, of appreciation, might we take an artistic value of this order either for produced or for recognised? We are, as a 'public,' chalk-marked by nothing, more unmistakeably, than by the truth that we know nothing of such values.[14]

The retort James gives to such an objection comes in his Preface to *The Lesson of the Master*, where he calls his creation of subtle artist-figures in his fiction who have no equivalent in the real world 'a campaign, of a sort, on behalf of the something better [...] that blessedly, as is assumed, *might* be'. Miriam embodies the part-cynical, part-idealistic artistic strategy that James in that Preface calls 'operative irony':

> It implies and projects the possible other case, the case rich and edifying where the actuality is pretentious and vain. So it plays its

lamp; so, essentially, it carries that smokeless flame, which makes clear, with all the rest, the good cause that guides it.[15]

James's cramped final chapter, though, hardly 'projects the possible other case, the case rich and edifying'. Only summarising, James announces a case where artistic and popular success go hand in hand:

> It is enough to say that these great hours marked an era in contemporary art [...] Miriam's Juliet was an exquisite image of young passion and young despair, expressed in the truest divinest music that had ever poured from tragic lips. The great childish audience, gaping at her points, expanded there before her like a lap to catch flowers. (p. 486)[16]

We may doubt that 'It is enough to say' no more than this. Whereas in Miriam's early display at Peter Sherringham's James described her playing of Juliet's last scene in some detail, here the closest we get to a rendering is that 'The curtain was rising on the tragic climax of the play. / Miriam Rooth was sublime [...]' (p. 490). This is a disappointment, but perhaps an inevitable one. The revival of Shakespearean performance in England, James's novel ends by saying, is something we will have to imagine for ourselves.

A few years later James went to see *Richard III* at the Lyceum and reported on it to the readers of *Harper's Weekly*. Though he was to write again on Shakespeare, and memorably so, in an extraordinary essay on *The Tempest* (1907),[17] these were his last published comments on Shakespeare in the contemporary English theatre. It was nearly a quarter of a century since he had started watching Sir Henry Irving, as he had now become, and his leading lady Ellen Terry. By 1897, after his own bruising experiences as a playwright of the conditions of the English stage, James had had enough. As Richard of Gloucester Irving was doing what he did best. James concedes that he 'makes, for the setting, a big, brave general picture, and then, for the figure, plays on the chord of the sinister-sardonic, flowered over as vividly as may be with the elegant-grotesque'. But for the wearied spectator nothing can obscure 'an acute sense that, after all that has come and gone, the represented Shakespeare is simply no longer to be borne' (*SA*, p. 287). The pictorial and spectacular Shakespeare with which Irving had dominated the English theatre of the end of the century had got hold of 'that' and crushed it. 'The more it is painted and dressed, the more it is lighted and furnished and solidified, the less it corresponds or coincides, the less it squares with our imaginative habits', James moaned. He was left with 'a sore sense that the more Shakespeare is "built in" the more we are built out' (*SA*, p. 288). James had been sounding this note back in 1882 when he complained of Irving's *Romeo and Juliet* that he had converted the play 'from a splendid and delicate poem into a gorgeous and over-weighted spectacle' (*SA*, p. 163). If Shakespeare was to be saved for the English stage, it would only be by a great disencumbrance, a demotion of the scene-painter, the carpenter and upholsterer that would allow the actor again to get hold of 'that', the poetry that had sustained Garrick and Mrs Siddons as they wandered over England, interpreting Shakespeare as they went, representing the visions of Hamlet and the sorrows of Constance 'with the assistance of a few yards of tinsel and a few dozen tallow candles' (*SA*, p. 168). But in James's own day it was no longer English actors who kept the spirit of the text alive. Now it was the 'immigrants' discussed by Jane Moody, including for James, above all, the Tommaso Salvini whose Othello had thrilled him in Boston in 1883, and again in London the following year.

Poor Miriam Rooth embodies a forlorn dream, for the English theatre, of a Shakespeare revitalised by French style and Italian passion. But by 1897 James wondered, and he was not alone in this, if the English stage might be better off leaving Shakespeare to his readers. *Richard III* itself seemed to him something of a loose baggy monster. In his piece for *Harper's Weekly*, it was with rising spirits and quickened interest that James turned from Irving's *Richard III* to a production by his friend Elizabeth Robins of Ibsen's *Little Eyolf*, and he voiced his eagerness to see *John Gabriel Borkman*, the most recent work of 'the wonderful old man of Christiania' *(SA*, pp. 288–9). Perhaps Miriam Rooth should have forgone the 'great childish audience' that was stuck in the past and focused instead on a small grown-up one that would do for the future.

Notes

1. Henry James, *The Scenic Art: Notes on Acting and the Drama 1872–1901*, ed. by Allan Wade (London: Rupert Hart-Davis, 1949), p. 125 (hereafter *SA*).
2. Henry James, *The Tragic Muse* (1890), in revised version of 1908, ed. by Philip Horne (London: Penguin Classics, 1995), pp. 88, 138 (hereafter *TM*; all references in text).
3. For a fuller account, see the classic essay by D. J. Gordon and John Stokes, 'The Reference of *The Tragic Muse*', in *The Air of Reality: New Essays on Henry James*, ed. by John Goode (London and New York: Methuen, 1973), pp. 81–167.

4. The earlier version has 'a kind of illuminated perseverance' instead of 'a blundering energy' (see 'Variant Readings', *TM*, 521).
5. 1 April 1882; quoted in George Rowell, 'Mercutio as Romeo: William Terriss in *Romeo and Juliet*', in *Shakespeare and the Victorian Stage*, ed. by Richard Foulkes (Cambridge University Press 1986), pp. 87–96 (p. 91).
6. *Ellen Terry's Memoirs*, ed. by Edith Craig and Christopher St. John (London: V. Gollancz, 1933), p. 162; quoted in 'Mercutio as Romeo: William Terriss in *Romeo and Juliet*', pp. 87–8.
7. Marion Jones, 'Stage Costume: historical verisimilitude and Stage Convention', in *Shakespeare and the Victorian Stage*, pp. 56–73 (p. 63).
8. Henry James, 'The Art of Fiction' (1884), in *Literary Criticism: Essays on Literature; American Writers; English Writers*, ed. by Leon Edel and Mark Wilson (New York: Library of America, 1984), pp. 44–65 (p. 48).
9. 'On Mr Fechter's Acting', *Atlantic Monthly* (August 1869), 243.
10. Miriam's comment looks forward to the end of the scene, where Constance declares, 'here I and sorrows sit; / Here is my throne, bid kings come bow to it,' (II. 2. 73–4).
11. And at the end of the novel Miriam indeed does what Mary Anderson did, starting in London with new, poorish plays, and *then* doing *Romeo and Juliet* – in her case after five months of rehearsals.
12. Henry James, Preface to *The Wings of the Dove*, in Henry James, *Literary Criticism: French Writers; Other European Writers; the Prefaces to the New York Edition*, ed. by Leon Edel and Mark Wilson (New York: Library of America, 1984), pp. 1287–303 (p. 1299).
13. Henry James, Preface to *The Aspern Papers, The Turn of the Screw, &c.*, in *Literary Criticism: Prefaces &c.*, p. 1188.
14. Henry James, Preface to *The Aspern Papers, The Turn of the Screw, &c.*, in *Literary Criticism: Prefaces &c.*, p. 1180.
15. Preface to *The Lesson of the Master &c.*, in *Literary Criticism: Prefaces &c.*, 1225–37, p. 1229.
16. We might notice from 'the great childish audience, gaping at her points', that James's revival doesn't seem to involve a serious challenge to the 'points' approach, unless there is some irony here about the unappreciative 'gaping'. An emphasis on clear communication is no more than we might expect from the writer who lectured the young women of Bryn Mawr on elocution as a mark of civilisation, who so passionately believed in articulation, form and expression. But the description of music pouring from Miriam's lips implies a 'passionate rapidity' in the performance which is a long way from Irving's, chopped up into tableaux.
17. *Literary Criticism: English Writers &c.*, pp. 1205–20.

7

Shakespeare's Weeds: Tennyson, Elegy and Allusion

Robert Douglas-Fairhurst

Stephen Greenblatt opens *Shakespearean Negotiations*, his seminal study of the reciprocal pressures which Shakespeare and his contemporaries exercised upon one another, by raising the idea of the literary critic as a type of cultural shaman: 'I began with the desire to speak with the dead.' However, critics are not alone in hoping that their writing will allow them to speak with the dead; nor are they alone in being aware that, in Greenblatt's words, 'works of art, however intensely marked by the creative intelligence and private obsessions of individuals, are the products of collective negotiation and exchange'.[1]

Take these lines from *In Memoriam*:

> How pure at heart and sound in head,
>   With what divine affections bold
>   Should be the man whose thought would hold
> An hour's communion with the dead.[2]

A brief communion with the dead is what Tennyson describes here, but also what he accomplishes, because – as Christopher Ricks points out in his great edition of the poems – the phrase 'communion with the dead' brings together a number of earlier writers (*TP*, II, 41 1n). There is Webster:

> O that it were possible we might
> But hold some two days' conference with the dead.[3]

There is Tennyson's early poem 'On Sublimity':

> For thou dost hold communion with the dead
>> (*TP*, I, 130)

– a self-allusion which reminds us that, for a poet, a dead voice could be his own earlier voice, the poems which no longer speak to him or for him, but also that in poetry, as in other human pursuits, 'men may rise on stepping-stones / Of their dead selves to higher things'.[4] Most strikingly, there are Arthur Hallam's lines on the 'Spirits that but seem / To hold communion with the dead' – a description which Tennyson's quatrain returns to and restores in a form of literary resurrection, as he catches Hallam's voice into his voice, and continues to speak alone as they might once have spoken together.[5]

Together, these allusions show Tennyson speaking not only about the dead, but with the dead, as one might speak with a foreign accent: by projecting their voices through his voice, he seeks out points of contact and contrast, give and take, exchange and blockage. Yet although this section of *In Memoriam* is especially haunted by the questioning presence of the dead, it also provides a representative sample of the poem's range and depth of literary allusion. Indeed, from its beginning (which refers to Goethe) to its end (which includes a grateful nod to Dante), so often do the lines of *In Memoriam* hum with earlier fragments of speech, that reading it can be like Tennyson's own experience once of stopping by a telegraph-pole 'to listen to the wail of the wires, the souls of dead messages'.[6] Many of these allusions seem to reflect self-consciously on the nature of allusion itself. This is especially true of Tennyson's borrowings from Shakespeare: an important writer for Hallam,[7] and an equally important presence in the poem which commemorates him by claiming that 'I loved thee, Spirit, and love, nor can / The soul of Shakespeare love thee more.'[8]

Tennyson was sensitive to the charge that he borrowed, or pilfered, some of his best lines from other writers. Commenting on his description of Melissa in *The Princess*, whose thoughts are 'as fair within her eyes, / As bottom agates seen to wave and float / In crystal currents of clear morning seas', Tennyson's explanation was characteristically tetchy: 'It has been said that I took this simile partly from Beaumont and Fletcher, partly from Shakespeare, whereas I made it while I was bathing in Wales.'[9] And yet, some of his early allusions to Shakespeare come close to acknowledging their source in ways that are playful, even jokey, in tone. For example, the unpublished political poem 'I loving freedom for herself', written between 1832 and 1834, concludes with two lines adapted from *Hamlet*:

> There lives a power to shape our ends
> Rough-hew them as we will!
>
> (*TP*, II, 46)

Lurking behind the cheery flourish of that exclamation-mark, the implication is that poems, too, have ends which can be shaped by a power outside the writer's conscious control. As Tennyson developed and revised *In Memoriam*, however, this idea that human lives can be mapped out according to the pre-existing co-ordinates provided by literature acquired a new gravity and pathos. Thus, 'who shall [...] reach a hand through time to catch / The far-off interest of tears?' (*In Memoriam*, I) is a question which contains its own answer, because Tennyson's lines are lent to him by Richard III:

> The liquid drops of tears that you have shed
> Shall come again, transform'd to orient pearl,
> Advantaging their love with interest [...]
>
> (*Richard III*, IV. 4. 322–4)

Tennyson glossed his lines as 'The good that grows for us out of grief' (*TP*, II, 319n), but his allusion also suggests what might grow out of an earlier description of grief, realising the process which Richard's lines imagine, advantaging their loan with interest.[10]

Even where Tennyson's allusions do not explicitly take the form of questions, they tend to treat Shakespeare's lines as questions, to which his own lines provide a reply, or retort, or reproof, as when he expresses the hope that 'from his ashes may be made / The violet of his native land' – a thoughtful translation of Laertes's words about Ophelia: 'Lay her i' th' earth, / And from her fair and unpolluted flesh / May violets spring!' (*Hamlet*, V. 1. 238–9).[11] By reappearing in Tennyson's elegy, like a belated floral tribute, Shakespeare's violets confirm that the belief expressed by a later section of *In Memoriam* can be as true of poems as it is of people: 'I know transplanted human worth / Will bloom to profit, otherwhere.'[12] Yet although this sort of allusion opens up a dialogue with the past, it is also solidly rooted in the present, because long before *In Memoriam* became a set of anthology pieces, a narrative poem reduced to a selection of free-standing lyrics, it tapped the Victorian fondness for anthologies: literally the 'flowers' of literature.[13]

By 1817, when Coleridge sourly described the 'shelf or two of BEAUT-
IES, ELEGANT EXTRACTS and ANAS' which comprised 'nine-tenths of
the reading of the reading public',[14] Shakespeare had already been put
through the mill of William Dodd's much-reprinted 1752 collection *The
Beauties of Shakespeare*. In the years that followed, Shakespeare would be
further 'collected' into *The Wisdom and Genius of Shakspeare* (1838),
Religious and Moral Sentences Culled from the Works of Shakespeare
(1843), *Sentiments and Similes of William Shakspeare* (1851), *Pearls of
Shakspeare* (1860), *Choice thoughts from Shakspere* (1861), *The Sweet Silvery
Sayings of Shakespeare on the Softer Sex. Compiled by an Old Soldier* (1877),
and many similar volumes. However, as Leah Price has pointed out in
her recent book on the rise of the anthology,[15] even in a period during
which many readers would have agreed, with Matthew Arnold, that not
to know Shakespeare was to be 'very imperfect and fragmentary',[16] there
was little consensus over what to make of a writer who himself appeared
more often in the form of parts than he did as a whole. At the same time,
there was varied and fertile disagreement over what a literary extract
was, and what it was for: should an extract be thought of as a fragment
taken out of context, like extracting a tooth, or the concentrated essence
of its source, like a plant extract?

The popularity of these anthologies can partly be attributed to individual literary habits. Edward FitzGerald, for instance, not only published a commonplace book entitled *Polonius*, but also studded his
poetic translation *Rubáiyát of Omar Khayyám* with allusions to his
other reading, including Shakespeare, in order to test his conviction
that the thoughts of writers separated by gaps of space and time continued to run along parallel lines.[17] Just as his commonplace book shed
each text's husk of historical specificity in order to expose its time-
travelling core, so his translation absorbed Shakespeare into a present
tense and epigrammatic style which freed each quatrain from the local
accidents of geography and history.

For FitzGerald, then, familiarity bred content. But the growing association of Shakespeare with all-purpose maxims and proverbs also
touched upon a broader range of Victorian cultural interests. Within
the field of textual theory, these include the early efforts of scholars,
attacked by F. E. Halliday as 'disintegrators',[18] to check how much of
Shakespeare was written by Shakespeare, and how much by other
writers, together with investigations into Shakespeare's own piecemeal
methods of composition, whereby, as Walter Pater put it, he 'refash-
ioned [...] materials already at hand, so that the relics of other men's
poetry are incorporated'.[19] Turning to theatrical practice, the same

interests also include the popularity of Shakespearean travesty, which often brought together parodies of lines from different plays within the spoofing of a single plot,[20] and the increasingly accurate attention to performance history which led Bulwer Lytton to contrast Elizabethan conventions of staging ('long and loose') with the 'close and hard [and] compact' style of contemporary productions.[21] There are even echoes of these debates to be found in the standard method of delivering dramatic speeches, which encouraged actors to pause over climactic 'points' and skim through the lines in between, just as anthologies encouraged a rhythm of reading which searched for highlights, alternately skipping and lingering.

In his 1860 collection *The Mind of Shakspeare*, A. A. Morgan sums up this popular cultural model of Shakespeare as a writer of general sayings rather than specific utterances: 'From that mind issued views, maxims and references time can never destroy [...] on upwards of five hundred subjects.'[22] Yet although the anthologist replaced each play's narrative continuity with a selection of free-standing fragments, not all Victorian allusions to Shakespeare assume a set of timeless truths. Some instead use the transmission of particular lines to reflect upon less orderly and predictable forms of historical development. For example, just as Darwin's reading of Shakespeare's history plays provided him with a set of ideas on which to model his own theories of succession, restoration, the spectacle of individuals conforming to type,[23] so George Eliot's tags from Shakespeare frequently resemble a running critical commentary upon the shifting moral demands which her narratives make on their characters and their readers. 'They'll take suggestion as a cat laps milk': the epigraph to chapter 32 of *Middlemarch* adapts *The Tempest* (II. 1. 288) to express the hope that human sympathies might 'take' as readily as her own literary graft; but then 'a world which has long been flat and stale to them', part of a description in *Brother Jacob* (ch. 2), uses its echo of *Hamlet* to admit, as if under its breath, that literature can make the world sound repetitive and routine, in addition to providing it with new shapes of understanding.[24] Two unconnected sentences from *Daniel Deronda* suggest something of Eliot's ambivalence towards the allusions which punctuate and structure her narratives. 'It is the curse of your life – forgive me – of so many lives, that all passion is spent in that narrow round, for want of ideas and sympathies to make a larger home for it' (ch. 36): allusion provides one textual model for that 'larger home' in which our minds and voices should move; but then, describing a broken plate, 'The story is chipped off, so to speak, and passes with a ragged edge into nothing' (ch. 37): allusion also reminds us of how partial and quickly exhausted our sympathies can become once they are drawn out over testing stretches of space and time.

A similar ambivalence is at work in Tennyson's use of Shakespeare. Lengthening and thickening his lines with phrases from individual plays, such as 'each particular hair', or 'yeasty waves', or 'out of joint' – or with phrases which have already been loosened from their source, such as 'thick night' (Shakespeare and Keats), or 'golden prime' (Shakespeare and Shelley), or 'guilty thing' (Shakespeare and Wordsworth) – means that even as a poem like *In Memoriam* is lamenting a unique loss, it is attuning our ears to the idea that grief can be shared, losses restored.[25] 'They know me not, but mourn with me',[26] remarks Tennyson of the voices which surround him in the countryside: rather a hopeful claim to make about cows and gnats, perhaps, but a reasonable one to make about the earlier human speakers whose voices are gratefully embraced by his poem: 'They know me not, but mourn with me.' That is, because allusion suggests two writers speaking with one voice, it can express a community of response to events which divide people from one another, such as death. However, its use in elegy can also be more equivocal, by bringing to our attention the way that a writer's voice is likely to be subject to the same forces of decline and decay as his body once it is released into the unpredictable world of print. Like people, poems can dwindle and die; as T. S. Eliot puts it in *Four Quartets*, 'Every poem an epitaph'.[27]

Consider, for instance, Tennyson's sharp-eyed and sharp-eared interest in weeds – a word whose meaning in *In Memoriam*, as in Shakespeare, hovers quizzically between 'plant-life' and 'clothing', natural circumstances and human responses to these circumstances:

> In words, like weeds, I'll wrap me o'er [...]

> I envy not [...]
> The heart that never plighted troth
> But stagnates in the weeds of sloth;

> We pass; the path that each man trod
> Is dim, or will be dim, with weeds [...] [28]

All three examples seem to be recalling the advice of Old Hamlet to his son: 'duller shouldst thou be than the fat weed / That roots itself in ease on Lethe wharf, / Wouldst thou not stir in this' (I. 5. 32–4).[29] (For the 'roots' of the Quartos, the Folio text has 'rots', a reading often accepted by later editions.) To some extent, therefore, like *In Memoriam*'s other references to *Hamlet*, these allusions are true to the play's own restless sense of delay, aftermath, what has been done but is not yet done with. Like the garlanded Ophelia, who sings 'snatches of old lauds' while she drowns, finding some company in her misery, we might then conclude that here Tennyson is confronting death with some 'weedy trophies' of his own (IV. 7. 174–7).

However, the allusions are also messier and more awkward than this. In Shakespeare's play, weeds are significant because they form part of a rich set of ideas and words associated with disgust. The 'unweeded garden / That grows to seed' (I. 2. 135–6), the poison which is a 'mixture rank, of midnight weeds collected' (III. 2. 257): when these weeds spring up between the cracks of speech, they serve to remind us of Hamlet's appalled fascination with corruption, contamination, the way that fertility and decay seem so easily mingled and muddled. As William Ian Miller describes it, in his wonderfully disturbing study of disgust:

> Rotting vegetation can be nearly as gorge raising as rotting flesh, and we are still wedded to folk beliefs that such vegetable muck spontaneously generates the worms, slugs, frogs, newts, mudpuppies, leeches, and eels we associate with it. [...] What disgusts, startlingly, is the capacity for life, and not just because life implies its correlative death and decay: for it is decay that seems to engender life. [...] Death thus horrifies and disgusts not just because it smells revoltingly bad, but because it is not an end to the process of living. [...] The having lived and the living unite to make up the organic world of generative rot – rank, smelling, and upsetting to the touch.[30]

In other words, what generates disgust is often generation itself, the fact that sometimes life doesn't seem to know where to stop. This provides a good model for Hamlet's speeches, which are repeatedly, compulsively drawn to and repelled by the physical world, much as the audience of *Hamlet* is asked simultaneously to approach the play with sympathy and recoil with alarm. It also provides a model of Tennyson's more general ambivalence over what to make of his own elegy: a poem which kept on growing, with no natural point of rest, but which also threatened a form of imaginative stagnancy and decay.

Of course, any poet with a distinctive style, recognisable speechtics, might be open to accusations of creative stuttering and brooding. Similarly, any popular or quotable poet might be enlisted in ongoing Victorian debates about the need for literature to flow between people if it is to avoid contributing to what Knox's eighteenth-century collection of literary extracts described as the 'stagnant pool' of unread works: 'large perhaps and deep, but of little utility'.[31] Thomas Hardy, for instance, is unlikely to have been surprised at T. H. Warren's complaint, in a review of *Poems of the Past and Present* (1901), that the 'prevailing note' of his verse was 'a morbid taste for the ghastly and gruesome'.[32] However, he might have been disappointed by Warren's conclusion that, whereas Tennyson had outgrown a youthful interest in the wormy circumstance of death, Hardy was still imaginatively trapped in the graveyard. After all, many of Hardy's poems do not only describe the transformations undergone by bodies in the earth, but also seek to make themselves complicit in the processes they describe: even those ideas which risk being exhausted through repetition retain a subterranean energy in his verse, spreading and sprouting like an old corpse. Thus, in 'Voices from Things Growing in a Churchyard', the seepage of human life into plant life, as 'Eve Greensleeves' is sucked up into fresh green leaves, or 'Thomas Voss' burrows his way into 'berries of juice and gloss', is carried in rhymes which remind the reader that our words, like our bodies, can enjoy unpredictable transformations, offshoots, and outgrowths.[33] Similarly, in 'The Levelled Churchyard', Hardy's claim that the dead do not rest in peace, but are instead forever rotting and blending into a 'human jam', is entertained in a stanza that adapts the common metre so popular with hymn writers in order to suggest teasingly that we may have more in common than we would wish once we can no longer fend off one another's attentions (a particular anxiety for the touch-sensitive Hardy).[34] Even Hardy's periodic returns to the subject of weeds (the 'weedy space' left by a removed building; 'sepulchres begirt with weeds'; the worry that an undefended country would be 'Untended as a wild of weeds and sand') come in lines which stretch out inquisitive fingers to one another across the years.[35] In all these examples, the 'prevailing note' of Hardy's verse can be heard sounding out not only the death that is in life, but also the life that continues to come out of death.

However, Warren's comparison with Tennyson is a helpful one, because Tennyson too was vulnerable to the charge that he confused development and degeneration. A number of Tennyson's contemporaries worried that his poetry was getting stuck in a rut; reading through the 1842 *Poems*, Leigh Hunt complained, 'We are oppressed as with a nook of Lincolnshire weeds [...] his luxury tends to rankness.'[36] The echo of *Hamlet* in Hunt's remark is especially suggestive, not only because Tennyson's poems are so variously attracted to decay, from the slow collapse of buildings to the piecemeal disintegration of human beings, but also because so many of his own allusions to Shakespeare emerge in a context of rottenness. From the early play *The Devil and the Lady*, which adapts *The Tempest* to consider whether 'the weeds of wanton Idleness / Have mantled his clear wit',[37] to the life of his Mariana in the moated grange, described as 'weeded and worn' ('weeded' so near to and so far from being 'wedded'),[38] there is a fertile creative overlap in Tennyson's mind between his subject-matter and his methods of composition. Repeatedly, scenes which centre on the rank and rotten bring together – in Miller's words – the 'having lived and the living' in a promiscuous tangle of voices. So, in *The Devil and the Lady*, when Amoret describes how Disappointment 'bears a charmèd life and will outlast me / In mustiness of dry longevity / Like some tough Mummy withered not decayed', she draws for support upon Macbeth ('I bear a charmed life') in a way that provides Tennyson's readers with the more cheering thought that even charmed lives must come to an end; even disappointment cannot always be successful.[39] Similarly, in *Merlin and Vivien*, when Vivien slyly urges that Merlin must trust her 'not at all or all in all', for doubt is the 'little pitted speck in garnered fruit, / That rotting inward slowly moulders all', there is a warning echo of Baptista's hope in *The Taming of the Shrew* that Petruchio will win more than a show of obedience from his daughter (a hope that Shakespeare's play never unequivocally fulfils): 'That is, her love; for that is all in all'.[40]

In this context, it is perhaps not surprising that *In Memoriam* is so animated by the worry that it goes on by going back, clogged up with bits of old verse, because one danger of writing within a recognisable genre, such as elegy, is that a unique and irreplaceable loss will itself be lost in stale conventions. 'So careful of the type she seems', writes Tennyson, 'So careless of the single life.'[41] He is describing the workings of Nature, but *In Memoriam* is among much else a set of troubled reflections on whether this is also true of the workings of poems like itself: so careful of a type of mourning, so careless of the single life it should be mourning.

> One writes, that 'Other friends remain,'
>   That 'Loss is common to the race' –
>   And common is the commonplace,
> And vacant chaff well meant for grain.[42]

The commonplace nature of this exchange is sunk into the texture of Tennyson's verse, because it remembers Gertrude's appeal to Hamlet:

'Do not for ever with thy vailed lids / Seek for thy noble father in the dust. / Thou know'st 'tis common, all that lives must die', and Hamlet's thin-lipped reply, 'Ay, madam, it is common' (I. 2. 70–4). And yet, the dangerous ease of such repetitions, forever threatening to die on the speaker's lips, could also serve Tennyson as a creative resource, as when he describes in *The Last Tournament* how Lancelot observes the bright white dresses put on in honour of the less than spotless Guinevere: 'He looked but once, and vailed his eyes again,' (*TP*, III, 513). The allusion looks forward as well as back; Lancelot lowers his eyes with a gesture which could be interpreted as a show of modesty, shame, or surrender, but the line which describes his action warns that by this stage in the story it is not only eyes which are falling: the faint but insistent reverberation of *Hamlet*, carried in Tennyson's sinking cadences, anticipates the death of another king, and with it the collapse of an entire culture.

Taken together, what these examples suggest is that the fragments of Shakespeare embedded in Tennyson's verse are in part a practical investigation into the equivocal nature of allusion, of literature's ongoing engagement with itself. Allusions can be read as equally convincing evidence of the redemptive power of art or the vanity of art; they can be used to welcome what we have in common or worry about the aimless commonplaces which lurk temptingly in the cracks of thought and speech; they can reflect upon the way that a piece of writing, as it travels through space and time, encounters pressures which make it more compact, more concentrated, more durable, or more fragile, more porous, more easily broken into pieces.

Any allusions might raise a similar set of questions, of course, but Victorian allusions to Shakespeare raise them with particular strength and urgency, because – especially towards the end of the century – Shakespeare was often enlisted in debates about cultural degeneration and decline, the pervasive worry that it was the weak who would inherit the earth. An 1867 essay on 'The Decay of the Stage' laments that the popular new emphasis on glamorous sets and stage trickery was ignoring the Shakespearean imperative of 'holding a mirror up to nature';[43] an 1884 article on 'The Decay of Genius' argues that 'Nothing is more remarkable [...] in a decaying civilisation' than its gradual loss of 'the power of producing individual genius' like Shakespeare's;[44] by the time we reach Arrigo Boito's libretto for Verdi's *Otello* (1887), it is no surprise to discover that an underlying cause has been found for what Coleridge famously described as Iago's 'motiveless malignity': 'Dalla vitta d'un germe o d'un atomo / Vile son nato', Iago sings, 'From baseness in the seed, or from one vile atom I was born'.[45] In this context, allusions to Shakespeare could be read as a symptom of cultural decline, audible evidence of the parasitical and withered nature of modern voices. But they could also be read as a form of cultural therapy, in the way that R. C. Trench imagined Shakespeare as a figure who should produce sturdy literary offspring, lines of writing as lines of descent, even in the thinning creative atmosphere of the nineteenth century: the writer whose work will last, he explains, is one whose 'words have past / Into man's common thought and week-day phrase [...] Such was our Shakespeare once, and such doth seem / One who redeems our later gloomier days.'[46]

Much of Tennyson's verse is suspended between these alternatives, which – to borrow another of *In Memoriam*'s allusions to Shakespeare – 'Contend for loving masterdom' throughout his career.[47] Part of this ambivalence can be traced to the mixed feelings which Shakespeare's own range of writings produced in his Victorian readers. Thus, while Matthew Arnold could celebrate Shakespeare's plays as an antidote to unhealthy, introspective brooding ('Shakespeare *animates*'),[48] Charles Kingsley was not alone in worrying that Shakespeare's *Sonnets* were 'the confession that over and above all his powers he lacked one thing, and knew not what it was, or where to find it – and that was – to be strong'.[49] In this context, Tennyson could use Shakespeare's unstable public reputation as a model for other, more private forms of doubt and self-doubt. For example, Shakespeare's plays are occasionally echoed in *Maud*, the poem which Tennyson referred to as his 'little *Hamlet*',[50] thereby providing *Maud*'s speaker with a critical gloss upon his own posturing and inertia. At the same time, Tennyson's carefully non-chalant description (how are we to read that 'little'?) should itself give a reader pause, given the diverse ways in which even a little allusion can be understood: as concentrated potential or shrunken lack, seed or relic.[51]

A similar ambivalence is central to *In Memoriam*, which often revolves thoughtfully around ambiguous words like 'mould' and its cognates ('moulded', 'moulder'd', 'moulding', 'mouldering'), to suggest both the shaping of a voice into a poem, and the possible decay of that voice once it is released into print.[52] Section LXXVI hints at the dilemma of the elegist who attempts to challenge the transience of nature with the permanence of his own poem:

> Take wings of fancy, and ascend,
>   And in a moment set thy face
>   Where all the starry heavens of space
> Are sharpened to a needle's end;

Take wings of foresight; lighten through
 The secular abyss to come,
 And lo, thy deepest lays are dumb
Before the mouldering of a yew;

And if the matin songs, that woke
 The darkness of our planet, last,
 Thine own shall wither in the vast,
Ere half the lifetime of an oak.

(*TP*, II, 389–90)

Tennyson glossed 'matin songs' as 'the great early poets', and these lines make explicit what is darkly hinted at in the second quatrain: a modern elegy may well be 'dumb / Before the mouldering of a yew', not just because the majestically slow-moving processes of nature should encourage a respectful silence in those who observe them ('before' being understood in the sense of 'confronted by'), but also because the elegy itself is likely to wither and fade much more quickly than the natural objects which it describes (here Tennyson's lines cast a retrospective accent of envy back into his earlier appeal to the '*Old* Yew').[53] And yet, the way in which Tennyson describes this sense of perspective also provides a clue that even those songs which are disappearing can still stubbornly remain in the sight of their readers, because his vision of space being 'sharpened to a needle's end' flickers with Imogen's yearning description of how she would have watched her beloved Posthumous disappear:

I would have broke mine eye-strings, crack'd them, but
To look upon him, till the diminution
Of space had pointed him sharp as my needle;
Nay, followed him till he had melted from
The smallness of a gnat to air, and then
Have turn'd mine eye, and wept.

(*Cymbeline*, I. 3. 17–22)[54]

The allusion suggests a larger imaginative pattern in Tennyson's poem, which frequently incorporates echoes of earlier writing (including Tennyson's own) in order to consider the possibility that expressions of mourning may not last much longer than the grief which occasioned them. That is, one question which *In Memoriam* repeatedly raises, and repeatedly recognises that it is not yet in a position to answer, is how far any elegy – given the unpredictable demands of the reading public, and the changing state of the language – may come to mourn those parts of itself that are dead or dying. Here Shakespeare provided Tennyson with both a vocabulary to express his fears and a timescale to test them against. For although an allusion like 'sharpened to a needle's end' warns his readers that even the 'deepest lays' can gradually fade from hearing, the resilience and adaptability of this fragment also reminds us that what Tennyson wished so passionately to believe was true of Arthur Hallam is also true of writers like Shakespeare: even speakers who have melted into air need not be altogether destroyed by time, as long as there are later speakers who can share the words which they left suspended in this air.

Benjamin Jowett recalled that Tennyson sometimes 'thought of Shakespeare as happier in having the power to draw himself for his fellow men, and used to think Shakespeare greater in his sonnets than in his plays'.[55] The *Sonnets* are, of course, an important structural model for *In Memoriam*, not only in their staggered narrative development and awkward blurring of private and public speech, but also because, more simply and painfully, the young man they address never answers back. But as the echo of *Cymbeline* suggests, Shakespeare's plays are equally important to Tennyson's attempts to 'draw himself' in his elegy, as both a set of self-portraits and a way of investigating his creative self-development. Section XIV imagines Hallam returning from a sea voyage:

> [If] I perceived no touch of change,
> No hint of death in all his frame,
> But found him all in all the same,
> I should not feel it to be strange.
>
> (*TP*, II, 333)

The rhymes 'change/strange', which chime throughout *In Memoriam*,[56] remember and reject the fate which Ariel imagines in *The Tempest*:

> Full fadom five thy father lies,
> Of his bones are coral made:
> Those are pearls that were his eyes:
> Nothing of him that doth fade,
> But doth suffer a sea-change
> Into something rich and strange.
>
> (I. 2. 397–402)

The enduring rhyme provides a verbal shape for Tennyson's hope that the frame of a person might continue to exist, in this life and the next, as recognisably as the frame of a poem. At the same time, because the rhyme which looks forward to his future reunion with Arthur Hallam is shared with another writer, it tactfully anticipates how they might encounter one another: not by exchanging words, but by exercising what Hallam once described as the 'penetrative mind' of the dead.[57]

As so often in Tennyson's writing, the allusion reveals 'Large elements in order brought, / And tracts of calm from tempest made'.[58]

Notes

1. *Shakespearean Negotiations: the Circulation of Social Energy in Renaissance England* (Oxford: Clarendon Press, 1988), pp. 1, vii.
2. *In Memoriam*, XCIV, in *The Poems of Tennyson*, ed. by Christopher Ricks, 2nd edn, 3 vols (Harlow: Longman, 1987), II, 410. All further references to Tennyson's poems will be to this edition (hereafter abbreviated to *TP*).
3. *The Duchess of Malfi*, IV. 2. 20–21. 'O that it were possible' was another charged phrase in Tennyson's mind and voice; see 'O that 'twere possible' in *Maud*, II. iv (*TP*, II, 571).
4. *In Memoriam*, I (*TP*, II, 318).
5. Fragment ('Who has not dreamt a lovely dream'), in *The Writings of Arthur Hallam*, ed. by T. H. Vail Motter (New York: Modern Language Association of America, 1943), p. 5. All further references to Hallam's writings will be to this edition (hereafter abbreviated to *Motter*).
6. *Alfred Lord Tennyson: a Memoir, By His Son*, 2 vols (London: Macmillan, 1897), II, 325.
7. Hallam's writings describe Shakespeare as the 'greatest of mankind' ('To One Early Loved, Now in India'), and praise him for possessing 'the most universal mind that ever existed' ('The Influence of Italian upon English Literature'), *Motter*, pp. 82, 29.
8. *In Memoriam*, LXI (*TP*, II, 378).
9. *TP*, II, 214 & n.
10. Ricks notes the echo (*TP*, II, 319n), and compares two further possible sources in Shakespeare: Sonnet 31 ('How many a holy and obsequious tear / Hath dear religious love stolen from mine eye, / As interest of the dead'), and *The Rape of Lucrece* ('do not take away / My sorrow's interest; let no mourner say / He weeps for her'). For Tennyson's debts to Shakespeare in the context of his other literary borrowings, see also Ricks's article, 'Tennyson Inheriting the Earth', in *Studies in Tennyson*, ed. by Hallam Tennyson (Basingstoke: Macmillan – now Palgrave Macmillan, 1981), pp. 66–104.
11. *In Memoriam*, XVIII (*TP*, II, 336 & n).
12. *In Memoriam*, LXXXII (*TP*, II, 394).
13. 'Anthology' is derived from 'anthos': the Greek for 'flower'.

14. *Biographia Literaria* (1817), ed. by James Engell and W. Jackson Bate, 2 vols (Princeton: Princeton University Press, 1983), I, 48.
15. *The Anthology and the Rise of the Novel: From Richardson to George Eliot* (Cambridge: Cambridge University Press, 2000).
16. Preface to Edmund Burke's *Letters, Speeches and Tracts on Irish Affairs*, repr. in *The Complete Prose Works of Matthew Arnold*, ed. by R. H. Super, 11 vols (Ann Arbor: University of Michigan Press, 1960–77), IX, 48.
17. I discuss this in more detail in *Victorian Afterlives: the Shaping of Influence in Nineteenth-Century Literature* (Oxford: Oxford University Press, 2002), pp. 270–341.
18. See Aron Y. Stavisky, *Shakespeare and the Victorians: Roots of Modern Criticism* (Norman: University of Oklahoma Press, 1969), p. 42.
19. *Appreciations* (London: Macmillan, 1889), p. 182.
20. See Richard W. Schoch's essay in the companion volume to this, together with his critical study *Not Shakespeare: Bardolatry and Burlesque in the Nineteenth Century* (Cambridge: Cambridge University Press, 2002).
21. Cited in *Shakespeare and the Victorian Stage* (Cambridge: Cambridge University Press, 1986), ed. by Richard Foulkes, p. 162.
22. *The Mind of Shakspeare: as Exhibited in His Works* (London: Chapman and Hall, 1860), cited in Foulkes, p. 195.
23. See Gillian Beer, *Darwin's Plots: Evolutionary Narrative in Darwin, George Eliot and Nineteenth-century Fiction* (London: Routledge & Kegan Paul, 1983), pp. 30–3.
24. 'How [weary], stale, flat, and unprofitable / Seem to me all the uses of this world!' (*Hamlet*, I. 2. 133–4).
25. TP notes the allusions: 'each particular hair' – *The Devil and the Lady* (TP, I, 57) and *Hamlet*, I. 5. 19; 'yeasty waves' – 'Timbuctoo' (*TP*, I, 191) and *Macbeth*, IV. 1. 53; 'out of joint' – 'Locksley Hall' (*TP*, II, 127) and *Hamlet*, I. 5. 188; 'thick night' – 'Timbuctoo' (*TP*, I, 196), *Macbeth*, I. 5. 50 and *Hyperion*, II.80; 'golden prime' – 'Recollections of the Arabian Nights' (*TP*, I, 226), *Richard III*, I. 2. 247 and *Epipsychidion*, l.192; 'guilty thing' – *In Memoriam*, VII (*TP*, II, 326), *Hamlet*, I. 1. 148 and 'Ode: Intimations of Immortality', l.151.
26. *In Memoriam*, XCIX (*TP*, II, 420).
27. 'Little Gidding', V, in *The Complete Poems and Plays of T. S. Eliot* (London: Faber, 1969), p. 197.
28. *In Memoriam*, V, XXVII, LXXIII, V (*TP*, II, 322, 345, 388).
29. Compare 'The Two Voices' on the dangers of 'rotting like a weed': 'Why, if man rot in dreamless ease, / Should that plain fact, as taught by these, / Not make him sure that he shall cease?' (*TP*, I, 578, 584).
30. *The Anatomy of Disgust* (Cambridge, MA and London: Harvard University Press, 1998), p. 40.
31. Vicesimus Knox, *Winter Evenings, or, Lucubrations on Life and Letters*, 2 vols (London: Charles Dilly, 1790), cited in Price, p. 73.
32. *Spectator* (5 April 1902), repr. in *Thomas Hardy: the Critical Heritage*, ed. by R. G. Cox (London: Routledge, 1979; repr. 1995), p. 333. Warren adds that 'Shakespeare, too, of course, knew the mood, as he knew every mood, and has rendered it with surpassing force in the well-known grave-digger's scene in *Hamlet*' (p. 333).

33. *The Complete Poetical Works of Thomas Hardy,* ed. by Samuel Hynes, 5 vols (Oxford: Clarendon Press, 1982–95), II, 395–7.
34. *Poetical Works,* I, 196–7.
35. 'Where They Lived' (II, 200), 'The Graveyard of Dead Creeds' (III, 33), 'A Call to National Service' (II, 300), in *Poetical Works.*
36. Unsigned review, in *Church of England Quarterly Review* (October 1842), repr. in *Tennyson: the Critical Heritage,* ed. by John D. Jump (London: Routledge & Kegan Paul, 1967), p. 132. Later in the century, weeds would provide a helpful metaphor in writings about cultural degeneracy: see, for example, the anonymous article 'Weeds', in *Cornhill Magazine,* NS, 13 (October 1889), 417–28, which quotes Tennyson in support of its claim (a thinly disguised argument against immigration) that 'the cosmopolitan weed is driving out the native vegetation all over the world' (428).
37. Compare *The Tempest,* V. 1. 67–8: 'the ignorant fumes that mantle / Their clearer reason' (*TP,* II, 65 & n).
38. *TP,* I, 206.
39. *TP,* I, 27 & n; *Macbeth,* V. 3. 12.
40. *TP,* III, 406 & n; II. i.130.
41. *In Memoriam,* LV (*TP,* II, 371).
42. *In Memoriam,* VI (*TP,* II, 323).
43. Anon., 'The Decay of the Stage', in *Saint Paul's,* 1 (November 1867), 173–81 (p. 179).
44. J. P. Mahaffy, 'The Decay of Genius', in *Macmillan's Magazine,* L (September 1884), 355–62 (p. 356).
45. See William Greenslade, *Degeneration, Culture and the Novel, 1880–1940* (Cambridge: Cambridge University Press, 1994), p. 25.
46. 'Sonnet', in *The Story of Justin Martyr, and Other Poems* (London: Edward Moxon, 1835), p. 127. It was frequently reprinted in subsequent editions of Trench's poetry, as for example in *Poems,* 2 vols (London: Macmillan, 1885). This stress on the value of commonplaces was itself a stock idea of the period: compare the anonymous article 'Some Commonplaces on the Commonplace', in *Macmillan's Magazine,* 52 (August 1885), 272–9.
47. 'Two spirits of a diverse love / Contend for loving masterdom', *In Memoriam,* CII; Ricks compares Shakespeare's Sonnet 144: 'Two loves I have of comfort and despair, / Which like two spirits do suggest me still' (*TP,* II, 423 & n).
48. *The Letters of Matthew Arnold to Arthur Hugh Clough,* ed. by H. F. Lowry (London and New York: Oxford University Press, 1932), p. 146.
49. 'The Limits of Exact Science as Applied to History', cited in Walter E. Houghton, *The Victorian Frame of Mind, 1830–1870* (New Haven and London: Yale University Press, 1957), p. 205. *TP,* II, 314 cites the influential opinion of Henry Hallam (Arthur Hallam's father), in his *Introduction to the Literature of Europe* (1839), that 'There is a weakness and folly in all excessive and mis-placed affection', and that 'Notwithstanding the frequent beauties of these sonnets, [...] it is impossible not to wish that Shakspeare had never written them.'
50. See *TP,* II, 517.
51. See, for example, Tennyson's introduction of the word 'little' into the mouth of his Boädicea, whose willingness to 'Chop the breasts from off the mother, dash the brains of the little one out' echoes Lady Macbeth's claim, after she

has unsexed herself, that she would have 'dashed the brains out' of her baby; 'Boädicea', *TP*, II, 617; *Macbeth*, I. 7. 54–8.

52. See, for example, *In Memoriam*, XXVI, LXIV, LXXVI, LXXIX, CXXIV (*TP*, II, 344, 380, 390, 392, 444).

53. *In Memoriam*, II (*TP*, II, 319); my emphasis.

54. Tennyson died with his copy of Shakespeare opened at *Cymbeline* V. 5. 263–4, 'Hang there like fruit, my soul, /Till the tree die!', which, according to his son, 'he always called among the tenderest lines in Shakespeare' (*Memoir*, II, 428). See Christopher Decker's 'Shakespeare and the Death of Tennyson', in the following chapter.

55. *TP*, II, 313.

56. Compare *In Memoriam*, XLI, LXXI, XCV (*TP*, II, 358–9, 386, 412).

57. 'To One Early Loved', in *Motter*, p. 82.

58. *In Memoriam*, CXII (*TP*, II, 434).

8

Shakespeare and the Death of Tennyson

Christopher Decker

The morning of 4 October 1892, a Tuesday, was clear and fine. The landscape fronted by Tennyson's house at Aldworth was illuminated by sunshine diffused across the weald of Sussex and the line of South Downs visible from the poet's window, as Hallam Tennyson tells us in his *Memoir* of his father.

> At noon he called out, 'Where is my Shakespeare? I must have my Shakespeare.' Then he said, 'I want the blinds up, I want to see the sky and the light.' He repeated 'The sky and the light!'[1]

In the closing moments of his life, Tennyson found Shakespeare much on his mind and wanted him close at hand. A day earlier he had asked his son for *Lear, Cymbeline*, and *Troilus and Cressida*, 'three plays which he loved dearly'.[2] The day of his death was compounded, as most such days are, with visits, physicians' ministrations, the blurred outlines of familial comfort and familiar words, much unease, and the consolation of a sacred text.

> He begged for his Shakespeare again. About 10.30 he called aloud, 'Hallam,' as I was leaving the room to fetch my mother. I questioned him as to whether he felt free from pain: he answered, 'Quite, but I shall not get better.'
> At 2 o'clock he again asked for his Shakespeare and lay with his hand resting on it open, and tried to read it.
> [...]
> His last food was taken at a quarter to four, and he tried to read, but could not. He exclaimed, 'I have opened it.' Whether this referred to the Shakespeare, opened by him at

'Hang there like fruit, my soul,
Till the tree die,'

which he always called among the tenderest lines in Shakespeare: or
whether one of his last poems, of which he was fond, was running
through his head I cannot tell:

Fear not thou the hidden purpose of that Power which alone is
great.
Nor the myriad world, His shadow, nor the silent Opener of the
Gate.[3]

In concluding his final diagnosis, Tennyson's doctor recorded the image
of the poet on his death-bed:

a figure of breathing marble, flooded and bathed in the light of the
full moon streaming through the oriel window; his hand clasping the
Shakespeare which he had asked for but recently, and which he had
kept by him to the end; the moonlight, the majestic figure as he lay
there, 'drawing thicker breath,' irresistibly brought to our minds his
own 'Passing of Arthur.'[4]

Into his coffin, before its transportation to Westminster Abbey,
Tennyson's family placed a laurel wreath from Virgil's tomb, a wreath
of roses, and a copy of *Cymbeline* – not Tennyson's own, on which his
large hand had lain so often and so heavily as to crack the spine, but
his daughter-in-law Audrey's – with his favourite passage marked.[5]

Hallam Tennyson would in due course complete the monumental
Eversley edition of his father's poetical works (1907–08), an *Ausgabe
letzter Hand* incorporating the poet's own explanatory notes – many of
which cite parallels with Shakespeare and the classical Greek and Latin
poets. But his first testamentary act in print was to be the two-volume
Memoir (1897), and it is here that I wish to consider the implications of
Shakespeare's presence in this crucial, final anecdote. More so than most
biographies, the *Memoir* is an archaeology and a tessellation of fragments. It gathers, arranges, and disposes (indeed, it disposes *of* much
that made Tennyson Tennyson) so as to procure a nobler monument to
the poet's character and achievements from amidst a welter of trivia,
untidy circumstance and dark family history.[6] The narrative of the
death-bed scene, in particular, is exemplary in its marshalling of detail
in the shaping of this monument, and it invites us to consider different

aspects of Shakespeare's significance for Tennyson and his literary reputation. For it is surely significant that a poet whose poems attend so
feelingly to endings – whether their own inconclusive narratives, the
latent metaphors in line-lengths and -endings, or the recurrent termin-
ations of rhyme – should wish to have Shakespeare attend at his own
ending. And it matters that the text in Tennyson's hand as he prepared
to face 'the goal of ordinance' was not the Bible (there is no mention of
it in Hallam's last pages on his father's life, nor in any other account) but
Shakespeare. Matthew Arnold may have recognised that both 'The Bible
and Shakespeare were imposed upon an Englishman as objects of his
admiration', yet it was Shakespeare's text alone that Tennyson insisted
on as a last right, and to which he seems to have been saying *abyssus
abyssum invocat.*[7]

Tennyson's gesture is complex and intensely private: its full import
was known only to him, and perhaps dimly at that, being so compounded of yearnings, compulsion and memories. Yet by offering this
private moment to be read, the *Memoir* obliges us to participate in an act
of commemoration, to negotiate between the public and the private in
our attempts to grasp the consequences of Tennyson's gesture. Three
salient aspects of Shakespeare's significance stand out distinctly from
Hallam's narrative and warrant closer attention here: public recognition, private affirmation and the allusive touch.

I

Hallam Tennyson understood that the Poet Laureate's calling repeatedly
for Shakespeare at the very end of his life would cement the public
recognition of Tennyson's cultural eminence. The last chapter of the
Memoir seems more loosely constituted than the preceding chapters, as
though it were disintegrating into fragments before our eyes. As an
artistic touch this is both masterful and natural: the contingency of
Tennyson's final moments and the intermittency of his consciousness
being reflected in the narrative's episodic quality. Hallam's resistance to
a more conspicuous rhetoric discovers a heroism in simplicity. The
Memoir also implicitly appeals to the monumental status of Shakespeare
in the creation of a comparable monument to Tennyson, and it is
Shakespeare that holds these final pages together. The Gothic quality of
the death-bed scene is developed in Dr Dabbs's account, which conjures
up 'a figure of breathing marble' immersed in moonlight which pene-
trates the room through an 'oriel window'. The volume of Shakespeare
in Tennyson's hand assumes a symbolic significance, as though sculpted

on a funerary effigy. In a characteristically Victorian association, arte-facts that bespeak a past greatness lend their power to present claimants. Readers of the *Memoir* would have recognised the depiction of this association as a granting of Shakespearean eminence to Tennyson, just as visitors to the British Museum would have recognised the ruined marbles of Greece and Assyria as tokens of modern imperial puissance (though some would have accepted them as merely Ozymandian re-minders of the transience of temporal power). This overt association of Shakespeare with Tennyson represents the gain of power and of influ-ence, not the loss. Hallam was well aware that the narrative of his father's last days would be read by most readers with consuming interest as an example of the familiar Victorian genre of the death-bed scene, or 'the good death'.[8] Not only would the scene in the *Memoir* unite Tennyson with Shakespeare in the public consciousness – as it were, canonically – but, as *In Memoriam* had done, it would show the nation a fit way to face the hour of death.

By 1897, when the *Memoir* first appeared, most of Tennyson's readers would have accepted unbegrudgingly the implied comparison with Shakespeare, but such recognition had been a long time coming. Re-viewers of Tennyson's early poetry had often adduced Shakespeare as an example of everything that Tennyson was *not*. In 1833 the *New Monthly Magazine*, reviewing Tennyson's most recent collection of poems, men-tioned Shakespeare as merely another victim of the young poet's pilfering of the English tradition. The reviewer complained that 'The newer aspirants to Parnassus', Tennyson among them, 'draw their in-spiration now from Keats, and now from Herrick, or copy one line from the Sonnets of Shakespeare, in order to pillage the next from the Frag-ments of Shelley'. Tennyson was guyed for having 'filled half his pages with the most glaring imitations, and the imitations have been lauded for their originality'.[9] Such imputations of plagiarism exacerbated Tennyson's touchiness about any criticism of his poetry, but although such charges were occasionally levelled at his later volumes, unfavour-able comparisons with Shakespeare tended to seize upon what were perceived to be more profound differences in their visions of life. When the 1842 collection of Tennyson's *Poems* was published by Moxon, the *Christian Remembrancer* judged that Tennyson needed to be evicted from the Palace of Art and brought down to earth:

> Mr. Tennyson has not yet become *human* enough for our cravings. [...] He is still too fantastic, – too removed from 'familiar matters of today' – from the ordinary fountains of mirth and woe, – still too

much a 'dweller in a baseless world of dream, that is not earth nor heaven'.

The reviewer's cavils here are already freighted with the argument shortly to follow: that Tennyson's poetry fell short of Shakespeare's because it did not reflect the congruence of life and literature as Shakespeare had. The reviewer's second quotation is from a sonnet on Shakespeare by Richard Chevenix Trench, published by Moxon, Tennyson's publisher, in 1835. Trench had, in effect, laid the cornerstone for Tennyson's 'The Palace of Art' by demurring, 'Tennyson, we cannot live in Art'.[10] In his sonnet Trench revived this earlier objection by praising the ideal poet as:

> A counsellor well fitted to advise
> In daily life, and at whose lips no less
> Men may inquire or nations, when distress
> Of sudden doubtful danger may arise,
> Who, though his head be hidden in the skies,
> Plants his firm foot upon our common earth,
> Dealing with thoughts which everywhere have birth, –
> This is the poet, true of heart and wise:
> No dweller in a baseless world of dream,
> Which is not earth nor heav'n: his words have past
> Into man's common thought and week-day phrase;
> This is the poet, and his verse will last.
> Such was our Shakspeare once, and such doth seem
> One who redeems our later gloomier days.[11]

Continuing in this strain, the reviewer in the *Christian Remembrancer* contrasted the arrant aestheticism proffered by Tennyson's poems with the stouter, *heartier* imaginations of Homer and Shakespeare, who were 'in a good sense, men of the world, – practical men, capable of ordinary business-like exertion of every sort'. Shakespeare, it seems, had differed very little from the robust Victorian bourgeois still earning dividends from a misspent youth, 'one who had not exactly lived the life of an ascetic – who had been loose on the world and had got soiled perhaps with a few of its stains [...] but who never seems to have fancied that either he or any one else could be a privileged person, exempt from ordinary rules or obligations'. Like Tennyson, Shakespeare had 'doubtless had his wayward moods and strange fancies, but the roots of [his] being were far from fantastic, but, on the contrary, energetic, human, and sympathizing, beyond the average degree. [...] it is precisely this deep fervent humanity that we miss in Mr. Tennyson. He brings visions of wondrous beauty before us, but all is icy cold.'[12]

The lances shivered on Tennyson's poetry before 1850 all tend to reflect disappointment that a poet perceived to be the younger Romantics' natural successor had not yet trained himself into the *métier* of being the great poet of his age, if not in fact its Shakespeare. In an unsigned review article on the fate of poetry in nineteenth-century Britain, John Sterling reflected that modern Britain seemed to lack sensibilities adequate to the turbulent phenomena of their nation. And yet, 'had we minds full of the idea and the strength requisite for such work,' he argued, 'they would find in this huge, harassed, and luxurious national existence the nourishment, not the poison, of creative art' in the same way that 'all bigotries, superstitions, and gore-dyed horrors were flames that kindled steady light in Shakespeare's humane and meditative song'.[13] But Sterling judged that Tennyson was not the great poet who could assume the task of producing a poetic monument to the Victorian age.

Not *yet*, according to Tennyson's Cambridge friend James Spedding, who praised him for having sounded the deepest pathos in 'the commonest incidents, told in the simplest manner' and for having shown that 'many a lighted drawing-room is doubtless the scene of tragedies as deep as *Hamlet*'. Spedding recognised that Tennyson's achievement partly consisted in his ability to make a 'tragic theatre', an external spectacle, of an internal mental tragedy. Yet Spedding felt that the powers revealed by the 1842 *Poems*, though 'adequate [...] to the production of a great work', were 'displayed in fragments and snatches, having no connexion, and therefore deriving no light or fresh interest the one from the other'. The comparison with Shakespeare was ready to hand:

Take the very best scenes in Shakspeare – detach them from the context – and suppose all the rest to have perished, or never to have been written – where would be the evidence of the power which created *Lear* and *Hamlet*? Yet, perhaps, not one of those scenes could have been produced by a man who was not capable of producing the whole. If Mr. Tennyson can find a subject large enough to take the entire impress of his mind, and energy persevering enough to work it faithfully out as one whole, we are convinced that he may produce a work, which, though occupying no larger space than the contents of these volumes, shall as much exceed them in value, as a series of quantities multiplied into each other exceed in value the same series simply added together.[14]

It is something of an irony that in later years Tennyson should so often be asked to verify the authenticity of certain plays of Shakespeare by weighing the merits of individual lines, snatches and fragments.

The decisive turning-point of Tennyson's critical fortunes – and it was a watershed in his life in every respect – was the publication of *In Memoriam A.H.H.* Its appearance in 1850 met with almost universal accolades, and the terms of its praise often included a Shakespearean comparison. Charles Kingsley thought they altogether rivalled the *Sonnets* of Shakespeare.[15] John Forster, writing in *The Examiner*, considered *In Memoriam* deserving of comparison not only with Shakespeare's sonnets but also with Petrarch's, with Milton's 'Lycidas', and even with the *Purgatorio* and *Paradiso* of Dante.[16] The anonymous reviewer for the *Guardian* joined the chorus of praise: 'Judged even by the standard of Shakespeare and Spenser, Mr. Tennyson will not be found wanting.'[17] Yet curiously, most reviewers failed to define which particular aspects or qualities of *In Memoriam*, if any, were peculiarly Shakespearean or responsive to the *Sonnets*. Instead, in a characteristically Victorian reification of Shakespeare's cultural prestige, Shakespeare's name was applied as a kind of standard or marque, like a royal appointment. Although *In Memoriam* was certainly influenced by the example of Shakespeare's *Sonnets* – as Tennyson himself acknowledged – it was the comparison in itself that conferred distinction. Those critics who did attempt to read the lineaments of Tennyson's affinity with, or indebtedness to, the sonnets tended to steer into perilous waters – as Hallam Tennyson recognised when, in the *Memoir*, he truncated Benjamin Jowett's revealing comments. Jowett had noted how Tennyson 'used to think Shakespeare greater in his sonnets than in his plays' and 'found the sonnets a deeper expression of the never to be forgotten love which he felt more than any of the many moods of many minds which appear among his dramas'. But Hallam silently omitted Jowett's further observation that the 'love of the sonnets which he so strikingly expressed was a sort of sympathy with Hellenism'.[18]

After *Maud* (1855) and late in Tennyson's career, Shakespeare continued to provide *points de repère* or touchstones for essays in appreciation. A critic like Walter Bagehot might distinguish sharply between the supposed compositional habits of Shakespeare and Tennyson as reflected in their respective styles: '[Tennyson's] genius gives the notion of a slow depositing instinct; day by day, as the hours pass, the delicate sand falls into beautiful forms – in stillness, in peace, in brooding. You fancy Shakespeare writing quick, the hasty dialogue of the parties passing quickly through his brain. we have no such idea of our great contemporary poet.'[19] Bagehot could not have known that Tennyson had written the 'Mad Scene' in *Maud* in only twenty minutes.[20] By contrast R. H. Hutton compared Tennyson's mastery with Shakespeare's 'over the power of real things [...] to express evanescent emotions that almost defy expression'. For Hutton, Tennyson possessed Shakespeare's great gift of negative capability: 'When Shakespeare gives us a character like Juliet's nurse, we feel somehow that Juliet's nurse was in him, that he needed as little study to enter into her and appropriate her as Tennyson needed to enter into the full ripe passion which breathes through "The Gardener's Daughter" or the gusty heroics of "Locksley Hall".'[21] Jowett added his own praise of *Maud*, exclaiming that 'No poem since Shakespeare seems to me to show equal power of the same kind, or equal knowledge of human nature. [...] I do not know any verse out of Shakespeare in which the ecstacy of love soars to such a height.'[22]

While Tennyson respected Shakespeare's range of experience and his moral authority, such respect did not inhibit his appreciation of the social discordancies that set Shakespeare at odds with his strait-laced heirs. When critics attacked *Maud* (Tennyson's 'little *Hamlet*' or 'pet bantling', as he called it), the poet expressed such shock as though Shakespeare himself had been impugned. Hallam recorded one critic saying that '"If an author pipe of adultery, fornication, murder and suicide, set him down as the practiser of these crimes." Thereupon my father twitted the editor, "Adulterer I may be, fornicator I may be, murderer I may be, suicide I am not yet." [...] "Good heavens! can this be the country of Shakespeare?"' On the other hand admirers of *Maud* were apt to praise the poem as the finest literary depiction of madness since Shakespeare's in *Hamlet*, *Lear*, or *Othello*. But to the author of the pamphlet *Maud Vindicated*, Tennyson complained, 'The prestige of Shakespeare is great, else Hamlet (if it came out now) would be treated in just the same way.'[23]

In fact such was the publicly recognised parity between Tennyson's prestige and Shakespeare's that Tennyson was the first to be asked by Frederick Furnivall to be the first President of the New Shakspere Society, in November 1873. He declined, 'hating to push himself forward as a learned Shakespearian', though he agreed to join as an ordinary member.[24] And such was the pre-eminence granted to Tennyson in the later decades of his life, that he was even called upon as an arbiter in questions of the performance of Shakespeare or the authenticity of

Shakespeare's texts. After seeing a performance of *Hamlet* at the Lyceum in late 1874 in which Henry Irving played the title role, Tennyson met with Irving and some of the other actors, who sought out his opinions on the playing of certain scenes. Annie Thackeray Ritchie, who accompanied Tennyson to this performance, recalled 'our own prince poet, in that familiar simple voice we all know, explaining the art, going straight to the point in his own downright fashion, criticising with delicate appreciation, by the irresistible force of truth and true instinct carrying all before him. "You are a good actor lost," one of them, the real actors, said to him, laughing as he spoke.'[25] Tennyson's feel for authentically Shakespearean language also won full-handed plaudits from one of the industrious members of the New Shakspere Society, Frederick Fleay. He dedicated his *Shakspere Manual* (London: Macmillan, 1878) to the Laureate who, 'had he not elected to be the greatest poet of his time, might easily have become its greatest critic'.[26] The letter on the 'authorship question' which Tennyson received a few days before his death, was only the last in a series of such letters regarding Shakespearean authenticity.[27] A typescript made by Hallam Tennyson of his father's 'chance remarks [...] about Shakespeare when he was seeing a play performed or reading it' includes many instances where Tennyson lays his finger on passages in *Pericles, Henry VI, Henry VIII*, or *The Two Noble Kinsmen* which he felt to be either 'glorious Shakespeare' or merely the work of a collaborator.

The public equation of himself with Shakespeare was certainly impressive enough for Tennyson occasionally to commiserate with his great precursor, especially over the relentless biographical interest of the reading public. Like Browning, Tennyson scorned the idea that it was desirable to know much about Shakespeare's personal life. 'He would have wished that, like Shakespeare, his life might be unknown to posterity,' Benjamin Jowett recalled.[28] Not that Tennyson objected to every enquiry for information about his own personal history: for example, he proffered a substantial note about the scenes of his early life to William Howitt for inclusion in the final article of the latter's two-volume *Homes and Haunts of the Most Eminent British Poets* (1847).[29] Yet in 1860 he fulminated to Julia Margaret Cameron, that:

he believed every crime and every vice in the world were connected with the passion for autographs and anecdotes and records, – that the desiring anecdotes and acquaintance with the lives of great men was treating them like pigs to be ripped open for the public; that he thanked God Almighty with his whole heart and soul that he knew nothing, and that the world knew nothing, of Shakespeare but his writings; and that he thanked God Almighty that he knew nothing of Jane Austen, and that there were no letters preserved either of Shakespeare's or of Jane Austen's, that they had not been ripped open like pigs.[30]

Such strong opinions and colourful language are characteristic of the private Tennyson, so little known even to the readers of Hallam's *Memoir*. So incensed could he be at the public revelations made about poets' private lives that in 1849 he committed his disgust to print in *The Examiner*. In 'To——, After Reading a Life and Letters', he calls down 'My Shakespeare's curse on clown and knave / Who will not let his ashes rest!' – alluding to his own epigraph, taken from the monument at Stratford: '"Cursed be he that moves my bones." – *Shakespeare's Epitaph*'.[31] And yet, when he looked on that monument with Edward FitzGerald in 1840, Tennyson could lament the fact that whitewashing had made it seem more monumental while obscuring the features of the living man: 'I should not think it can be a good likeness. That foolish fellow painted it white all over. [...] I suppose from a notion that so painted [it] would look more classic, but [...] we have in all probability lost the colour of Shakespeare's hair and eyes, which perhaps would do the world very little good to know, but would have been a little satisfaction to poor physiognomists like myself.'[32] A similar criticism could be made of the *Memoir*, with its emphasis on monumentality and its whitewashing.

Yet as much as we owe to the restoration of Tennyson undertaken by his grandson Sir Charles Tennyson in his 1949 biography, Hallam Tennyson's *Memoir*, like Pope's 'Epistle to Dr Arbuthnot', is a masterpiece of concealing *and* revealing that should not be unjustly undervalued. The *Memoir* deserves our interest not only for its 'breathing a sense of what it was like in the immediate vicinity of Tennyson' but also for its honourable aim of achieving for Tennyson a monumentality to which Shakespeare's frequent appearances contribute defining accents.[33] Every insight into Tennyson's private life that Hallam provides is always already wearing a public face, the public face of Victoria's Laureate. Almost everything of importance stands comparison to Shakespeare: from Tennyson's politics ('I am of the same politics as Plato, Shakespeare, and Bacon, and every sane author') to his commonsense ('This gift [...] is in reality nothing less than a minor form of inspiration. [...] It is often, as obviously in the case of Shakespeare, united with the highest genius').[34] Tennyson appears in print so regularly in the same character that one has the impression of his being typecast:

> Fanny Kemble says of him when at College, 'Alfred Tennyson was our hero, the great hero of our day.' Another friend who knew him then, describes him, as 'six feet high, broad chested, strong limbed, his face Shakespearian with deep eyelids, his forehead ample, crowned with dark wavy hair, his head finely poised, his hand the admiration of sculptors, long fingers with square tips, soft as a child's but of great size and strength. What struck one most about him was the union of strength with refinement.'[35]

From this description, Tennyson would appear to have been tailor-made by his Creator for the part of the Hero as Poet – if Carlyle had not already given public notice that Shakespeare was best suited to play that role.[36]

II

The private significance of Tennyson's repeated calling for Shakespeare on his death-bed and his insistent attempts to read from his own favourite edition of the plays is more difficult to discern. One would wish to have the 'magnifying-glasses for secret feelings, and doubts, and fears, and hopes, and trusts' that R. H. Hutton found so abundant in *In Memoriam*.[37] Tennyson's fondness for Shakespeare had been enduring, lifelong; and Shakespeare had been present at so many moments of Tennyson's life that it can seem unremarkable to find him also presiding over Tennyson's passing.

From his earliest years, Tennyson encountered Shakespeare often on the printed page. He and his brothers, when still living in the rectory at Somersby, had 'the run of their father's excellent library. Their favourite books were Shakespeare, Milton, Burke, Rabelais, and the works of Sir William Jones, the Arabian Nights and Don Quixote.'[38] Later, Tennyson acquired many editions of Shakespeare, including the successive 'standard editions' of Johnson and Steevens, Dyce, and the Cambridge editors Clark, Glover, and Aldis Wright; miscellaneous separate editions of the plays and sonnets; and two 'travelling' Shakespeares which he took with him on holiday.[39] From Johnson and Steevens or from Dyce, he would often read aloud: to his mother when still at home ('with passion and the flexible voice of a born tragedian'), and to his wife and sons in later life.[40] Emily Tennyson's journal teems with references to Tennyson reading Shakespeare to the family or to her alone. 'A. has a romp with the boys & reads bits of "Sir Launcelot" to me. Some of *Julius Caesar* after dinner & scraps of *Noctes Ambrosianae* after tea' is a typical entry.[41] Hallam Tennyson recalled how Shakespeare was much a part of the family's daily life, so that 'When we were old enough, we were allowed to have luncheon with our parents; and when guests were there he called us "Bardolphs" and bade us pour out the beer and make it foam well!' And although Shakespeare may have been a familiar, quotable presence in the Tennyson household, 'he would never teach us his own poems, or allow us to get them by heart'.[42]

Tennyson had learned Shakespeare off by heart not only from his private reading but also from performances. Whenever in London for an extended stay, Tennyson made time to see Shakespeare on the stage, and he appraised many of the leading lights of the Victorian period: Macready, Fanny Kemble, Helen Faucit, Salvini, Henry Irving and Ellen Terry. In the late 1820s and early '30s, when at Cambridge, Tennyson and his friends regaled each other with their own quasi-pantomime versions of the plays – very often travesties in all senses of the word, of *Much Ado*, for instance: 'Kemble as Dogberry, Hallam as Verges, Milnes as Beatrice. When Beatrice sat down, her weight was so great that she crashed through the couch on which she sat, and sank on the floor, nothing to be seen but a heap of petticoats, much to the discomfiture of the players and to the immeasurable laughter of the spectators.' (The travesties were easily reversed: 'To someone playing the part of Falstaff, "Pooh," said Kemble, "you should see my sister, she does Falstaff better than any other man living." ') Tennyson himself 'was famous in certain parts of Shakespeare, particularly in Malvolio'.[43] Some are born great, some achieve greatness.

The enjoyment that Tennyson found in Shakespeare throughout his life was common to many of his contemporaries. Yet, as the last scenes of the *Memoir* suggest, there are intimations that Tennyson's need for Shakespeare also betokened an intense private affirmation, whether of Shakespeare's absolute importance as a creative power (Tennyson's last look on life is on Shakespeare's page as well as the dark world where he was born) or of Tennyson's sense of indebtedness and homage to his great precursor (recorded in the act of reading, of holding and behold-ing). Laying his hand on Shakespeare's text at the end of his life was like the touching of a relic or touching the living man from the past through his own pages. In *In Memoriam*, Tennyson had left the record of his own response to reading Arthur Hallam's letters from days that were no more:

So word by word, and line by line,
The dead man touched me from the past,
And all at once it seemed at last
The living soul was flashed on mine[44]

For Tennyson knew that 'an hour's communion with the dead' happened not only through the commingling of voices, in conversation or in metaphor, but also in the contact and pressure of human touch through the medium of writing.

The long moment of Shakespeare's presiding over Tennyson's death links hands across the years to another moment five decades earlier, a pilgrimage to Stratford with Edward FitzGerald in June 1840. The visit was one of many literary tours that Tennyson had made or would make – to Kenilworth with its associations of Sir Walter Scott, to Lyme Regis where he exclaimed immediately on arrival, 'Now take me to the Cobb, and show me the steps from which Louisa Musgrove fell.'[45] But the brief trip to Stratford was of greater significance. After a visit to Warwick Castle where they admired portraits by Rembrandt and Titian, Tennyson and FitzGerald went into Stratford to look at the Shakespeare Monument. Afterwards they were admitted to the Birthplace. 'We went also into the room where they say he was born. Every part of it is scribbled over with names. I was seized with a sort of enthusiasm and wrote mine, though I was a little ashamed of it afterwards: yet the feeling was genuine at the time, and I did homage with the rest.'[46]

Tennyson's graffito and the impulse that moved him to write his name were both commonplace and highly personal, which could equally be said of almost every name inscribed in that room. Each person would have had some reason, devotional or otherwise, to write his or her name, and in choosing a spot to write, each person would be aware of the many others who had already done so. The gesture is, in a sense, the opposite of taking a photograph or even a piece of the site as a souvenir. As a writing act it is also the opposite of allusion or plagiarism, being related instead, indirectly, to forgery and similar kinds of scriptural impositions or impostures.[47] Nothing is taken away, whole or in part or in reflection. The potency of the act, as with most graffiti, lies in its self-conscious transformation of the space in which it occurs, however negligible its physical manifestation (even to the point of illegibility, since many signatures are illegible to anyone but their authors). Tennyson's gesture does not incorporate Shakespeare's text, Shakespeare's writing, within his own, but inscribes the emblem of himself onto the surface of the material remains that stand for Shakespeare. Tennyson acknowledged his writing as 'a sort of enthusiasm' – an expression of intense personal devotion – and a homage he performs with others in a collective epigraphy. It was not an act that he intended as a gesture to be recognised by others, but an entirely personal and private one.[48]

Tennyson well knew that visits to great men may be something finer than mere tourism or indexing one's own self-importance. They can mark a kind of fealty. Not always an easy thing: Tennyson's encounters with living greatness (or mere prestige) – with Wordsworth, Carlyle, or Samuel Rogers – were fraught with awkwardness and spikiness. Shakespeare, however, fared far better in Tennyson's affections than Wordsworth, or indeed any of the poet's intimate friends. There was little sense of active rivalry. Tennyson's comments on Shakespeare differ markedly from Goethe's: one senses that Tennyson never thought of himself as Shakespeare's competitor. Rather, as was true for most Victorians, Shakespeare was a guarantor of literary value – which meant also moral value, human value, personal and social principle.

Tennyson's inscription in the room where Shakespeare was born and the laying of his hand on Shakespeare's text as he lay dying in his own room are friendly gestures of poetic affinity, of drawing strength and confidence from poetic authority – not the contesting of an inheritance, of which Tennyson had had already too much with his own family. More than friendship, Shakespeare and his work represented for Tennyson an extraordinary and exorbitant love, Shakespeare's love of his fellow creatures. Thinking of Arthur Hallam passing upward through higher stages of existence, Tennyson offered him again the benediction of earthly love:

> If, in thy second state sublime,
>   Thy ransomed reason change replies
>   With all the circle of the wise,
> The perfect flower of human time;
>
> And if thou cast thine eyes below,
>   How dimly charactered and slight,
>   How dwarfed a growth of cold and night,
> How blanched with darkness must I grow!
>
> Yet turn thee to the doubtful shore,
>   Where thy first form was made a man;
>   I loved thee, Spirit, and love, nor can
> The soul of Shakspeare love thee more.[49]

Hallam had said, in praising the *Sonnets*, that Shakespeare was 'the most universal mind that ever existed'.[50] It would be fairer to say the *second-most universal mind*. But the confusion here of love, the creation, and the creator could not be more joyously compact. As he himself faced the doubtful shore of his own dying, Tennyson's gestures across the years should be seen as devotional acts of a certain catholicity – the pilgrimage to a shrine, the laying of a hand upon a reliquary in which precious remains are kept.

III

Among Tennyson's last words were Shakespeare's words. It remains, finally, to attend to the quotation that Tennyson singled out from so many, Posthumus's reply to Imogen in the last scene of *Cymbeline* (V. 5. 263–4):

> Hang there like fruit, my soul,
> Till the tree die!

which Tennyson considered 'One of Shakespeare's wonderful rejoinders', observing also that 'Posthumus asks no word of forgiveness'.[51] The lines preceding it belong to Imogen:

> Why did you throw your wedded lady [from] you?
> Think that you are upon a rock, and now
> Throw me again.
>
> (V. 5. 261–3)

Posthumus's reply has an ambiguity within the play itself, attracting critical attention to the generous aptness of 'soul' in its referring equally to Imogen and to Posthumus himself.[52] Posthumus may be speaking directly to Imogen, his wife, as 'his soul', whom he bids never to part from him again till death, the untying of all marriage bonds. At the same time, he pledges his renewed fidelity and confidence by bidding his soul never to depart from Imogen – a pledge made to himself but which, because it is heard by another person, like a marriage vow, is simultaneously a commitment made that other person. This is not the only ambiguity in these lines, or surrounding them. As in allusion, there is a furtive, transitory union or confusion of voices. It is difficult to say who is speaking at the moment in which the lines from *Cymbeline* involved themselves in Tennyson's dying, if not Shakespeare, Posthumus, and

Tennyson all together. Posthumus's words assume new life beneath Tennyson's touch, itself like a voice. Tennyson in the act of allusion is speaking at once to himself, soon to be posthumous (puns were never lost on him, not even in this moment) – 'Linger on, my soul, until this dying trunk at last releases you' – and to Emily Tennyson (his wedded lady and his soul in the sense that Imogen is Posthumus's, 'fruit' in being flesh of his flesh) – 'Stay with me until the very end.' *Cymbeline* was perhaps the first of Shakespeare's plays that Emily Sellwood had read at the age of eight, and Tennyson may well have known this, having it in mind for her at this moment, a joining of her early days with his last.[53]

But there is uneasiness here, too, in yet another twist in the sense of these lines. Just as the very inclusion of this book with Tennyson in his grave breathes a deep nostalgia, an incurable fondness for the written word and, by extension, for the life in which poetry happens (and makes things happen), so the words themselves spell out a hope that knows it cannot be granted by its own terms. For it is natural, simply, for fruit to ripen, fall, and cease long before the tree itself perishes. To 'hang there like fruit' until 'the tree die' is to do something very *un*like fruit, something very unnatural. This contradiction is pained with the sense that loved lives and love-lives perish. Tennyson's taking of these lines with him, to him, against their better logic, is saturated (it had soaked his heart through) with a longing for fidelity to last beyond its natural span. It is the embodiment of the principle of marriage at the heart of the matter – of the passage in Shakespeare, of Tennyson's lived experience – and a telling instance of the power of Shakespeare's words to touch life and to touch us into new life.

Notes

1. Hallam Tennyson, *Alfred Lord Tennyson: a Memoir by His Son*, 2 vols (London: Macmillan, 1897), II, 426. Hereafter, *Memoir*.
2. *Memoir*, II, 425.
3. *Memoir*, II, 427–8.
4. *Memoir*, II, 428–9.
5. For two finely balanced accounts of Tennyson's death and its immediate aftermath, see Robert Bernard Martin, *Tennyson: the Unquiet Heart* (Oxford: Oxford University Press, 1980), pp. 580–2; and Ann Thwaite, *Emily Tennyson: the Poet's Wife* (London: Faber & Faber, 1996), pp. 1–37.
6. On Hallam Tennyson's composition of the *Memoir*, see Philip L. Eliot, *The Making of the Memoir* (Lincoln: Tennyson Society, 1993) and Michael Millgate, *Testamentary Acts: Browning, Tennyson, James, Hardy* (Oxford: Clarendon Press,

1992), pp. 48–60. In particular, Millgate writes tellingly of 'Hallam's determination to impose upon the characterization of his father an almost novelistic or fabular consistency' and his 'almost lifelong experience of intimate and intensive participation in the construction of his father as both a public and a private figure' (pp. 54, 59).

7. Matthew Arnold, 'A French Critic of Milton' (1877) in *The Complete Prose Works of Matthew Arnold*, ed. by R. H. Super, 11 vols (Ann Arbor: University of Michigan Press, 1960–77), VIII, 170. In his own final hours, Thomas Hardy asked for FitzGerald's *Rubáiyát of Omar Khayyám* and Browning's 'Rabbi ben Ezra' to be read to him, no doubt relishing the antithetical tension between them.

8. On the Victorian death-bed scene and the 'good death', see especially John R. Reed, *Victorian Conventions* (Athens, Ohio: Ohio University Press, 1975), pp. 156–71; Garrett Stewart, *Death Sentences: Styles of Dying in British Fiction* (Cambridge, MA: Harvard University Press, 1984), pp. 101–38; Michael Wheeler, *Death and the Future Life in Victorian Literature and Theology* (Cambridge: Cambridge University Press, 1990), pp. 28–47; and Pat Jalland, *Death in the Victorian Family* (Oxford: Clarendon Press, 1996), pp. 17–58.

9. *New Monthly Magazine*, 37 (1833), 69–74 (p. 70); cited in Edgar Finley Shannon, Jr., *Tennyson and the Reviewers: a Study of His Literary Reputation and of the Influence of the Critics upon His Poetry 1827–1851* (Cambridge, MA: Harvard University Press, 1952), p. 38.

10. See *Memoir*, I, 118; and *The Poems of Tennyson*, ed. by Christopher Ricks, 2nd edn, 3 vols (Harlow: Longman, 1987), I, 436. All further references to Tennyson's poems will be to this edition (hereafter abbreviated to *TP*).

11. The text of Trench's sonnet is taken from Richard Chevenix Trench, *The Story of Justin Martyr, and Other Poems* (London: Edward Moxon, 1835), p. 127. The likeliest candidate for the 'redeemer' of the final line is presumably Wordsworth.

12. Francis Garden, unsigned article, *Christian Remembrancer*, 4 (July 1842), 42–58; repr. in *Tennyson: the Critical Heritage*, ed. by John D. Jump (London: Routledge & Kegan Paul, 1967), pp. 98–102 (pp. 98, 99, 100).

13. John Sterling, unsigned review article, *Quarterly Review*, 70 (September 1842), 385–416; repr. in *Critical Heritage*, pp. 103–25 (pp. 103, 111).

14. James Spedding, unsigned review, *Edinburgh Review*, 77 (April 1843), 373–91; repr. in *Critical Heritage*, pp. 139–52 (pp. 151–2).

15. Charles Kingsley, unsigned review, *Fraser's Magazine*, 42 (September 1850), 245–55; repr. in *Critical Heritage*, pp. 172–85 (p. 183).

16. John Forster, unsigned review, *The Examiner*, 8 June 1850, pp. 356–57; cited in Shannon, *Tennyson and the Reviewers*, p. 142.

17. Unsigned review, the *Guardian*, 26 June 1850, p. 477; cited in Shannon, *Tennyson and the Reviewers*, pp. 142–3.

18. The full text was printed in *Materials*, 4: 460.

19. Walter Bagehot, unsigned review of *Idylls of the King* (1859), *National Review*, 9 (October 1859). 368–94; repr. in *Critical Heritage*, pp. 215–40 (p. 230–1).

20. See Hallam Tennyson, *Materials for a Life of A. T.: Collected for My Children*, 4 vols (London: Macmillan [limited run], 1895), II, 108 (hereafter *Materials*). Hallam Tennyson seems largely to have re-edited this entry for February 1855

148   *Victorian Shakespeare: Literature and Culture*

in his mother's journal, interpolating the time it took to compose the 'Mad Scene' and generally condensing. For the full entry, see Emily Lady Tennyson, *Lady Tennyson's Journal*, ed. by James O. Hoge (Charlottesville: University of Virginia Press, 1981), pp. 42–3.

21. Hutton in *Critical Heritage*, pp. 363–4.
22. Quoted in *Materials*, II, 128.
23. *Materials*, II, 129; *Memoir*, I, 406 (a slightly different text of the same letter, excerpted by Hallam Tennyson); and *The Letters of Alfred Lord Tennyson*, ed. by Cecil Y. Lang and Edgar F. Shannon, Jr., 3 vols (Oxford: Clarendon Press, 1981–87), II, 127 (hereafter, *Letters*).
24. *Memoir*, II, 152; he advised Gladstone, 'I think you cannot do better than subscribe and have no more to do with it' (*Letters*, III, 69). Tennyson had no later cause for regret. Browning was offered the Presidency in 1879 and had no sooner accepted the largely titular post than he found himself embroiled in an ungentlemanly slanging match in print between Furnivall and A. C. Swinburne (the 'Pigsbrook' controversy).
25. *Memoir*, II, 151.
26. Cited by J. M. Robertson; see *Critical Heritage*, p. 426. Fleay notes that the manual was dedicated with Tennyson's permission, 'however he may differ from some of its opinions' (dedication).
27. And not only Shakespeare: when a controversy arose in 1868 over an epitaph then recently discovered in a copy of Milton's *Poems* (1845) and believed by some to be in Milton's hand, FitzGerald wrote to Tennyson, '*you* would settle it by a word, my old Alfred' (*Letters*, III, 106).
28. Hallam Lord Tennyson, *Tennyson and His Friends*, (London: Macmillan, 1911), p. 186.
29. William Howitt, *Homes and Haunts of the Most Eminent British Poets*, 2 vols (London: Bentley, 1847). For the text of Tennyson's note see *Letters*, I, 254–5 n.
30. Henry Taylor, *Autobiography of Henry Taylor, 1800–1875*, 2 vols (London: Longmans, Green, and Co., 1885), II, 193; cited in Martin, *Tennyson*, p. 552.
31. *TP*, II, 297–8.
32. Letter of [*c.* 8 June 1840] to Emily Sellwood; *Memoir*, I, 176; *Letters*, I, 182.
33. 'breathing a sense ... ', *TP*, I, p. vii.
34. *Materials*, I, 54; 'Recollections of Tennyson by Aubrey de Vere, 1832–1845', *Materials*, I, 268–9.
35. *Materials*, I, 49.
36. Thomas Carlyle, 'The Hero as Poet' in *On Heroes, Hero-Worship, and the Heroic in History* (London: James Fraser, 1841).
37. Hutton in *Critical Heritage*, p. 364.
38. *Materials*, I, 33–4.
39. William Shakespeare, *The Plays*, ed. by Samuel Johnson and George Steevens, 3rd edn, 10 vols (London: Bathurst, 1785); *Works*, ed. by Alexander Dyce, 6 vols (London: Moxon, 1857); *Works*, ed. by William George Clark and George Glover, 9 vols [vols 2–9 ed. by Clark and William Aldis Wright] (Cambridge: Macmillan, 1863–6). The travelling editions were *Dramatic Works* (London: Tilt, 1838), only vols 1 and 4–8 surviving; and *The Handy-volume Shakspeare* (London: Bradbury, Evans, and Co., 1866–7; the later being a popular edition, of which both A. C. Swinburne and Pen Browning (son of Robert and

Elizabeth Barrett Browning) had copies (now in the Folger Shakespeare Library, Washington DC). On Tennyson's portable reading, see *Materials*, II, 53.

40. *Materials*, I, 94.
41. *Lady Tennyson's Journal*, p. 125. Tennyson had by now largely forgiven John Wilson ('Christopher North') his review of *Poems, Chiefly Lyrical* (1830), hence the *Noctes*.
42. *Materials*, II, 98.
43. *Materials*, I, 60.
44. *In Memoriam A. H. H.*, XCV, 33–6; *TP*, II, 413.
45. *Memoir*, II, 47.
46. *Letters*, I, 182.
47. One might compare a curious item in the Folger Shakespeare Library, a bound collection of lines from Shakespeare's plays written out by Charles and Ellen Kean (Folger: S. a. 15). Each page contains a single quotation written out by either of the two Keans, each with the autograph of either one signed above or below the quotation. The impression created is that the actors are laying claim to these particular lines, even ascribing their own authorship, though the book may only have been intended as an autograph book. The quotations are not necessarily related to roles played by either ·actor, since Charles Kean signs his name beneath a quotation, slightly altered, of Lady Macbeth ('Things without remedy / Should be without regard.') and of Portia ('I never did repent for doing good, nor shall not now.').
48. On the history of public inscription, see Armando Petrucci, *Public Lettering: Script, Power, and Culture*, trans. by Linda Lappin (Chicago: University of Chicago Press, 1993), esp. pp. 117–29.
49. *In Memoriam A. H. H.*, LXI; *TP*, II, 378.
50. A. H. Hallam, 'The Influence of Italian upon English Literature' (1831) in T. H. Vail Motter, *The Writings of Arthur Hallam* (New York: Modern Language Association of America, 1943), p. 229.
51. Hallam Tennyson, typescript 'Alfred Tennyson on Shakespeare', p. 36. In the *Memoir*, Hallam reports that 'he always called [these lines] among the tenderest lines in Shakespeare,' – *Memoir*, II, 428.
52. See Eric Griffiths, *The Printed Voice of Victorian Poetry* (Oxford: Clarendon Press, 1989), pp. 171 ff.
53. Ann Thwaite, *Emily Tennyson: the Poet's Wife* (London: Faber & Faber,), p. 48.

9

'The Names': Robert Browning's 'Shaksperean Show'

Danny Karlin

> Shakespeare! – to such name's sounding, what succeeds
> Fitly as silence? Falter forth the spell, –
> Act follows word, the speaker knows full well,
> Nor tampers with its magic more than needs.
> Two names there are: That which the Hebrew reads
> With his soul only; if from lips it fell,
> Echo, back thundered by earth, heaven and hell,
> Would own 'Thou did'st create us!' Nought impedes
> We voice the other name, man's most of might,
> Awesomely, lovingly: let awe and love
> Mutely await their working, leave to sight
> All of the issue as – below – above –
> Shakespeare's creation rises: one remove,
> Though dread – this finite from that infinite.
>
> ('The Names')

'The Names' shares in the general neglect of Browning's later work to an extreme degree. Until recently it received virtually no critical attention, whether from Browning scholars or those interested in the Victorian reception of Shakespeare. There is no separate mention of it in the standard Browning bibliographies.[1] Biographers make nothing of it: Mrs Orr (1891) gives it a passing mention, Griffin and Minchin (1910), Ward (1967–69), Irvine and Honan (1974), and Ryals (1993) are representative in not mentioning it at all.[2] Berdoe's *Browning Cyclopædia* (1891; 1912) has a brief entry glossing the Hebrew name of God; DeVane's *Handbook* (1937; 1955) is anodyne ('Browning's praise of Shakespeare is very pleasant') and gets some details wrong.[3] In a long and still very useful article on Browning and Shakespeare published in

1909, G. R. Elliott quotes the poem as exemplifying Browning's belief that 'the poet's creative power, although limited, [is] essentially the same in nature as that of the Divinity'.[4] John Maynard, in *Browning's Youth* (1977), is the first modern critic to take the poem seriously: he places it in the context of Browning's knowledge of Shakespeare and participation in (or resistance to) Victorian 'bardolatry', and (more accurately than Elliott) draws the parallel with 'Coleridge's idea that Shakespeare's imagination is the secondary power closest to God's own primary creative force'.[5] Sarah Wood, in *Robert Browning: a Literary Life* (2001) acutely and suggestively links the poem to Milton's 'Epitaph on the admirable Dramatic Poet W. Shakespeare' (one of the dedicatory poems in the Second Folio of 1632), as part of a wider argument about the 'fragmenting and monumentalizing [of] the names of poets'; she also points out that the conjunction of 'finite' and 'infinite' in the last line connects the poem to 'Popularity' and to Browning's good-humoured but sharp exchange with Ruskin about that poem, and about the poetics of *Men and Women* generally, in which Browning declared that 'all poetry [was] a putting the infinite within the finite'.[6] In an equally valuable article, 'The Allure of Supernatural Language: the Ineffable Name in Robert Browning's Poems' (1998), Gal Manor focuses on the significance to Browning of the tetragrammaton, the Hebrew name of God which cannot be spoken, which I discuss below.[7]

The poem's long neglect is, in one respect at least, no great mystery. Browning offered posterity little incentive. The poem, a sonnet, was published in a booklet issued for a charity fair, and appeared simultaneously in a magazine. Browning did not collect it. He disliked the sonnet form, disliked writing to order, and especially disliked periodical verse.[8] He was persuaded – importuned – by his inveterate admirer, Frederick J. Furnivall, founder of the New Shakspere Society in 1873 and the Browning Society in 1881, to do what he detested. 'I have a true regard for [him],' Browning wrote, 'in spite of the most teasing tactlessness that ever plagued a man's would-be esteemers.'[9]

Compressed, disjunctive, allusive; its power shadowed by conscious ironies of text and voice; its extreme modernity rooted in primitive dread; its intellectual grasp twined with kabbalistic fantasy: the poem is truly 'occasional', the product of a forced response to a demand which is both emotionally compelling and fiercely resented. 'What succeeds / Fitly as silence?' If the poem succeeds, it does so in defiance of its author's impulse to tell Furnivall where to shove it.

'It is the shortest poem, for the stuff in it, I ever wrote,' Browning remarked of *The Ring and the Book*.[10] Of 'The Names' – 21,120 lines shorter – he might have said that it was the longest. The poem's relations really and truly end nowhere; my problem is the Jamesian one of circumscription. Also, the poem's strands are tightly interwoven; they must be disentangled, otherwise nothing will be clear. In turn, then: the poem's locality, its time and place; Browning's Shakespeare; magical language; the name of God and the poetics of vision.

The Shaksperean Show Book[11]

The Shaksperean Show was held at the Royal Albert Hall on 29–31 May 1884. It was a charity event in support of the Chelsea Hospital for Women (specifically to pay off a mortgage of £5,000). *The Shaksperean Show Book* functioned as prospectus for the hospital, official programme for the event, souvenir booklet and advertising supplement.[12] The hospital was a typical Victorian good cause, with 63 beds 'for the reception and treatment of respectable poor Women and Gentlewomen in reduced circumstances, suffering from those many distressing diseases to which the female sex is liable, irrespective of character or social position' – a rider which was presumably meant to reassure benefactors that they were not contributing to the treatment of alcoholism or sexual immorality. The President was the Earl of Cadogan, and the prospectus lists the many aristocratic Patronesses, the eminent and respectable members of the Board of Management, and the Ladies' Committee (presided over by Lady Cadogan). There is a page of royal, noble and professional endorsements of the hospital's work, headed by the Prince of Wales. The British Library copy still has the banker's order pasted to the verso of the front page for the use of potential donors.

The second section of the booklet consists of the charitable contributions by writers, artists and musicians. Browning has pride of place, on page 1, probably because of Furnivall's partisanship. But it is also the case that his is the only contribution of any distinction. Perhaps the fact that he hated making such gestures meant that he took them more seriously than others to whom they were a matter of routine, or who judged their desk-sweepings good enough for charity. Tennyson contributed four lines from the unpublished poem 'Hail, Briton', which he had originally drafted in 1831–33 and which he used as a quarry for several later poems, including some from the 1880s.[13] When readers turned over the page after reading 'The Names', they were greeted by a drawing by W. Weekes called 'The Sleeping Beauty', which shows two pigs woken from their slumbers by a crow on a fence-rail; the motto is from *A Midsummer Night's Dream*: 'What angel wakes me from my flowery bed?' (III. 1. 129).[14] In 'Somebody's Story' by Hugh Conway, a farmer casts out his daughter for her idle love of Shakespeare; she becomes a famous actress ('one, moreover, against whom slander had breathed no breath') and rescues her repentant parent from destitution. There is a feeble sketch in which Shakespeare tries to sell *Hamlet* to a modern theatrical manager, mediocre illustrations ('Touchstone and Audrey', 'Falstaff the Brave', 'Orlando and Rosalind'), some musical settings of Shakespeare songs, etc. etc. Several items besides Tennyson's have no connection with Shakespeare; perhaps the most baffling is Lady Brassey's 'A Ride to Ronda and Back', which describes a ride to Ronda and back ('It was a bright, clear moonlight morning, and myriads of stars were visible, though their light was somewhat paled by that of the more prominent orb'), concluding with a table of distances and time taken. Violet Fane and Oscar Wilde contributed best-forgotten poems (though both the *Pall Mall Gazette* and *The Times* singled out Wilde's contribution as an example of fashionable decadence).[15] Shakespeare himself is not spared: in 'A Voice from the Tomb' he appears in woeful mock-Tudor to support the Show. Of the literary contributions, in fact, only one beside Browning's is worth respect, for its unpretending honesty: it is Mary Grace Walker's poem, 'The Chelsea Hospital for Women: an Appeal'.

The *Times* report on 29 May gives the following account of the layout and character of the Show itself:

> On entering the Albert-hall to-day at 3 o'clock, when the show commences, the visitor will find that familiar building transformed. The area is cleared, and down the centre, running north and south, are erected stages facing outwards towards the stalls, and each exhibiting a scene from one of the great master's plays. The orchestra, opposite the principal entrance, is occupied by three more Shakespearian scenes, displayed somewhat in the form of a triptych, and Shakespeare's house and Anne Hathaway's modest little cottage, with its thatched gables, fill in the background. Stratford Church towers above all, and its elegant spire finds its way far aloft among the galleries. [...]
>
> The Prince of Wales has specially deputed Lord Cadogan to open the proceedings in his unavoidable absence. At the blast of a trumpet the curtains will fall disclosing the several Shakespearian scenes to view, the characters will pose in their costumes for a few moments after the fashion followed by *tableaux vivants*, and then descend from the stages and adopt the *rôle* of *dames vendeuses*, in which character we trust they may succeed in disposing of their wares at the most

exorbitant prices. Besides the tableaux and the purchase stalls there are abundant other attractions. There are concerts of Shakespearian songs, to which Madame Antoinette Sterling, Mr. Maas, and other distinguished professional and amateur singers contribute their services; Shakespearian recitals under Miss Cowen's direction; an exhibition of Shakespearian relics, presided over by Mr. F. J. Furnivall, founder of the New Shakespeare Society, and Mr. J. W. Jarvis; an organ recital by Mr. Tamplin, and other amusements for those who, having partaken of the above, are still unsatisfied.[16]

The *Show Book* adds a few other details, such as the fact that the refreshments stall was named for *The Merry Wives of Windsor*, and that ladies 'attired in the Costume of a Serving Maid of Shakspeare's time' sold the *Show Book* itself, along with raffle tickets for the 'Black and Gold Pianoforte' which had been donated by Messrs Collard and Collard, and which was used for the song recitals. Promenade concerts were given each afternoon by the Band of the 2nd Life Guards. Two 'extra shows' are listed: 'The Shy of the Show' and 'An Angle in the Avon'. I do not know what they were, but I like to think they were fairground attractions for younger visitors.

The *Times* report catches the very Victorian enjoyment which the participants and patrons of the Show felt in play-acting and dressing up. Homage to Shakespeare is subsumed in pastiche; the 'show' is given a self-conscious modern twist by the transmutation of Shakespeare's stage into the fashionable entertainment of *tableaux vivants*, and his wenches into *dames vendeuses* (even their acting is denominated by another modish French term, *'rôle'*). The prominence of high society masks, but does not really disguise, the economic basis of the event, which works in two directions: the selling of Shakespeare, and Shakespeare's selling power, his ability to shift 'wares at the most exorbitant prices'. The *Show Book*, too, accurately reflects this double appropriation (Shakespeare as Victorian 'property'). It begins with institutional charity and aristocratic patronage and ends with commerce: 68 pages of advertisements for firms which had donated goods or services to the Show. The page design is uniform throughout, having a border at the left margin in an abstract or floral pattern, with a Shakespearean motto in its centre. These mottoes are sometimes apt to whatever material is on the page – one of the poems pleading for charitable donations has 'When maidens sue men give like Gods' from *Measure for Measure* (I. 4. 80–1) – but sometimes they are quite arbitrary – Browning, for example, gets a quotation from *Richard III*, 'For God's sake entertain good comfort' (I. 3. 4). The advertisements, however, all have mottoes chosen to reflect (with varying degrees of wit) on the product being advertised.[17] Oetzmann & Co., for example, a furniture and household goods retailer, has 'Fit it with such furniture as suits' from *Henry VIII* (II. 1. 99); Brand & Co. (purveyors of restoratives for invalids – 'Essence of Beef, Turtle Soup, Calf's Foot Jelly') has ''Tis not enough to help the feeble up, but to support him after' from *Timon of Athens* (I. 1. 107–8). Some advertisements play the tradition card: Keen's Mustard has 'What say you to a piece of Beef and Mustard?' (*The Taming of the Shrew* (IV. 3. 23), proving the ancient worth of the product: 'Shakspere shows that mustard was in use 300 years ago. Keen's Mustard was first manufactured 125 years after Shakspere's death.' More modern inventions resorted to wordplay: the London Stereoscopic & Photographic Co. has 'That I may see my shadow as I pass' from *Richard III* (I. 2. 263); The 'Piston' Freezing Machine & Ice Co. has 'Able to freeze the God Priapus' from *Pericles* (IV. 6. 4) (perhaps in the hope that ladies would not get the joke). The advertisement for Sewell's 'Rival' Corset is especially ingenious (or shameless): its motto is 'Thy shape invisible retain thou still' from *The Tempest* (IV. 1. 185). Only Liberty bucks the trend by preferring the Laureate to the Bard: though its advertisement for Art Fabrics has a Shakespearean motto ('Of very reverent reputation', from *The Comedy of Errors* (V. 1. 5)) it is eclipsed by a bold quotation from *Idylls of the King* across the top of the page: 'And Enid fell in longing for a dress.'

When he wrote the poem, which is dated 12 March 1884 in the fair copy MS,[18] Browning could not of course have foreseen the exact mode of its appearance. He owned a copy of the *Show Book*, but what he felt on seeing his poem in such company is not known; nor is it known if he attended the Show itself.[19] Yet it is as though he had anticipated the noisy soundings of Shakespeare's name, the impudently witty travesties of his words, the multiple appropriations of him for charity, for vanity, for piety and for money. 'What succeeds / Fitly as silence?' What succeeds Browning's poem is the Shakespearean babble of the Victorian age, to which Browning was adding his voice even as he declared he would rather withhold it.

Browning's Shakespeare

'After God, Shakespeare has created most.'[20] 'The Names' accepts Victorian bardolatry in an obvious, even blatant way. Shakespeare's name is 'man's most of might', his 'creation' takes on cosmic dimensions, he is closer to us than God, as 'this finite' (here, now) is closer than 'that infinite' (there, beyond; the name of God is 'That'). The extent and depth of Browning's familiarity with Shakespeare, and the pervasiveness of Shakespearean quotation and allusion in his poetry and letters, are well documented, and, in terms of cultural milieu, typical – much more so than his knowledge of the Talmud and of occult philosophy.[21] The 'voice' of the poem, at any rate in its closing movement, is a collective one: 'Nought impedes / We voice the other name [...].' Conventional tributes to Shakespeare are not hard to find in his writing, though since many of them are voiced by dramatic characters their status is often problematic, and there are also strong traces of vitiation. At the same period as he solicited Browning's contribution to the Shaksperean Show, Furnivall attacked his treatment of Shakespeare's Caliban in 'Caliban upon Setebos' (*Dramatis Personae*, 1864), and though Browning defended himself from the charge the defence itself has traces of irony.[22] One whole poem, 'At the "Mermaid"' (*Pacchiarotto* [...] *with Other Poems*, 1876), is supposedly spoken by Shakespeare himself, but to paraphrase Chesterton it is a much better guide as to what Shakespeare thought of Browning than vice versa.[23] I am holding in reserve the earliest tribute of all, in Browning's first, anonymous publication, *Pauline* (1833), for reasons which will become evident; but we can take as representative a cluster of references to Shakespeare, in poems, letters and critical writing, from the 1850s. In the *Essay on Shelley* (1852), Shakespeare does not stand alone: he is the supreme exemplar of the 'objective' mode of vision and poetry, as Shelley is of the 'subjective'. In 'Bishop Blougram's Apology', the worldly Catholic bishop imagines his idealistic opponent Gigadibs urging him to a higher ambition than the 'status, entourage, worldly circumstance' of an ecclesiastical potentate.[24] Why not write *Hamlet* or *Othello*? 'I can't – to put the strongest reason first', is Blougram's sardonic reply. Gigadibs doesn't give up: '"But try," you urge, "the trying shall suffice; / The aim, if reached or not, makes great the life: / Try to be Shakespeare, leave the rest to fate!"' Blougram makes fun of this, too: 'Spare my self-knowledge – there's no fooling me!' He can't be Shakespeare in the spiritual sense ('His power and consciousness and self-delight'); on the other hand he already surpasses Shakespeare in the material sense: Blougram, who is well versed in nineteenth-century Shakespearean biography, points out that Shakespeare didn't consider his 'soul's works' to be the end and aim of life: 'He leaves his towers and gorgeous palaces / To build the trimmest house in Stratford town', and measured his worth according to 'a coat of arms' and 'Successful dealings in his grain and wool'. Blougram concedes Shakespeare's genius but, good mid-Victorian that he is, debunks its Romantic associations with an ethereal spirit above the base desires of mankind: the author of *The Tempest* retires to Stratford. In this respect at least Blougram is probably voicing Browning's opinion, or one opinion of Browning's. The opposition between Shakespeare and Shelley is implicit here, as it was explicit in the *Essay*; but Blougram has another touch, towards the end of the poem, which introduces a different topic. He finds a neat reversal of Gigadibs's (presumed) exalted view of Shakespeare in a belittlement of Gigadibs himself; far from being one of those 'exceptional / And privileged great natures that dwarf mine', he is no more than a derivative hack:

> You, Gigadibs, who, thirty years of age,
> Write statedly for Blackwood's Magazine,
> Believe you see two points in Hamlet's soul
> Unseized by the Germans yet – which view you'll print –
> Meantime the best you have to show being still
> That lively lightsome article we took
> Almost for the true Dickens [...]

Blougram knows that German critics are top of the heap, as they are in George Eliot's *Middlemarch* (written twenty years after *Men and Women* but set in the 1830s), where Mr Casaubon's ignorance of German scholarship is a sign of his intellectual sterility; Blougram knows, too, that the psychology of Hamlet is both an extremely popular, and an over-populated field, so that Gigadibs can be stigmatised for being both trendy and outmoded. The competition for critical insight into 'Hamlet's soul' is in any case ignoble and futile; Shakespeare, in the Victorian age, is 'the true Dickens', and in that light Gigadibs can produce only pastiche.[25]

The topic of critical appreciation of Shakespeare (and, implicitly, of his own poetry) is fiercely taken up by Browning himself, in an exchange of letters with Ruskin following the publication (and disastrous reception) of *Men and Women* in 1855. 'There are truths and depths in it,' Ruskin declared, 'far beyond anything I have read except Shakespeare – and truly, if you had just written *Hamlet*, I believe I should have written to you, precisely this kind of letter – merely quoting your own Rosencrantz against you – "I understand you not, my Lord."' To this Browning responded:

> Do you believe people understand *Hamlet*? The last time I saw it acted, the heartiest applause of the night went to a little by-play of

the actor's own – who, to simulate madness in a hurry, plucked forth his handkerchief and flourished it hither and thither: certainly a third of the play, with no end of noble things, had been (as from time immemorial) suppressed, with the auditory's amplest acquiescence and benediction.[26]

The contempt which Blougram shows for literary criticism, Browning here shows for the vulgar theatrical audience. Again, it would be wrong to think of this as an absolute judgement. Browning longed desperately for popularity and had deluded himself that *Men and Women* was accessible to a wide readership and would actually make money. His ferocious scorn for the book-buying or theatre-going public is in part a reaction against the failure not just of his best work, but his most determined effort to please. Comparison with Shakespeare was rubbing salt in the wound; the true comparison, once more, was with Dickens.

Although these allusions to Shakespeare in the mid-1850s confirm Browning's familiarity with Shakespeare's life and work, and with the literary and cultural dissemination of his fame, they suggest, too, that Browning's admiration for the former was tempered by his revulsion at the latter. A comment he is reported to have made on the Shakespeare Tercentenary in 1864 sums up this dual view and points directly towards the opening gesture of 'The Names': 'Here we are called upon to acknowledge Shakespeare, we who have him in our very bones and blood, our very selves. The very recognition of Shakespeare's merits by the Committee reminds me of nothing so apt as an illustration, as the decree of the Directoire that men might acknowledge God.'[27]

The spell

Shakespeare's name is a word of power. Like a magic spell, when you speak it, 'Act follows word'; in this instance, 'Shakespeare's creation rises' (a creation made up of dramatic 'Acts', as Gal Manor points out).[28] Browning's interest in the occult goes back a long way, and its origins are close to those of his poetry. There is no evidence that he believed in magic – on the contrary, he thought of it as a form of charlatanism – but then, in his poetry, the liar is often the greatest, the most compulsive truth-teller (think of Mr Sludge, or Guido, or Don Juan). In any case Browning does not need to affirm or deny his own faith in what 'the speaker knows full well'. Dramatically, the spell works (as it does in *The Tempest*). Why should it be 'faltered forth'? Perhaps because this fits the fearfulness which pervades the poem, affecting the

'Hebrew' who dare not speak the name of God aloud, and marking the difference between divine and human as 'dread'. Magic is not to be taken lightly, as the Arab physician Karshish recalls: when Lazarus shows unaccountable anger at a 'word' or 'gesture' of one of his children,

> Demand
> The reason why – "tis but a word,' object –
> 'A gesture' – he regards thee as our lord
> Who lived there in the pyramid alone,
> Looked at us (dost thou mind?) when, being young,
> We both would unadvisedly recite
> Some charm's beginning, from that book of his,
> Able to bid the sun throb wide and burst
> All into stars, as suns grown old are wont.[29]

The effect of the spell in 'The Names' is as world-encompassing as this, though in the opposite direction: instead of cataclysmic destruction, 'creation rises'. But the element of danger, of fear and trembling, is just as apt. Long ago, in *Pauline* (1833), Browning had placed as a preface to the poem a long passage from the *De Occulta Philosophia* of Cornelius Agrippa, one of the most famous of the Renaissance mages whose works he knew (great charlatans and truth-tellers, another of whom, Paracelsus, became the hero of his next poem); and in this preface the terror of meddling with the dark arts, whether of magic or poetry, is strongly voiced: 'quibus et ego nunc consulo, ne scripta nostra legant, nec intelligant, nec meminerint: nam noxia sunt, venenosa sunt: Acherontis ostium est in hoc libro, lapides loquitur, caveant, ne cerebrum illis excutiat' [Whom therefore I advise that they read not our writings, nor understand them, nor remember them. For they are pernicious and full of poison; the gate of Acheron is in this book; it speaks stones – let them take heed that it beat not out their brains].[30]

Even taken by itself, the fact that Cornelius Agrippa introduces Browning's first published poem would tell us something about the importance of magic to 'The Names'; but we need also to look at the very last words of the poem, not those of the speaker but the author, and which consist of a place-name and date: 'Richmond, October 22, 1832'. Browning did not live in Richmond, and the date is not, as you might suppose, that on which the poem was completed. It is a private notation – or rather, an occult one, since it is 'published' but remains unintelligible without a key. We possess the key because of a complicated exchange between Browning and John Stuart Mill, which there isn't space to describe in full; suffice it to say that Browning was driven to give the following explanation: '[Edmund] Kean was acting there [at Richmond]: I saw him in Richard III that night, and conceived the childish scheme already mentioned' – this 'scheme' involved an elaborate fantasy-life as universal artist, of which *Pauline* was the first (and abortive) production.[31] My point is that magic and Shakespeare link hands across the body of Browning's first work. In connecting the name of Shakespeare with a magic spell, Browning is returning to his own origins as a poet. The collective voice, the *we* of the poem, conceals a private, jealously guarded *I*. In turn, the deliberate choice of the sonnet form, and Browning's magnificent handling of it, acquire a deeper significance. The sonnet is not 'Shakespearean', but nor does it obey the conventional 'Petrarchan' division between octave and sestet. Line 8, instead of concluding the octave, begins the syntactic movement of the sestet; the word 'impedes' is not an impediment but a prompt, the phrase 'Nought impedes' swings open like a gate as the 'voice' of the poem pronounces its spell: 'Awesomely, lovingly', the rhythm of the poem creates the 'awe and love' it celebrates; the *fiat* of God becomes the 'awe and love' of human worship. Not 'let there be light', but 'let awe and love / Mutely await their working'. Enjoining silence at the end as at the beginning, the poem 'leave[s] to sight / All of the issue', yet what can be seen is only in the mind's eye, an imagined world which is also a world made out of language.

The name of God and the poetry of vision

'That which the Hebrew reads / With his soul only': the allusion is to the tetragrammaton, YHVH, consisting of the Hebrew letters *yud, heh, vav, heh*, one of the two principal names of God in the Hebrew bible (the other is 'Elohim'). 'The holiest of names was never pronounced (the 'Ineffable Name', *Shem ha-Meforash*), except once a year by the high priest in the Holy of Holies [in the Temple] on Yom Kippur [the Day of Atonement]. According to a rabbinic tradition, once (or twice) in seven years the sages entrusted to their disciples the pronunciation of the tetragrammaton, but the original pronunciation is now unknown; it is read as Adonai (my Lord) which was already used in the second century BCE. The combination in the Hebrew Bible of the consonants *y, h, v, h* and the vocalisation for Adonai gave rise to the misnomer Jehovah.'[32]

Browning knew all this; he is the most Hebraising of our post-Renaissance poets. His knowledge of Jewish religion, legends and scholarship probably came to him, like so much else, from his father, and included not just the Talmud but the Kabbala, which tied in with his general interest in the occult. The title of his series *Bells and Pomegranates* (1841–46) drew on a knowledge of biblical hermeneutics which defeated even Elizabeth Barrett. He studied Hebrew at one time well enough to regret losing it, and he returned to it in the 1870s and 1880s; he wrote poems with Jewish characters from the bible and from rabbinical stories, and quoted a well-known rabbinical saying, in Hebrew, in a note to 'Jochanan Hakkadosh', one of the poems of *Jocoseria* – the volume which he published in 1883, the year before 'The Names'. His interest in Hebrew was especially active in this period: in May 1883 he acquired a Hebrew grammar and a 'Hebrew Family Bible'.[33]

Browning's apprehension of the significance of the 'Ineffable Name' would have been heavily influenced by its connections with Jewish mysticism, with Kabbala and with Renaissance occult philosophy. Abraham Ibn Ezra, the twelfth-century Spanish poet and philosopher who is Browning's 'Rabbi Ben Ezra' (*Dramatis Personae*, 1864), wrote that the four letters of the name of God were the most spiritual of the alphabet and symbolised the presence of the divine in the body of the world. Kabbala claimed that all existing things were formed by God using the creative aspect of the 22 Hebrew letters; Kabbala itself reaches back to earlier rabbinical commentary on the creative power of language, such as the statement that the universe was created by ten divine utterances, or that Bezalel ben Uri, the builder of the Tabernacle, was given 'the knowledge of the letters by which the heaven and earth were created'.[34]

The manipulation of language was a source of power, and the name of God conferred this power in its highest form, since the tetragrammaton contained the quintessence of the divine nature. Renaissance mages such as Pico della Mirandola, Marsilio Ficino, and Paracelsus, all of whose works Browning knew, took up this extraordinarily suggestive idea: it forms part of Paracelsus's doctrine of 'signatures' which influenced eighteenth-century mystics such as Christopher Smart – another favourite of Browning's and the subject of one of his *Parleyings* (1887). In *De natura rerum* (1537) Paracelsus re-stated the kabbalistic belief that Adam in the Garden of Eden understood the signs within things, and was thus able to give each thing its proper name; he believed that this originary language was Hebrew, a belief which lasted into the eighteenth century and beyond. The clergyman and theologian George Benson confidently affirmed in 1754 that in Hebrew 'the true sense of a word is better secured than is possible to be in any other language', and that 'the structure of the Hebrew language is an internal evidence, that the Hebrew scriptures are of God's own inditing, who only knows the resemblance between the *natural* world and the *spiritual*, and who only is able to give the information this language affords'.[35]

Besides 'The Names', Browning refers to the tetragrammaton four times in his poetry, but only one of these instances, 'Abt Vogler' (*Dramatis Personae*, 1864) refers to its creative power.[36] In the opening lines of this poem, the composer and musician Abt Vogler compares his genius to that of Solomon, who possessed the power of the 'ineffable Name', and by using it could compel 'Armies of angels that soar, legions of demons that lurk' to do his bidding – to 'Pile him a palace straight, to pleasure the princess he loved'. Abt Vogler's 'palace' is 'the structure brave, the manifold music I build': the 'ineffable Name' in this image gives access to a genie out of the Arabian Nights – or the Talmudic legends which they so resemble. However, just as Shakespeare's authority is at 'one remove' from that of God, so Abt Vogler's power is at one remove from Solomon's. He speaks the poem, as the subtitle tells us, 'After he has been extemporizing upon the musical instrument of his invention'. Abt Vogler can rival Solomon, but only for the duration of his performance. 'Would that the structure brave, the manifold music I build [...] Would it might tarry like his [...].' But an extemporised performance will not tarry – the word *build* is deceptive. As Browning's readers well knew, even Solomon's structures hadn't 'tarried', whether pleasure-palaces or the great Temple (which, according to another Talmudic legend, his command of the 'ineffable name' had also enabled him to build). Abt Vogler learns this lesson of transience: later in the poem he rejects Solomon, the magician and manipulator of the Name, in favour of the Name itself: 'Therefore to whom turn I but to thee, the ineffable Name? / Builder and maker, thou, of houses not made with hands!' (ll. 65–6). He no longer conjures with the name, but invokes its transcendent immaterial power as a guarantor of eventual salvation: 'On the earth the broken arcs; in the heaven, a perfect round' (l. 72).

Thinking about 'Abt Vogler' in relation to 'The Names' brings into focus, from another perspective, what Sarah Wood so persuasively argues – the significance to Browning's poetics of the opposition between 'finite' and 'infinite'.[37] If 'all poetry', as Browning wrote to Ruskin, is 'a putting the infinite within the finite', then all poetry must fail, or succeed only by the very gaps and flaws which result from its impossible effort. The true sublime is a gesture *towards* transcendence, man's 'reach' which, in Browning's most famous formulation, should always 'exceed his grasp'.[38] But to understand 'The Names' we must take account of the dimension of *time* in this contrast between finite and infinite, since it is not only a contrast between imperfect and perfect, but also a contrast between mortal and immortal, change and permanence. Abt Vogler's desire is for a 'structure' which is time-bound to become timeless, in a heaven where 'eternity affirms the conception of an hour' (l. 76). The metaphor of the building or palace is not accidental: it strengthens the pathos of Abt Vogler's realisation that his music is evanescent, despite its visionary solidity. When, therefore, Browning says in 'The Names' that 'Shakespeare's creation rises', in all its seeming perfection and god-like completeness ('below – above'), the reminder of 'Abt Vogler' is clear: Shakespeare's work is as time-bound as that of the musician, as liable to dissolution. And this connection is sealed by the passage which Browning surely had in mind when he wrote both these poems, and which is spoken by Shakespeare's own mage and conjuror:

> Our revels now are ended. These our actors,
> (As I foretold you) were all spirits, and
> Are melted into air, into thin air,
> And like the baseless fabric of this vision,
> The cloud-capp'd tow'rs, the gorgeous palaces,
> The solemn temples, the great globe itself,
> Yea, all which it inherit, shall dissolve,
> And like this insubstantial pageant faded,
> Leave not a wrack behind.
> *(Tempest,* IV. 1. 148–56)

This is, if you like, the true 'Shaksperean Show', whose dissolution 'The Names', like 'Abt Vogler', evokes even as it affirms Shakespeare's enduring power over his own creation, and his influence over 'all which it inherit'. For Browning, one of the greatest of Shakespeare's inheritors, the 'dread remove' which separates finite from infinite measures the 'insubstantial pageant' of his own work, not to mention the spectacle in the Albert Hall at which, in the end, you don't know whether to laugh or weep.

Notes

1. L. N. Broughton, C. S. Northrup, and R. B. Pearsall, *Robert Browning: a Bibliography, 1830–1950*, rev. edn (Ithaca: Cornell University Press, 1953); W. S. Peterson, *Robert Browning and Elizabeth Barrett Browning: an Annotated*

Bibliography 1951–1970 (New York: Browning Institute, 1974); annual bibliographies from 1971 in *Browning Institute Studies* and its continuation, *Victorian Literature and Culture*.

2. Mrs [Alexandra] Sutherland Orr, *Life and Letters of Robert Browning* (London: Smith, Elder, 1891), p. 358 ('A complete bibliography would take account of three other sonnets...'); W. H. Griffin and H. C. Minchin, *The Life of Robert Browning* (London: Methuen 1910, rev. edn 1938); M. Ward, *Robert Browning and His World*, 2 vols (London: Cassell, 1967, 1969); W. Irvine and P. Honan, *The Book, the Ring, and the Poet: a Biography of Robert Browning* (London: Bodley Head 1974); C. de L. Ryals, *The Life of Robert Browning* (Oxford: Blackwell 1993).

3. Edward Berdoe, *The Browning Cyclopædia*, 7th edn (London: George Allen & Unwin, 1912), pp. 282–3; originally published in 1891. W. C. DeVane, *A Browning Handbook*, 2nd edn (New York: Appleton-Century-Crofts, 1955), p. 567; originally published in 1937. DeVane's acts of inattention are small: he mis-spells the *Shaksperean Show Book* as *Shakespearean Show-Book* and implies that 'The Names' was published there with a subtitle, '(To Shakespeare)', which in fact appears neither there nor in the text printed in the *Pall Mall Gazette*.

4. G. R. Elliott, 'Shakespeare's Significance for Browning', *Anglia. Zeitschrift für Englische Philologie*, 32 [n.s. 20] (1909), 90–161; 'The Names' is quoted on p. 110.

5. J. Maynard, *Browning's Youth* (Cambridge, MA: Harvard University Press, 1977), p. 322.

6. S. Wood, *Robert Browning: a Literary Life* (Basingstoke: Palgrave – now Palgrave Macmillan, 2001), pp. 133–4.

7. For Manor's article, see *Browning Society Notes*, 25 (December 1998), 6–17; her article was later revised and incorporated into her doctoral thesis, *Supernatural Language in the Poetry of Robert Browning* (University of London, 2000). My debt to the work of both Wood and Manor will be obvious in the course of this essay.

8. Of Browning's eleven sonnets only three were collected, or published originally in book form. He associated the form with personal effusions: 'Shall I sonnet-sing you about myself?' begins the poem 'House' (*Pacchiarotto [...] with Other Poems*, 1876), which attacks Wordsworth's claim in 'Scorn not the sonnet' that 'with this key / Shakespeare unlocked his heart': 'Did he? if so, the less Shakespeare he!' the poem concludes. Browning's reluctance to 'unlock his heart' in sonnet form was probably intensified, if not caused, by his wife having famously done so in *Sonnets from the Portuguese*. On periodical publication, William Allingham records Browning asking his advice on how to publish *The Ring and the Book*: 'I want people not to turn to the end, but to read through in the proper order. Magazine, you'll say: but no, I don't like the notion of being sandwiched between Politics and Deer-Stalking, say,' (26 May 1868; *William Allingham's Diary*, ed. by G. Grigson (Fontwell: Centaur Press, 1967), p. 181). In 1886 he wrote to the editor of a Boston magazine: 'I cannot bring myself to write for periodicals. If I publish a book, and people choose to buy it, that proves they want to read my work. But to have them turn over the pages of a magazine and find me – that is to be an uninvited guest,' (*Letters of Robert Browning collected by Thomas J. Wise*, ed. by T. L. Hood (London: John Murray, 1933), p. 244).

9. Letter dated 27 January 1884, in *More than Friend: the Letters of Robert Browning to Katharine de Kay Bronson*, ed. by M. Meredith (Waco: Armstrong Browning Library of Baylor University, and Winfield: Wedgestone Press, 1985), p. 39. The occasion for this remark was not the Shakespearean request, but other Furnivallesque behaviour. Four months earlier Furnivall had tried to get Browning to write a commemorative poem following the death of his secretary (and mistress) 'Teena' (Miss Mary Lilian Rochfort-Smith), representing the request as coming from Teena's parents. Browning refused: 'I should hate any mechanical attempt to do what would only acquire worth from being a spontaneous outflow,' (letter of 17 September 1883, in *Browning's Trumpeter: the Correspondence of Robert Browning and Frederic J. Furnivall, 1872–1889*, ed. by W. S. Peterson (Washington, DC: Decatur House Press, 1979), p. 77). You could never quite get the better of Furnivall, though. In the memoir of Teena that he wrote and privately printed, he included a photograph of Browning, to Browning's annoyance.

10. Letter of 19 July 1867, in *Letters*, ed. by Hood (see note 8), p. 114. The text in the final collected edition of 1888–89 is 21,134 lines (technically this should be a hundred or so lines less, but all editions of the poem follow the first edition of 1868–69 in counting half-lines as full lines).

11. Furnivall insisted on the spelling 'Shakspere', and the official title of the show and book conform to his demand; but most contributors, Browning included, continued to spell 'Shakespeare' (occasionally 'Shakspeare'). The copy I have used for this essay is in the British Library (11763.de.4).

12. The booklet is in album format (10" × 5"), originally paper-wrapped. The hospital's prospectus occupies pp. i–iv of the booklet; pp. v–xii have the title page, contents, and other prefatory matter; the writers' and artists' contributions occupy pp. 1–81; the official programme of the show itself (with some further illustrations) is on pp. 82–124; last comes the advertising supplement, separately numbered in roman, pp. i–lxviii. The booklet was edited by J. S. Wood, the secretary of the Chelsea Hospital.

13. Tennyson's contribution is headed 'Stanza, by Lord Tennyson' and runs as follows: 'Not he that breaks the dams, but he / That thro' the channels of the State / Convoys the people's wish, is great; / His name is pure, his fame is free.' The provenance is 'Hail, Briton!', ll. 145–8: see *The Poems of Tennyson*, ed. by Christopher Ricks, 2nd edn, 3 vols (Harlow: Longman, 1987, II, 528, and the headnote to the poem on pp. 521–2. I am very grateful to Professor Ricks for pointing out this reference. The *Pall Mall Gazette*, after printing Browning's poem, remarked: 'Lord Tennyson's stanza is shorter, and apropos of nothing in particular'. The stanza form is that of *In Memoriam*; the sentiment reflects some of Tennyson's political poems of the 1880s, e.g. 'Compromise' (1884), which was addressed to Gladstone and uses river-imagery: see Ricks's edition, III, 128.

14. I discuss these mottoes later on in the essay, pp. 154–5.

15. 'After these contributions from masters in the art of song [Browning and Tennyson], we come upon one of Mr. Oscar Wilde's poems, in which he sings from under the balcony to crimson-mouthed stars, golden-browed moons, &c.' (*Pall Mall Gazette*); 'Mr. Oscar Wilde provides, for the satisfaction of those who admire what now passes for poetry in certain quarters...' (*The Times*, 29

May 1884, p. 10). Reports on the Shakespearian [*sic*] Show appeared in *The Times* on 29, 30 and 31 May.

16. *The Times*, 29 May 1884, p. 10a. A plan of the show appears on p. 83 of the *Show Book*; the stalls are described on pp. 111–22, the *tableaux* on p. 95; a catalogue of the relics (many of them staggeringly inauthentic) appears on pp. 97–108. The Prince of Wales's regrets at being unable to attend the show were reiterated in the *Times* report on the following day (30 May 1884, p. 6c), which also reveals that the opening spectacle did not quite come off: some of the curtains around the *tableaux vivants* did not fall at the right moment, and the 'general effect of several was spoiled by the movement of the figures'. The costumes, however, were 'without exception good, in many cases magnificent'. The trial scene in *The Merchant of Venice* had Shylock (Mr E. Brocklehurst) in puce gabardine and yellow shoes ('in obedience to the Venetian sumptuary laws'), while 'Antonio (Mr A. Stopford) certainly showed no signs of his fallen fortunes in his dress. He was magnificently attired in a shirt and trunk-hose of blue Venetian brocade, slashed with cream-coloured satin, a cloak of pale salmon-coloured plush, with a hat of the same material'.

17. It is not clear whether individual firms were asked to provide a Shakespearean motto with their advertising copy; my guess would be rather that the mottoes were provided by someone who knew his Shakespeare (again, Furnivall is the obvious candidate: he would have enjoyed the challenge).

18. The MS is in the Aldrich Collection (Historical Department, Des Moines, Iowa); see *The Browning Collections*, ed. by P. Kelley and B. Coley (Winfield, KS: Wedgestone Press, 1984), #E278, p. 421. On 27 March 1884 Browning wrote to Furnivall: 'I indited a Sonnet for the Fair – too hastily perhaps, but it may do' (*Browning's Trumpeter* (see note 9), p. 94).

19. Browning's copy is recorded in *Browning Collections* (see n. 18), #A2085, p. 176. It was bought by a dealer at the Sotheby sale of Pen Browning's estate in 1913 but has not been traced. Browning was in London from late April to August 1884 but I have found no references to the Show in extant letters from this period.

20. Alexandre Dumas *père*, 'How I Became a Playwright' (1863), cited in *After Shakespeare*, ed. by John Gross (Oxford: Oxford University Press, 2002), p. 3.

21. Maynard (see note 5) has a good summary, pp. 321–4, drawing in part on Elliott's article (see note 4).

22. Letter of 25 April 1884; *Browning's Trumpeter* (see note 9), pp. 95–6.

23. In a recent doctoral thesis, *A Poet's Self-Presentation: Robert Browning's Poems In Propria Persona* (University of London, 2002), Britta Martens brilliantly demonstrates the rashness of taking this poem at face value, a lesson which Browning never tires of teaching even those critics who think they know his work backwards. Of course there are clear enough examples of Browning's unaffected admiration of Shakespeare: Mrs Bronson records him rebuking her for not having any Shakespeare on her shelves, and vigorously rebutting a flattering comparison between Shakespeare and himself: 'No, no, no; I won't hear that. No one in the world will ever approach Shakespeare; never,' (*More than Friend* [see n. 9], pp. 142, 158).

24. The quotations which follow are taken from the passage which begins at l. 485 of the poem and runs to l. 554.

25. Blougram may be remembering this bit of *Hamlet*-baiting from chapter 24 of *Nicholas Nickleby* (1838–39): '"As an exquisite embodiment of the poet's visions, and a realisation of human intellectuality, gilding with refulgent light our dreamy moments, and laying open a new and magic world before the mental eye, the drama is gone, perfectly gone," said Mr. Curdle. – "What man is there now living who can present before us all those changing and prismatic colours with which the character of Hamlet is invested?" exclaimed Mrs. Curdle. – "What man indeed – upon the stage;" said Mr. Curdle, with a small reservation in favour of himself. "Hamlet! Pooh! ridiculous! Hamlet is gone, perfectly gone."'

26. Ruskin's letter, and Browning's reply, are reprinted in J. Woolford and D. Karlin, *Robert Browning* (Harlow: Longman, 1996), pp. 252–9; the Ruskin extract quoted here is on p. 255, the Browning on p. 258. Five years later how must Browning have relished Mr Wopsle's Hamlet in *Great Expectations*!

27. From a diary entry by Thomas Richmond, dated 12 February 1864, quoted by Mrs Orr (see n. 2), p. 268.

28. *Supernatural Language* (see n. 7), p. 232.

29. 'An Epistle containing the Strange Medical Experience of Karshish, the Arab Physician' (*Men and Women*, 1855), ll. 165–73.

30. Text and translation from *The Poems of Browning*, ed. by J. Woolford and D. Karlin, 2 vols (Harlow: Longman, 1991), I, 27–8.

31. For a full account of the extraordinary 'dialogue' between Browning and Mill, in which Mill annotated a copy of *Pauline* which Browning then counter-annotated, see either the Longman edition (see n. 30), or the Oxford English Texts edition by Ian Jack and Margaret Smith (vol. 1, 1984). The critical implications of this dialogue are extremely suggestive: Browning in effect reveals that a performance not just of Shakespeare but of this particular play, *Richard III*, lay behind his first, unbridled creative fantasy; not only did the occasion feature one of the last appearances of the great Romantic icon Edmund Kean, but the place where Kean was acting, Richmond, is also the name of a character in *Richard III*, indeed the name of his successor, Henry VII. For the young poet is both usurper and true heir, king and king-killer.

32. *Oxford Dictionary of the Jewish Religion*, general eds. R. J. Zwi Werblowsky and G. Wigoder (Oxford: Oxford University Press 1997), s.v. God, Names of, p. 277.

33. I repeat my debt to Manor (see n. 7) who draws in turn on Judith Berlin-Lieberman, *Robert Browning and Hebraism* (Jerusalem: Azriel Press, 1934). Robert Browning Sr compiled an annotated nomenclature of the Hebrew Bible, and owned what was probably the specific source for Browning's knowledge of the 'Ineffable Name', a translation by an eighteenth-century clergyman, the Rev. B. Gerrans, of *The Travels of Rabbi Benjamin, Son of Jonah of Tudela* (London, 1783), a book which Browning inscribed in 1882 (see *Browning Collections*, #A192, pp. 18–19). For Browning's early knowledge of Hebrew, see Elizabeth Barrett's letter to him of 22 November 1845 and his reply of 23 November, in *The Brownings' Correspondence*, ed. by P. Kelley and S. Lewis, vol. 11 (Winfield, KS: Wedgestone Press, 1993), pp. 191, 192n.5, and 196. The Hebrew saying in the note to 'Jochanan Hakkadosh' is in praise of the philosopher Moses Maimonides: meaning 'from Moses to Moses arose none like Moses'. In a letter of 24 March 1883 to Mrs FitzGerald, Browning

glosses a phrase from 'Jochanan Hakkadosh' in Hebrew and comments on the Hebrew meaning of his son's name; in another letter of 5 May 1883, he thanked her for sending him a card with a Hebrew blessing written by a Jewish friend of hers: 'I get more and more attached to that grand language' (*Learned Lady: Letters from Robert Browning to Mrs Thomas FitzGerald*, ed. by E. C. McAleer (Cambridge, MA: Harvard University Press, 1966), pp. 158, 162–3, 164nn.1, 11). Browning's Hebrew grammar and Bible are now both in the Armstrong Browning Library at Baylor University.

34. The ten utterances are alluded to in a Mishnaic tractate, *Avot* (5.1); the *Oxford Dictionary of the Jewish Religion* (see n. 23) comments that this 'postulates that language is first and foremost a divine tool of creation rather than a human means of communication' (s.v. Alphabet, Hebrew, p. 39) – another very suggestive thought for students of Browning. The story about Belzalel is in the tractate *Berakhot* (55a); it is a gloss on Exodus 31: 3, where God tells Moses, 'I have filled him [Belzalel] with the spirit of God, in wisdom, and in understanding, and in knowledge, and in all manner of workmanship.' For more on the subject of Hebrew as the divine language, and on kabbalistic creation theory, see Umberto Eco, *The Search for the Perfect Language*, trans. by J. Fentess (Oxford: Blackwell, 1995).

35. George Benson, *A Summary View of the Evidences of Christ's Resurrection* (London: J. Waugh, 1754); cited in Manor (see n. 7), pp. 49–50. Manor points out that the transformation of the idea of Hebrew as a divine or primary language into its modern classification took place in Browning's lifetime. She compares, for example, the entry for Hebrew in the *Encyclopaedia Britannica* of 1791 with that of 1880: in the former Hebrew 'appears to be the most ancient of all the languages in the world, at least we know of none older, and some learned men are of opinion, that this is the language in which God spoke to Adam in Paradise'; in 1880 'Hebrew is a language of the group which since Eichorn has generally been known as Semitic, and of which Arabic and Ethiopic (Southern Semitic), the various dialects of Aramaic, and the language of the Assyrian and Babylonian inscriptions are the other chief representatives'.

36. The other three are 'Mr Sludge, "the Medium"' (also *Dramatis Personae*, 1864), *The Ring and the Book* (1868–69), and 'Solomon and Balkis' (*Jocoseria*, 1883). In 'Mr Sludge', Sludge refers to 'the Great and Terrible Name' (a phrase from Psalm 99, v. 3: 'Let them praise thy great and terrible name; for it is holy') in the course of countering the argument that the spiritualist's 'signs and omens, raps and sparks' are too trivial for God to bother with. The occult power of God's name was associated in primitive times with 'thunders, lightnings, earthquakes, whirlwinds, dealt / Indisputably on men whose death they caused', which led men to tremble 'at the breath / O' the Name's first letter; why, the Jews, I'm told, / Won't write it down, no, to this very hour, / Nor speak aloud' (ll. 1080–1, 1085–7). But modern science, Sludge goes on, has revealed that the power of the 'Name' extends in the opposite direction: 'The small becomes the dreadful and immense!' (l. 1122). In Book 6 of *The Ring and the Book*, Caponsacchi recounts how the ignorant, worldly Bishop who ordained him persuaded him that he need not take his vow of chastity literally: ' "Mark what makes all smooth, / Nay, has been even a solace to myself! / The Jews who needs must, in their synagogue, / Utter sometimes the

holy name of God, / A thing their superstition boggles at [...] How does their shrewdness help them? In this wise; / Another set of sounds they substitute, / Jumble so consonants and vowels – how / Should I know? – that there grows from out the old / Quite a new word that means the very same – / And o'er the hard place slide they with a smile".' (Bk 6, ll. 278–89). 'Solomon and Balkis' is founded on an old Talmudic legend about the visit of the Queen of Sheba to Solomon: the Name is inscribed on Solomon's ring, and compels whomever looks at it to reveal their true thoughts – a power which backfires on the king and his guest.

37. For Wood's book, see n. 6.
38. 'Andrea del Sarto' (*Men and Women*, 1855), l. 97.

10

Mary Cowden Clarke: Marriage, Gender and the Victorian Woman Critic of Shakespeare

Ann Thompson and Sasha Roberts

> Together roaming through the world of books,
> Together writing for our daily bread.
> (Mary Cowden Clarke, *A Score of Sonnets to One*
> *Object* (1884), Sonnet XX)

Mary Cowden Clarke was the first woman to make a profession of writing about Shakespeare. Unlike female critics today she did not hold a university post – indeed it was not possible for women to attend universities at all when she was growing up – but she was a freelance writer living by her pen. In so far as she is remembered at all today it is for *The Girlhood of Shakespeare's Heroines* (1850–52), occasionally cited (usually by people who have not read it) as an example of a naive Victorian novelistic approach to the plays. *The Girlhood* is however representative of only one strand in Mary's long and prolific writing career;[1] she published voluminously on Shakespeare, both as a solo author and in collaboration with her husband Charles. In the mid-nineteenth century, when Mary Cowden Clarke began writing, Shakespeare scholarship was not yet institutionalised within British universities; how did Mary establish herself among contemporary circles of Shakespeare scholars, particularly as the female member of a literary couple? Our intention in this essay is twofold: we want to consider the nature of the collaboration and how it was seen by the Clarkes themselves and by others at the time and subsequently, but we also want to look at how their work on Shakespeare – particularly their analysis of marriage and gender in Shakespeare – was shaped by the fact of their collaboration.

The collaborative relationship between husband and wife bears with it, in the case of the Cowden Clarkes, a problematic legacy. For the Cowden Clarkes' work has been regarded in terms of *domestic*, rather than *literary* production – and this emphasis upon the domestic becomes a means of denigrating their literary achievements, either as individual writers or when working together on joint projects. Thus Richard D. Altick, author of the only book on *The Cowden Clarkes* (London: Oxford University Press, 1948), describes their work as 'not intrinsically important' (p. xi), and locates their collaboration in the context of sentimental Victorian domestic values rather than serious scholarly endeavour:

> There was something of a fashion for literary couples in the time of Victoria; the pervasive ideal of harmonious domesticity extended even to the production of literature. The Victorians were particularly pleased by the idea of a loving husband and wife sitting on opposite sides of a cluttered work table, each busy with his or her new essay or poem or novel. (p. ix)

He continues in this condescending vein about the Clarkes: 'the story of their personal lives, first in London, then in Nice and finally at Genoa, affords a revealing instance of how the romantic ideal, somewhat vulgarized, was subtly and gradually transformed into the sentimental outlook so characteristic of the Victorians' (pp. x–xi), and refers later to their way of life as 'a sort of domesticated romanticism' (p. 82). In some respects the Cowden Clarkes do lay themselves open to others' condescension: they refer constantly to the strength and importance of their personal and professional partnership in ways that may seem complacent, even irritating, to those not blessed with such happiness. Their self-conscious idealisation of their collaboration as 'married lovers' and Shakespeare scholars invokes contemporary ideals of domestic bliss and industry, and promotes an image of the home as a source of comfort, pleasure and productivity. But does 'domestic collaboration' (as the Cowden Clarkes' partnership might be termed) preclude serious or significant critical activity? In the case of Mary Cowden Clarke, we think not: rather, we want to re-evaluate her contribution to Shakespeare scholarship, and the ways in which that contribution was supported and shaped by her partnership with Charles.

The Cowden Clarkes were literary and scholarly collaborators who self-consciously idealised the process of collaboration. After Charles died in 1877 at the age of 89, Mary, who was 67, took over his projected book of *Recollections of Writers* and memorialised their joint work in her Preface as a loving, literary partnership:

> Charles and Mary Cowden Clarke may with truth be held in tender remembrance by their readers as among the happiest of married lovers for more than forty-eight years, writing together, reading together, enjoying together the perfection of loving, literary consociation; and kindly sympathy may well be felt for her who is left singly to subscribe herself,
>
> Her readers' faithful servant,
>
> MARY COWDEN CLARKE.

The intensity of Mary's grief testifies to the sincerity of these remarks; three years later she wrote to James and Annie Fields, 'Oh, my dear friends! I try hard never to break down and utter a syllable that may hurt those who would grieve to see me grieve – but often, often, I feel that I would give all that may remain to me of life to be only one simple quarter of an hour with him again.'[2] In 'Two Lovers of Literature and Art', her own memorial of Charles and Mary Cowden Clarke written for *The Century Magazine*, after Mary's death in 1898, Annie Fields quotes a letter Charles wrote to his sister when he was seventy in which he says of his wife 'My soul seems daily more and more knit with hers; and I do not conceive how there can be a happier being in existence than your brother Charles.'[3] The sonnets Mary wrote to Charles after his death (*A Score of Sonnets to One Object*, 1884), might, as Fields says 'have been dedicated to a young lover' (p. 128). She refers to him as 'my lover-husband', a phrase she had used in 1873 on the title-page of *The Trust and The Remittance* ('Two Love Stories in Metred Prose'): 'To the lover-husband of eighty-five, these love stories are dedicated by the lover-wife of sixty-three' (Title-page, *The Trust and The Remittance*, 1874). The words 'husband' and 'wife' were, it seems, insufficient to describe the passion and commitment Mary and Charles felt for each other. Indeed, the terms they used to describe each other repeatedly evoke a sense of heightened mutuality in which the self is shared with and belongs to another: Mary calls herself 'thy second self' (*A Score of Sonnets*, Sonnet XIX), a phrase they both used frequently, along with 'other self'.

The fact that the Cowden Clarkes had no children may have intensified their relationship; this is never discussed explicitly by either of them, but Mary came from a large, happy, talented family, Charles was famous for his love of children, and they both took great pleasure in the company of their various nieces and nephews. Annie Fields hints at another significant factor in the Cowden Clarkes' relationship when she writes of their engagement: '[Charles] now felt that the moment when he could ask for the woman of his choice had arrived, although she was still very young. [John] Keats [Charles' former pupil and protégé] had already died, leaving a gap never to be filled in the loving heart of his friend.'[4] The Cowden Clarkes spent their honeymoon in Enfield, revisiting places Charles had been to with Keats, but Mary herself never seems to have felt she was in any way a substitute in Charles' affections.

Although the Cowden Clarkes published separately on various topics, they concentrated their joint energies on Shakespeare from about 1845 to 1877. Mary's single-authored works included a number of essays in both general and specialist periodicals, and three mammoth works: her *Concordance to Shakespeare* (1844–45), the first of its kind; her *The Girlhood of Shakespeare's Heroines* (1850–52), and her unannotated edition of *Shakespeare's Works* (1860). Charles was less prolific in his single-authored work on Shakespeare, publishing an article on 'Shakespeare's Women; Considered as Philosophers and Jesters' for *The Gentleman's Magazine* (1873) and a volume of his collected lectures, *Shakespeare-Characters* (1863). They collaborated on two projects: an annotated edition of *Shakespeare's Works* (1865) and an analytical and critical study, *The Shakespeare Key* (1879), 'the last Shakespearian labour we achieved / Together' as Mary wrote in her Added Preface to *The Shakespeare Key*.

The actual process and nature of the Cowden Clarkes' collaboration is described by Mary in her correspondence with her American 'fan', Robert Balmanno, from 1850 to 1861, published in 1902 as *Letters to an Enthusiast*. In response to his request, she details the domestic circumstances of their work at this time in Craven Hill Cottage in Bayswater, London, where they lived with her brother Albert. On 4 August 1850 she describes how 'our own snuggery – our own room, part sleeping-room, part scribbling room – is behung' with no fewer than 47 paintings, sketches, daguerrotypes, lithographs and miniatures mainly of literary figures and including a bust of 'our Idol' Shakespeare (pp. 48–50). On 23 April 1851 she writes 'I am up at six [...] Charles is sitting beside me at the same table, writing away at his new course for the London Institute' (pp. 62–3). In the same letter she describes how Charles always reads aloud for 15 or 20 minutes before breakfast: Bacon, Milton or Wordsworth (pp. 66–7). By 12 July 1852 the pace has increased: 'Charles and I are up at five o'clock, take a shower-bath, and then repair to the den to work together till breakfast time. So hard do we work just now, that sometimes of an evening he gets through a second day's labour here, after having done a fair day's clerkifying at Dean Street' (p. 150). And on 28 April 1858 she writes from Nice that work on the Shakespeare edition keeps them occupied from before five until well into the night – fortunately, she remarks, 'Shakespeare and mutual love make the time pass happily, and console us for giving up all holidays. [...] He is fully worth any amount of pains taken for him; and the delight of re-reading and re-considering him amply counterbalances the fatigue and solicitude,' (pp. 269–73).

The specific readerly and writerly nature of their 'consociation' (another favourite word) is revealed by Mary in her own poetry. She celebrated Charles's 88th birthday with a sonnet 'Together, hand-in-hand, we've been allowed / To work, to write, to read, to pass through life' (*Honey From the Weed*, Sonnet V). In the third of Mary's *Score of Sonnets* to Charles she writes 'I keep thee with me still, by conning o'er / And o'er each word that thou hast said or penn'd', while in Sonnet VII she seeks consolation in 'Re-reading books that thou and I once read / Together'. Elsewhere she longs 'Oh, that my Charles had lived to read this book / With me', while in a poignant sonnet called 'Widowed' she describes herself as

> A torn half-sheet of paper thrown away,
> Disfigur'd, crumpled, meaningless, and blurr'd,
> With scarce one clear intelligible word [...]
> A script inscrutable, a song unheard.[5]

Mary imagines herself as the very materials of collaboration: paper, script, and words, that require the 'other self' to make them meaningful. The collaborative paradigm of authorship that Mary and Charles Cowden Clarke repeatedly invoke – with the emphasis upon romantic and scholarly companionship or 'consociation' – represents a striking alternative to the *Romantic* paradigm of the author as 'solitary genius', working in isolation and solitude.[6]

During her lifetime, Mary's work was considered to be scholarly and serious – and was clearly appreciated by her contemporaries, as her own collection of reviews (now at the Brotherton Library, University of Leeds) amply demonstrates. While Richard Altick patronises Mary as a 'modest lady' who 'spent her best years' (p. 120) on her *Concordance* to Shakespeare's plays – 'a monument of feminine tenacity' (p. 122) – he does not note that it was reprinted in ten editions between 1845 and 1875 or that the *Times* obituarist of Mary in 1898 remarked that 'it has not even now been superceded' (despite the publication of John Bartlett's *Concordance* in 1894).[7] Mary's *Concordance*, which took 'sixteen years of assiduous labour' to complete and was published in no less than eighteen monthly parts in 1844–45, was a massive contribution to Victorian Shakespeare studies.[8] It was widely praised both in Britain and America, and hailed by the press as a 'great national work'.[9] 'It is a perpetual monument of the mental powers, the taste, skill, and indefatigable industry of its accomplished author', concluded the Rev. N. J. Halpin, author of *The Dramatic Unities of Shakespeare*: 'the suitable inscription on its base, DUX FEMINA FACTI, should imperishably record our homage to her genius, and our admiration of her achievement'.[10] In 1852 American Shakespeareans acknowledged Mary's work on the *Concordance* by presenting her with a Testimonial Chair, elaborately carved with the head of Shakespeare between two swans on the back and masks of Tragedy and Comedy below the seat. The 64 listed subscribers came from all over the States (Alabama, California, Florida and New Mexico as well as from New England and the Mid-West); they included the actress Charlotte Cushman, the writers Washington Irving and Henry Longfellow, Secretary of State Daniel Webster, numerous professors and clerics, a sprinkling of judges and state officials.[11] Mary never went to America (she hated sea-voyages and always approached even a cross-Channel journey with trepidation), and it may be that the Clarkes' removal to Nice in 1856, then to Genoa in 1861 kept them somewhat detached from the circles of Shakespeare scholars in England, despite their prolific correspondence and contributions to journals. Mary did not join the New Shakspere Society which flourished in London from 1873 to 1892, although when she reflected in her autobiography *My Long Life* (1896) on a visit she had made to the Shakespeare Library in Birmingham in 1885 she commented 'I may here be permitted to mention that I have ever felt grateful for the liberal way in which distinguished Shakespearians have treated me with a cordial *fraternity* as one of their brotherhood,' (pp. 226–7).

How did Mary approach her position as a woman critic of Shakespeare – an anomalous 'sister' within the brotherhood of Victorian Shakespeare scholarship? In the preface to her *Concordance* she thanks John Payne Collier for entrusting her with the unpublished manuscript of the final volume of his edition of Shakespeare, and in so doing aligns herself with the male Shakespeare establishment:

> Such a mark of confidence was a worthy type of the fraternity of feeling inspired by a close study of our immortal Poet [...] [Compiling

the *Concordance*] has been the means of my receiving generous testimonies of sympathy and encouragement from many of the cleverest men of our age, between whom and myself I could never have hoped for any assimilation, had it not been for the mutual existence of profound veneration and love for the genius of Shakspere. (p. vii)

The study of Shakespeare becomes Mary's means of 'assimilation' into an otherwise exclusive group, 'the cleverest men of our age'. She goes on to thank 'my co-mates and brothers in "labour" – the Printers' (preface, vii), while the *Shakespeare Key* (1879), jointly authored by Charles and Mary, was dedicated to 'The True Shakespearian all over the world [...] in token of cordial fraternity'.

But the discourse of brotherhood and fraternity surrounding Shakespeare scholarship and publication is interrupted by Mary in a footnote to the preface of her *Concordance*:

I cannot refuse myself the pleasure of mentioning that the day which witnessed the conclusion of this task, was the birth-day of the best of mothers – Mary Sabilla Novello; she who forms the glory and happiness of her children; she who first inspired me with a love for all that is good and beautiful, and who therefore may well be said to have originated my devotion to Shakspere. (Preface, v)

While Mary utilises the discourse of brotherhood to position herself within the fraternity of Shakespeare scholarship, here she locates her passion for Shakespeare in her mother's inspiration and constructs herself as a daughter.[12] Mary's preface registers the tensions and contradictions of her anomalous position as a Victorian woman scholar of Shakespeare, included in an elite group 'I could never have hoped' to join under ordinary circumstances – part of the brotherhood and yet still a daughter.

The Concordance established Mary as a Shakespeare scholar in her own right – not as a wife of a lecturer on Shakespeare – and led to another landmark text in Victorian women's publication on Shakespeare: *Shakespeare's Works, Edited, with a Scrupulous Revision of the Text, by Mary Cowden Clarke* (London and New York, 1860). 'I may be allowed to take pride', wrote Mary in the preface to her edition of *Shakespeare's Works*, 'in the thought that I am the first of his female subjects who has been selected to edit his works; and it is one of the myriad delights I owe to him [Shakespeare], that I should be the woman upon whom so great a distinction is conferred' (p. v; understandably, Mary was unaware of the work of Henrietta Bowdler, whose expurgated edition of Shakespeare was published under her brother's name in 1807).[13] In her edition Mary eschewed commentary – the characteristic feature of previous Shakespeare editions by male editors – as intrusive, tedious, and aggressive in spirit: footnotes are 'mere vehicles for abuse, spite and arrogance' (p. vii). She also drew attention to the positive images of women found in Shakespeare, hopefully attributing this to the influence of Anne Hathaway:

> From the uniformly noble way in which Shakespeare drew the wifely character, we may feel certain of the esteem as well as affection with which his own wife inspired him; and the advantage in generosity which he has always assigned to women over men when drawing them in their mutual relations with regard to love, gives us excellent warrant for supposing that he had reason to know this truth respecting her sex from the mother of his children [. . .] (p. x)

Mary seeks to recognise in Shakespeare's works a respect for 'married lovers' and for women, particularly wives. In terms of her stated views both on Shakespeare's characterisation and on editorial format, Mary's edition of *Shakespeare's Works* displays an attention to gender issues.

As the 'first' woman editor of Shakespeare, Mary Cowden Clarke faced prejudice. Though she never drew attention to sexual discrimination in the reception of her work, her husband Charles did. In a letter to the reviewer of Mary's edition of *Shakespeare Works* in the *Daily News*, 1862, he commended the reviewer for his unbiased approach:

> That which has mainly gratified us both, and herself especially, is the tone in it [the review] taken towards her by the Examiner as well as yourself; – that of ignoring all distinction with regard to sex in a question of literary judicature: – 'No mere courtesy due to her sex, will avail her here: she is to be estimated on independent grounds' [. . .] your very differences with her in her readings of passages furnish a tacit proof that you have deemed her judgment worthy of impugnment.[14]

But Charles objected to the reviewer's assumption that part of the scholarly apparatus attached to the edition – a Glossary – was the work of the husband, not the wife. Such an assumption was perhaps understandable, given Mary's comment in the preface that 'I owe this Glossary to the same other-self; although his own unwillingness to diminish the

Editor's credit for the whole work would fain have made him forbid this acknowledgement' (p. vii). Anxious to stress the insignificance of his contribution to the Glossary of the 1860 edition, Charles instructed the reviewer to annotate Mary's acknowledgement with the remark 'if the erecter of the scaffolding can claim to be designated the Architect of a Building, the above statements are correct'.[15] Charles went on to locate the reviewer's readiness to accept Mary's self-effacing comments at face value in the wider context of patriarchal prejudice against her:

> I have but one objection to make against your 'review'; and that is, your having named me at all in reference to the 'Glossary' [...] I know that the *male* world will give me credit for being the compiler of that Glossary; as I know of those who said of the 'Concordance' – 'Of course, her husband helped her'. (original emphasis)

Charles demonstrates considerable awareness of the gender-bias in Victorian Shakespeare studies, and his comments reveal how 'the *male* world' was inclined to privilege the male rather than female collaborator. Charles points to an important dynamic of collaboration in the context of Victorian patriarchal values: while a man may gain prestige from a male–female literary partnership and be credited with playing a decisive role, a woman's literary reputation is compromised by working with a man – she becomes relegated to the position of needing 'help' or becoming a 'helpmate'. Conversely, when criticism is levelled against the work of a male–female partnership, it is the woman who is blamed for bringing standards down. This is the case in the reception of Mary's second edition of Shakespeare, which she co-edited with Charles for *Cassell's Illustrated Shakespeare* (1865). Designed for 'family reading', this annotated, expurgated, and illustrated edition sought to provide a serious volume for the popular market, and Mary and Charles were commended for their 'shrewd insights' into the plays and 'admirable Shakespearean criticism'.[16] But in 1869 one critic of the edition, writing under the pseudonym 'Jaques', attributed the edition's faults to Mary:

> The work [...] is, we are informed, 'Edited, with Notes, by Charles and Mary Cowden Clarke', who must, of course, take responsibility of the numberless alterations, mutilations, corruptions, or whatever we may choose to call them, which deface these noble dramas. If the lady editor had refrained from thus tampering with our great poet's language, she would not have marred the praises justly awarded her for the compilation of her excellent 'Concordance'.[17]

'Jaques' associates textual tampering with 'the lady editor', not the male collaborator. Notions of 'responsibility' in a literary male–female literary partnership thus become the arena for gender bias.

But the Cowden Clarkes tended to stress instead their mutual responsibility for joint works, conceiving of themselves as an 'author-pair'.[18] And clearly they influenced each other's scholarly output, not just in the works that appeared under both their names. It was Mary's suggestion that Charles should exploit his good speaking voice by undertaking a career as a public lecturer on literary topics and he rehearsed his lectures by reading them aloud to her (*My Long Life*, pp. 120–6). She regretted his absences (*Letters to an Enthusiast*, p. 243), but revelled in his success (ibid., pp. 134–6, 192, 196–7, 213–14), and records that whenever he was away they always wrote to each other at least once and sometimes twice a day (*Recollections of Writers*, p. 305). Charles organised a subscription list to publish the *Concordance* and dealt with the associated correspondence (Folger letters). He was delighted with the Testimonial Chair and wrote 'I am three hundred and sixty degrees – the entire circle – more cordially happy at the honour having been paid to her than if three hundred and sixty times its amount in applause and pecuniary value had been paid to myself' (quoted by Mary in *My Long Life*, pp. 135–6). And while Mary acknowledged the influence of 'the same other-self' in the Glossary of her 1860 edition of *Shakespeare's Works*, three years later Charles acknowledged the influence of the 'better part of me' in his volume of lectures which he had been giving and revising over a 20-year period:

> An addition to my pleasure – and I think it will likewise be one to my old hearers and new readers – is in the occasion afforded me of mentioning, that my affectionate study of Shakespeare has always been shared by one whom it were scant praise to pronounce the 'better part' of me, and that to her feminine discrimination are owing many of the subtlenesses in character-development that we traced together, and which form part of this volume. (Preface, *Shakespeare-Characters*, 1863)

That 'feminine discrimination' perhaps encouraged Charles to take a pro-women line in the lectures; indeed, he announced on the volume's title-page that Shakespeare was a 'champion' of women. His lecture on *Much Ado About Nothing* begins 'I never knew anyone object to the nature and conduct of Beatrice in "Much Ado About Nothing" who was not either dull in faculty, ill-tempered, or an overweening assertor of the exclusive privileges of the male sex' (p. 295), while he described Bertram, Posthumus Leonatus, Leontes, Othello, Proteus and Claudio as characters who appear at a disadvantage by and 'are unworthy of the women with whom they are consorted' (pp. 306–7). He is also undoubtedly thinking of his own happy marriage when in his lecture on *The Merry Wives of Windsor* he objects to the use of the word 'uxorious' as one of contempt (as applied to Master Page): 'so far from seeing any disgrace in a man being thoroughly in love with his wife, I only hope the complaint may become more and more epidemic' (p. 145). Charles's lectures acknowledge the fact of gender-bias in Victorian culture, promote the prestige of women via an analysis of Shakespeare's female characters, and champion women as worthy of men's love and respect.

Mary and Charles both took a pro-women line in their Shakespeare studies – one which in part can be located in the Victorian tendency to idealise Shakespeare's heroines.[19] But in her single-authored work for a popular, female readership, Mary developed her attention to gender issues far more extensively. In her mammoth *The Girlhood of Shakespeare's Heroines* (1850–52), a series of fictional tales describing the childhood and early lives of Shakespeare's heroines, Mary considers the status and condition of women in more depth than in any of her other work. The 'design' of the book, she explained, was 'to trace the probable antecedents in the history of some of Shakespeare's women; to imagine the possible circumstances and influences of scene, event [...] surrounding the infant life of his heroines', and to place them 'in such situations as should naturally lead up to, and account for, the known conclusion of their subsequent character and afterlife' (I, iii–iv). This novelistic format allowed Mary to explore women's abilities – particularly in the realm of work and education – and the limitations placed upon women in society. Her tale, for instance, on Portia, includes a discussion of the suitability of women as lawyers: 'Might not we women make good advocates, then, cugino mio?' asks the child Portia (reprinted in *Women Reading*, p. 87). Portia grows to be 'a profound lawyer' – a woman 'capable of bearing her part in the great drama of life, and of influencing the destinies of others by her intellect, her sentiment, her actions' (*Women Reading*, p. 88) – and contemporary reviewers recognised that Mary's tale bore relevance to contemporary society: the *Hull Advertiser*, for instance, remarked that 'the education of the youthful Portia affords Mrs. Clarke an opportunity of giving some precepts on the early training of children, which deserve to be held in remembrance'.[20] Similarly, Mary's account of Katherine the Shrew's childhood contains a damning critique of Victorian girls' education, 'mostly held to be comprised in the teaching of knick-knack making, accomplishments, and housewifery [...] their intellects had been put under glass cases with artificial flowers' (*Women Reading*, p. 93).

When we turn to Mary's examination of marital relations in *The Girlhood of Shakespeare's Heroines*, the key values which Mary repeatedly emphasises are collaboration, trust, respect and equality between husband and wife. Her analysis of Desdemona's childhood emphasises the 'intolerable bondage' and 'thraldom of spirit' suffered at the hands of a tyrannical father (*Women Reading*, p. 88). 'Accustomed to see her mother yield in silence even to things in which she did not acquiesce', Desdemona follows her mother's example of 'submission', 'passiveness' and 'subserviency' to patriarchal rule (*Women Reading*, p. 89). Mary commends instead 'the honest remonstrance, the modest yet plain representation, – which surely beseem a wife, when reasoning a point with a husband', concluding that 'perfect love, must be free, unreserved, unfearing, equal' (*Women Reading*, p. 89). Mary's positive personal experience as a 'married lover' fuels her analysis of gender relations in Shakespeare; her partnership with Charles shapes her reading of Shakespeare.

Mary published in a variety of genres and for a diversity of readers – including Shakespeare scholars and enthusiasts, general readers of Shakespeare, families, women readers of periodicals, and young girls. The range of her work enabled (or perhaps forced) Mary to take different approaches to marriage, gender and the role of the Victorian woman critic of Shakespeare. Mary's attention to issues of gender in the *Girlhood* is not simply a function of her being the work's sole author; her single-authored *Concordance* and 1860 edition of *Shakespeare's Works* do not dwell on women's position in marriage or society in anything like as much detail as the *Girlhood* – nor of course do the genres of concordance and edition give her the same opportunities. Rather, genre and readership play a crucial role in the approaches and interests of Mary's work. Written in a fictional, often romantic and sometimes sensationalist mode, the novellas that make up *The Girlhood of Shakespeare's Heroines* were primarily aimed at a young, female readership, a quite different audience to the 'fraternity' of Shakespeare scholars Mary addressed in the *Concordance* and the *Shakespeare Key*. The *Weekly News* described the *Girlhood* as 'an agreeable introduction for young ladies to the works of the great dramatist', and Mary's 'womanly nature' was seen to make her particularly 'competent' to tackle the subject of young women's development.[21] There seems to be little evidence that Mary was (or felt) freer to tackle gender issues when working on her own, without her 'other self'; rather, when writing for a 'popular', primarily female readership, she paid particular attention to gender issues. In the Introduction to a series of articles on 'Shakespeare – Studies of Women' for *The Ladies Companion* (1849–54), for instance, Mary argued that:

> In Shakespeare's page, as in a mental looking-glass, we women may contemplate ourselves. Of all the male writers that ever lived, he has seen most deeply into the female heart; he has most vividly depicted it in its strength, and in its weakness. (1849, 1st series, I, 25)

She took up the point again in 'Shakespeare as the Girl's Friend', originally published in *The Girl's Own Paper* in 1887 but also carried by the Philadelphia-based journal *Shakespeariana*. Mary commends Shakespeare for depicting women 'with full appreciation of their highest qualities': he has 'vindicated their truest rights and celebrated their best virtues [and] may well be esteemed a valuable friend of womankind'. On Desdemona she remarks 'Shakespeare has read all gentle-charactered women a lesson on the danger of allowing gentleness to merge into timidity, and timidity into untruthfulness', while 'in Paulina he has given a specimen of womanly ardor in advocating a friend's cause – boldly confronting her royal master himself with plain-spoken remonstrace and rebuke' (pp. 360–1). Co-opting Shakespeare as what might be termed a proto-feminist dramatist, Mary credits him with exceptional insight into women:

> he, the most manly thinker and most virile writer that ever put pen to paper, had likewise something essentially feminine in his nature, which enabled him to discern and sympathize with the innermost core of woman's heart. (p. 356)

Shakespeare is feminised in Mary's account, but also speaks to and for women. But Mary did not restrict her discussion of Shakespeare's representation of women to the primarily female audience of *The Girlhood of Shakespeare's Heroines, Ladies Companion*, or *Girl's Own Paper*. For instance, in the article 'Shakespeare's Self as Revealed in his Writing' on male characters and Shakespeare's literary style for the specialist journal *Shakespeariana* (1886), she points out that

> Shakespeare had the most exalted ideal of womanhood, painting it in vividest colors and with a wondrous insight into the very core of

feminine feeling such as no male writer save himself ever had (making every woman bound in gratitude to him eternally) [...] he gave way to none of the vulgar general flings at womens' inferiority, and never joined in the too-common attribution to them of weakness, pettiness, or worthlessness. (p. 155)

For Mary Cowden Clarke, Shakespeare takes the woman's part. Indeed, Shakespeare himself becomes a vicarious collaborator – 'a valuable friend of woman-kind' ('Shakespeare as the Girl's Friend', p. 355), helping to promote women's 'rights' and 'virtues'. In turn, Mary was credited with unique insight into and intimacy with Shakespeare: 'she has treasured up every work of Shakespeare, as if he were her lover and she were his', remarked Mrs Balmanno.[22]

Mary did not, however, always take what might be described as a 'progressive' stance on the representation of women in Shakespeare. In 'Shakespeare as the Girl's Friend', for instance, she praises Virgilia's silence in *Coriolanus* as 'a model of discreet conduct for a daughter-in-law' (p. 368), and describes *The Comedy of Errors* (which centres upon a husband's adultery) as a 'demonstration of how it may be a wife's own fault if her husband prove neglectful and driven to distraction' (p. 366). In *The Girlhood*, Mary is suspicious of intellectual women who intimidate, neglect their 'feminine' sympathy for others, or bear an 'aversion to matrimony' (such as Rosaline in *Romeo and Juliet*);[23] Portia's complete happiness is to be found not in the legal profession but in marriage, and Katherine the Shrew discovers that it is 'not altogether painful' to be '*mastered*' by the 'strong, manly arms' of the young Petruchio (*Women Reading*, pp. 95–6; original emphasis). The tensions in Mary's work around women's empowerment, independence, and submission perhaps point to the difficulties for a woman critic conforming to Victorian notions of femininity. Mary was not an outspoken feminist or suffragist, and in many respects her work attempts to reconcile rather than contest conflicting notions of Victorian womanhood – especially in promoting the education, achievements and status of women while privileging the 'duties of wife and mother'. Such a reconciliation is not easily achieved, even for someone with as supportive a partner as Charles. And to an extent, the difficulties of reconciling the positions of wife and critic also penetrated the Cowden Clarkes' home life. Mary is at times touchingly anxious to reassure her readers that she is a 'proper wife' despite her increasingly professional status as a freelance writer. In *My Long Life* she writes of her pleasure in preparing meals for Charles and in making all her own clothes and his dress waistcoats: 'I mention these particulars in order to show that a woman who adopts literary work as her profession need not either neglect or be deficient in the more usually feminine accomplishments of cookery and needlework,' (p. 107). But in other ways Mary was not an orthodox Victorian wife: from the age of nineteen she was determined to contribute to the couple's income 'knowing that my betrothed was not a rich man' (*My Long Life*, p. 47), and given the success of her publications she probably earned far more than he did. Annie Fields records that 'Every guinea that Charles gained he brought to his wife. He confided to her from first to last the entire management of whatever money they earned,' (pp. 125–6).

The Cowden Clarkes were one among several collaborating couples in the nineteenth century, and they recognised other 'married lovers' and collaborators in real life as well as in literature. In her biography of her father, the musician Victor Novello, Mary described her mother, Mary Sabilla Hehl, as 'one of the most perfect companions and "other-selfs" to her husband that it is possible to conceive' (*The Life and Labours of Vincent Novello*, pp. 47–8), and she said of their friends the Lambs that 'In a more than usual degree was Charles Lamb's sister, Mary Lamb, blended with his life, with himself – consociated as she was with his every act, word, and thought, through his own noble act of self-consecration to her' (*Recollections*, p. 176). Recalling that Mary Lamb taught her Latin, Mary Cowden Clarke made an explicit link between the Lambs' personal and literary partnership and her own:

> This Victoria Novello [i.e. Mary Cowden Clarke] was a namesake of the honoured Mary Lamb, having been christened 'Mary' Victoria. When she married, she abided by her first and simpler baptismal name, as being more in consonance with the good old English (plain but *clerkly*) surname of her husband, and became known to her readers as their faithful servant, MARY COWDEN CLARKE. (p. 189)

Mary corresponded with Horace Howard Furness, Philadelphia-based editor of the Variorum Shakespeare series, and with his wife Helen Kate Furness. Unlike Mary, Helen was usually content with 'helping' her husband without getting title-page credit but she published a *Concordance to Shakespeare's Poems* under her own name in 1875 with a deferential reference to Mary's work in the Preface: 'I would not have it thought that any imperfection is hereby imputed to Mrs. Clarke's invaluable Concordance to the Dramas. The bulk of that work was a sufficient bar to the plan I have been enabled to follow in the lesser task which was before me' (p. iii). The two women never met, but Mary published an elegy for Kate in the first volume of *Shakespeariana* (1883–84), hailing her as 'My sister in concordant deed' and expressing sympathy for Furness, deprived like herself of collaborator as well as spouse.[24]

Late in her life, Mary's correspondence with Annie Fields suggests her identification with Annie who (like Mary) was nearly twenty years younger than her husband who (like Charles) had known his wife from her childhood.[25] Annie too had collaborated in her husband's life of writing and publishing until his death in 1881. Mary singles out for praise a moment in Annie's memoir of her husband when she quotes him as saying 'I hold that husband and wife should be *lovers* all their days', recalling the Cowden Clarks' terminology of 'married lovers', 'lover-husband' and lover-wife'.[26] She is generous in her joy when Annie secures what she calls the 'permanent companionship' of the writer Sarah Orne Jewett, though she continues to assume that Annie understands her own loneliness in widowhood.[27]

When Mary Cowden Clarke began her career as a Shakespeare scholar, with the publication of the *Concordance* in 1845, there were comparatively few women writing on Shakespeare; by the time of her last publication on Shakespeare in 1887 ('Shakespeare as the Girl's Friend') the opportunities for women as both critics and editors of Shakespeare had increased dramatically. Mary's work not only coincided with but helped to shape a period of unprecedented change for women's Shakespeare criticism in the nineteenth century. In 1845 only one monograph on Shakespeare by a woman had been published in the century, Anna Jameson's enormously popular *Characteristics of Women* (1832) – which, like the *Girlhood*, used Shakespeare criticism as an opportunity to investigate 'the condition of women in society'.[28] By 1887 there were no less than eight monographs on Shakespeare by women (Delia Bacon, Henrietta Palmer, Frances Kemble, Mary Preston, Dorothea Beale, Kate Richmond-West, Helena Faucit, Mrs Elliott), several editions of Shakespeare and specialist journals on Shakespeare edited by women (notably the Philadelphia-based *Shakespeariana* edited by Charlotte Porter from 1883 to 1887), and numerous critical articles in both general periodicals and scholarly journals (such as the work of Annette Handcock, Grace Latham, Constance O'Brien and Emma Phipson in the *Transactions of the New Shakespere Society*); in addition, women's study clubs on Shakespeare flourished both in Britain and America.[29] Mary Cowden Clarke, as the first female editor of an unabridged Complete Works and a prolific and renowned writer on Shakespeare, partly enabled the sea change in Victorian women's Shakespeare criticism to take place by providing women with a precedent. And by the 1880s, the work of women critics on Shakespeare was acknowledged to make a significant contribution to Shakespeare studies. In 1884, for instance, Professor William Taylor Thom took issue with the *New York Tribune* for its 'thoroughly Philistine view' that few women 'understand' Shakespeare:

> the brilliant and solid work in recent years on Shakespeare [by women] – both as writers and as interpreters of his gracious heroines – gives a curious inappropriateness to the *Tribune's* censure, and constitutes of itself a very patent answer thereto. Mrs. Cowden Clarke, Mrs. Furness, Lady Helen Faucit Martin, Mrs. Siddons, Mrs. Jameson, and many others, can be most worthily cited and compared with the best workers among the men.[30]

Mary's 'other self', her husband Charles, enabled rather than restricted her work on Shakespeare and the international reputation as a Shakespeare scholar which resulted from it. The dynamics of collaboration, in the case of the Cowden Clarkes, supported the wife as much as the husband; indeed, in contrast to other nineteenth-century male–female collaborators working on Shakespeare, Mary Cowden Clarke emerges as the equal if not leading parter. The example the Cowden Clarkes provide of a Victorian male–female literary partnership perhaps represents an exception to a rule which was more generally dominant in the nineteenth century – that of privileging the male collaborator.

Appendix: a chronological list of works referred to by Charles Cowden Clarke (CCC) and Mary Cowden Clarke (MCC)

1844–45 MCC *The Complete Concordance to Shakespeare: Being a Verbal Index to all the Passages in the Dramatic Works of the Poet*, revised edition: London: W. Kent & Co.

1849–54 MCC 'Shakespeare – Studies of Women', series of essays for *The Ladies Companion* (London), 1st series, vol. I

1850–52 MCC *The Girlhood of Shakespeare's Heroines* (5 vols), London: W. H. Smith & Son, Simpkin, Marshall & Co.

1860 MCC (ed.), *Shakespeare's Works, Edited, with a Scrupulous Revision of the Text*, London and New York: Trübner, Appleton & Co.

1863 CCC *Shakespeare-Characters, Chiefly Those Subordinate,* London: Smith, Elder & Co.

1864 MCC *The Life and Labours of Vincent Novello,* London: Novello & Co.

1865 CCC and MCC (eds), *Shakespeare's Works,* London: Cassell (Illustrated Edition)

1873 CCC 'Shakespeare's Women; Considered as Philosophers and Jesters', *The Gentleman's Magazine* X (January to June), 514–39

1873 MCC *The Trust and The Remittance,* London: Grant

1878 CCC and MCC *Recollections of Writers,* London: Sampson Low, Marston, Searle & Rivington

1879 CCC and MCC *The Shakespeare Key,* London: Sampson Low, Marston, Searle & Rivington

1881 MCC *Honey From the Weed: Verses,* London: C. Kegan Paul & Co.

1884 MCC *A Score of Sonnets to One Object,* London: Kegan Paul, Trench & Co.

1886 MCC 'Shakespeare's self as revealed in his writings', *Shakespeariana,* 3 (1886), 145–57

1887 MCC 'Shakespeare as the Girl's Friend', *The Girl's Own Paper* (London) June; repr. in *Shakespeariana,* 4 (Philadelphia, 1887), 355–69

1896 MCC *My Long Life: an Autobiographical Sketch,* London: T. Fisher & Unwin

1902 MCC *Letters to an Enthusiast* (edited by Anne Upton Nettleton), London: Kegan Paul, Trench, Trubner & Co.

Notes

1. While we would not normally adopt the habit of using a first name for a female author, it seems sensible here in order to distinguish her from her husband.
2. Mary Cowden Clarke to James Thomas Fields and Annie Adams Fields, 17 February 1880, Huntington Library, San Marino.
3. Mrs James T. [Annie] Fields, 'Two Lovers of Literature and Art: Charles and Mary Cowden Clarke', *The Century Magazine,* 58 (1899), 122–31 (p. 128).
4. 'Two Lovers of Literature and Art', 124–5. On the Cowden Clarkes' visits to the favourite haunts of Charles and John Keats, see Mary Cowden Clarke, *My Long Life: an Autobiographical Sketch* (London: T. Fisher & Unwin, 1896), pp. 65–6.

5. 'On Reading George H. Calvert's *Shakespeare: a Biographical and Aesthetic Study*' and 'Widowed', in *Honey From the Weed* (London: C. Kegan Paul & Co., 1881), pp. 323–4.
6. See Jack Stillinger, *Multiple Authorship and the Myth of Solitary Genius* (Oxford: Oxford University Press, 1991). The creative conjugal partnership of the Cowden Clarkes recalls the Wollstonecraftian ideal of companionate marriage.
7. See W. M. Parker, 'Shakespeare Concordances', *Times Literary Supplement* (12 May 1945), 228.
8. See *Women Reading Shakespeare, 1660–1900: an Anthology of Criticism*, ed. by Ann Thompson and Sasha Roberts (Manchester and New York: Manchester University Press, 1997), p. 81; hereafter abbreviated to *Women Reading*.
9. Review from *The Liverpool Chronicle*, 21 February 1844, in Mary Cowden Clarke's scrapbook, Novello–Cowden Clarke Collection, Brotherton Library, Leeds.
10. Review in the *Dublin Evening Mail*, 4 Feb 1846, in Mary Cowden Clarke's scrapbook, the Novello–Cowden Clarke Collection, Brotherton Library, Leeds.
11. See *A Testimonial to Mrs. Mary Cowden Clarke. Author of the Concordance to Shakespeare* (New York: privately printed, 1852).
12. What Mary did not reveal in the preface is that the idea for the *Concordance* came to her in Mary Lamb's garden; at the home of a long-standing female friend, not within an educational institution (Anne Upton Nettleton, Prefatory Note to *Letters to an Enthusiast*, p. 9). Conversely, in her preface to *Shakespeare's Works* (1865), Mary attributes her passion for Shakespeare not to her mother but to her father: 'My affectionate veneration for Shakespeare began in childhood when – a little girl – my father brought me home a new book, – "Lamb's tales from Shakespeare", and showed me the pictures, and told me something of each,' (p. vi).
13. *Women Reading Shakespeare*, pp. 46–8.
14. Letter from Charles Cowden Clarke to the reviewer of the *Daily News*, 15 April 1862, from Villa Novello, Genova. Cowden Clarke Papers, Folger Library.
15. Charles made the same remark in a copy of the proofs of Mary's Preface to the 1860 American edition of *Shakespeare's Works*, now in the Folger Shakespeare Library (PR 2976 C44 As. Col.). At Mary's acknowledgment of the Glossary 'to the same other-self' Charles adds the marginal note: 'If the man who raises the scaffold may be termed the Architect of a building, the above statement is accurate,' (p. vii).
16. 'Gossip about books and the arts', unsourced review article in Mary Cowden Clarke's Scrapbook, the Novello–Cowden Clarke Collection, Brotherton Library, Leeds.
17. *Modern Corruptions of Shakespeare's Text. a Letter to a Friend on the Subject of 'Cassell's Illustrated Shakespeare'*, 2nd edn (London: privately printed, 1869), pp. 3–4. This volume, incidentally, found its way into the library of the eminent nineteenth-century Shakespeare scholar, Edward Dowden (Folger Shakespeare Library copy).
18. Mary Cowden Clarke, Added Preface, *The Shakespeare Key* (1879).
19. See *Women Reading Shakespeare*, p. 5.
20. Anonymous review article, *The Hull Advertiser*, 14 December 1850, in Mary Cowden Clarke's Scrapbook, the Novello–Cowden Clarke Collection,

Brotherton Library, Leeds. For further discussion of some aspects of *The Girlhood*, see also Ann Thompson, 'Pre-Feminism or Proto-Feminism?': Early Women Readers of Shakespeare', *Elizabethan Theatre*, 14 (1996), 195–211.

21. Anonymous review article, *Weekly News*, 28 December 1850; unsourced article, *CXIX Times*, 14 December 1850; in Mary Cowden Clarke's Scrapbook, The Novello–Cowden Clarke Collection, Brotherton Library, Leeds.

22. Mrs (Mary) Balmanno, *Pen and Pencil* (New York: Appleton & Co., 1858), p. 150.

23. *The Girlhood of Shakespeare's Heroines*, Everyman edn, 4 vols (London: J. M. Dent & Co, and New York: E. P. Dutton & Co., n. d.), IV, 128–9.

24. Mary Cowden Clarke, 'Helen Kate Furness', *Shakespeariana*, I (1883–84), 71. The increasing role of women as critics and scholars of Shakespeare in the nineteenth century has parallels with women's increasing involement in Browning scholarship: in 1889 for instance, Charlotte Porter launched the journal *Poet-Lore* 'devoted to Shakespeare, Browning, and the Comparative Study of Literature' with Helen Clarke, and continued to collaborate with Clarke on Browning and Shakespeare studies and editions (see *Women Reading Shakespeare*, pp. 160–1).

25. James T. Fields, *Biographical Notes and Personal Sketches* (Boston: Houghton Mifflin & Co., 1881), p. 51.

26. See Annie Fields to 'Frank', 7 June 1882, Huntington Library, and James T. Fields, *Biographical Notes*, 59.

27. On Annie Fields and Sarah Orne Jewett's association, see Margaret Roman, *Sarah Orne Jewett: Reconstructing Gender* (Tuscaloosa: University of Alabama Press, 1992), 142–6.

28. Anna Jameson, *Characteristics of Women, Moral, Poetical and Historical*, 2 vols (London. Saunders & Otley, 1832), I, viii; see *Women Reading Shakespeare*, p. 5.

29. See *Women Reading Shakespeare*, pp. 1–7, 132, 154, 160, 196–8, 213–14. For an account of one rather tragic tale of a young woman's encounter with Victorian Shakespeare scholarship, see Ann Thompson, 'Teena Rochfort Smith, Frederick Furnivall, and the New Shakspere Society's Four-Text Edition of *Hamlet*', *Shakespeare Quarterly*, 49 (1998), 125–39.

30. William Taylor Thom, 'Shakespeare Study for American Women', *Shakespeariana*, 1:4 (1844), 97–102 (p. 99).

11
Shakespeare, the Actress and the Prostitute: Professional Respectability and Private Shame in George Vandenhoff's *Leaves from an Actor's Notebook*

Pascale Aebischer

The mid nineteenth century saw the circulation of a number of urban legends concerning the over-identification of actors and actresses with their Shakespearean roles. *Othello*, in particular, seems to have inspired this type of mythologisation: Edmund Kean died a few days after collapsing on-stage while playing the Moor of Venice opposite his son Charles as Iago at the line 'Farewell, Othello's occupation's gone!', and there are reports of Junius Brutus Booth and Ira Aldridge getting carried away in their performances of Othello and nearly suffocating their respective Desdemonas.[1]

A peculiarly drawn-out version of this myth, in which (as in Scott's *Kenilworth*) the focus rests more on the idealised Desdemona-figure than on the male hero,[2] resurfaces in George Vandenhoff's theatrical memoirs. In the middle of *Leaves from An Actor's Notebook, With Reminiscences and Chitchat of the Green Room and the Stage* (published in America in 1860), Vandenhoff tells his readers about an eventful starring engagement at a theatre on the British provincial circuit in 1842. On the night he played Othello there, the following happened to Coralie Walton, his local Desdemona:

> The last scene, in the chamber, she played with terrible earnestness: her asseverations of innocence, her prayers for mercy, her agonized

supplications, her heart-rending shrieks, and her convulsive death-struggle, tore my heart, and made me really

> 'call that a murder which
> I thought a sacrifice'.

The death-calm into which she fell, when the deed was completed, was no less terrible to me. I could not help fearing that she *was* dead; a chill came over me; for if so, 'twas I that had killed her! When I put my hand on her heart, in the action of the scene, as she lay there more white than snow,

> 'and smooth as monumental alabaster',

there was no throbbing; her pulse seemed motionless, her breath would not have stirred a feather! Oh, how I longed for the scene to end!

The knocking at the door came; Emilia entered, and, at the proper time, approached the bed where Desdemona lay; how eagerly I listened for the dying words –

> 'A guiltless death I die. Commend me to my kind lord!' –

but they came not. To Emilia's question,

> 'Who hath done this?'

she returned no answer; all was silent, still as the grave!

Good God! *Could she be really dead?* There was no time for thought; I hurried through the scene. [...] At last, Iago has left the stage; one more speech; Othello strikes the poniard to his heart, and, thank God! The curtain is down.

I sprang up from the stage; rushed to the bed; but she, she moved not, stirred not; there she lay pale as her sheets, unconscious as the grave![3]

If Vandenhoff is to be believed, Coralie Walton died within eight days of this performance.

Vandenhoff's account of Coralie Walton's life and death sheds an interesting light on early Victorian provincial theatre practice, the end of the era in which independent Shakespearean productions by provincial stock companies coexisted with the company providing the supporting cast for a visiting London 'star'.[4] In particular, it confirms Leman Rede's 1827 estimate of sixteen working hours a day for young country actors by illustrating the punishing demands this system made on the repertory theatre companies, with intensive last-minute rehearsals to prepare for the performance of a different play every night.[5] In relation to Shakespeare's standing in the mid nineteenth-century theatre and early Victorian culture in general, Vandenhoff's narrative (and indeed, his autobiography as a whole) constitutes strong evidence of the centrality of Shakespeare in the theatrical repertoire alongside more contemporary so-called 'legitimate' theatre such as Sheridan Knowles's *Virginius* and Edward Bulwer Lytton's *The Lady of Lyons*.[6] More crucially, for my argument, Vandenhoff's account of the young performer's hysteric identification with Desdemona is suggestive of the cultural power of Shakespeare in providing a template according to which mid nineteenth-century subjects could model their experience. Like the young Ruskin,[7] Vandenhoff, Coralie Walton and their fellow actors are deeply absorbed in Shakespeare's works and structure their views of gender differences and personal relations according to Shakespearean plot structures and characters. Specifically, I want to suggest, Shakespeare is used by both the author of the memoirs and the individuals he writes about as a smokescreen for deep interlocked anxieties about professional respectability and private shame.

During Vandenhoff's week-long starring engagement at the 'S——Theatre', Coralie, as the company's leading lady, plays Knowles's chaste Virginia and Shakespeare's Desdemona and Ophelia, all of whom she identifies with 'beyond the limits of the mimic scene' (p. 137). Throughout the narrative, Coralie appropriates the words of Shakespeare's betrayed heroines to give expression to her own suffering, madness and eventual death. As Vandenhoff soon finds out from the company's manager, a certain Mr Henderson, Coralie's identification with Shakespearean heroines started months before his arrival, when she fell in love with her stage Romeo, a young man of the name of Lionel Ransom who had become an actor in order to be able to court her and show her and '*everybody*, that [he was] not ashamed of the profession [he] adopt[ed]' (p. 145; original emphasis). Lionel then deserted her all of a sudden in mysterious circumstances and emigrated to America. Thereafter, Coralie seems to have sickened and become increasingly unable to distinguish between her own experience and that of Desdemona and Ophelia – which is the point at which Vandenhoff joins the company. Before she dies in a hysterical identification with both of these characters, she entrusts Vandenhoff with a package (containing a brief note and a few tokens) for her lover in America. In a last emulation of Desdemona, she asks Vandenhoff to 'Tell [Lionel], I forgive him and bless him, and shall do so with my last sigh. Farewell!' (p. 160). Her last words to the manager's wife, who has taken on the role of Shakespeare's outspoken and protective Emilia both on- and off-stage are: '*Tell Hamlet not to forget*' (p. 161) – an injunction that identifies Vandenhoff with Hamlet and Coralie both with Ophelia and, bizarrely, the otherworldly paternal voice of Old Hamlet's ghost.

Incredibly, Vandenhoff claims that a few years later he did come across Lionel Ransom in a St Louis hotel and delivered Coralie's message and her package to him. This is when Vandenhoff finally manages to pluck out the heart of Coralie's mystery. Apparently, when, at the height of their romance, Lionel asked Coralie to marry him, the girl insisted that he first meet her mother. The existence of a mother was news to Lionel and there was something distinctly ominous about the words half-borrowed from Juliet that Coralie sent him off with: 'I have an ill-divining soul! I feel, Lionel, as if this were our last parting. [...] Remember you sought the love of the poor, unfriended girl, who shunned all notice save that which gave her bread,' (p. 171). Suspecting that 'her mother [was] some very strict old lady, with very strong prejudices against the Theatre' (p. 172), Lionel immediately left for London and sought out the address Coralie had given him. To his horror, he found out there that Coralie's mother, Mrs Wilton, was the loud, brash, self-displaying Madam of a sizeable brothel, the 'moral monster' hidden behind the angelic surface of the virginal Coralie.[8] In a sort of uncanny double vision, Lionel now suddenly recognised his cherished virgin in the whore:

> 'Who wants me?' a loud, coarse voice asked, from the stair-head; and a large, bold-looking woman, about forty years of age, descended, excessively over-dressed, with bare neck and bosom, her cheeks evidently made up with white and red paint, but with a fine, and even classic contour of features, in which, as she stood in the light, I was horror-struck to trace a resemblance to Coralie's sweet and innocent face! (p. 175)

Unwilling to respond to the mother's desperate plea for news of her long-lost daughter and to reconcile himself to the blot on Coralie's character, Lionel took the next boat to America, joined the army and never entered another theatre.

When Vandenhoff tells Lionel of Coralie's death-bed forgiveness, Shakespeare once more, and this time explicitly, provides the template for extreme emotional turmoil. With 'such a look as Romeo might have worn just before he drank the fatal draught, at Juliet's tomb' (p. 165), Lionel indulges in a series of self-accusations: 'Was ever a villain black as me? Have I not "killed the sweetest innocent that e'er did lift up eye?".' It is at this point that Vandenhoff's narratorial voice intrudes to provide his rationale for the overwhelming presence of Shakespeare's voice in his account: '([Lionel] quoted unconsciously: Shakespere supplying, (as he never fails to do those who love him,) the very fittest language for his impassioned thoughts),' (p. 166).

I want to suggest that Vandenhoff's comment only gives us a partial explanation for the pervasive presence of Shakespeare in his narrative. Lionel and especially Coralie certainly do pluck from Shakespeare 'the very fittest language for [their] impassioned thoughts'. But in the case of Coralie, the invocation, appropriation and performance of Shakespeare additionally provide the vehicle by which she can assert her innocence and openly show her grief. It is through the performance of Shakespeare's plays that the girl can give public expression to sexual awareness and extreme emotions which have no place in her impeccably respectable private life. Shakespeare's Desdemona, even more than Knowles's Virginia, provides the shield that enables her publicly to declare her inability to pronounce the word 'whore' and refuse to accept the very possibility of unchastity. Reflecting Anna Jameson's stress on Ophelia's love for Hamlet, her youth, helplessness, innocence and the way 'love and grief together rend and shatter the frail texture of her existence',[9] Coralie's absorption in the role additionally allows her to give vent to her distress at the insinuation of falseness, to reveal the depth of her love for the unfaithful Lionel, and to let her grief drive her into madness and death. Even Coralie's first Shakespearean model Juliet, with her constancy and determination 'to live an unstained wife', fits into this pattern.

With the help of Shakespeare's plots of unjustly slandered women, Vandenhoff's account of Coralie's life and death thus seems to play out a refutation of the popular association of the professional actress with the prostitute.[10] It is helpful at this point to glance sideways at two other texts. The first is Geraldine Jewsbury's 1848 novel *The Half-Sisters*, which includes so many parallels with Vandenhoff's narrative that I suspect the novel may well be a source for it. In *The Half-Sisters*, a young man's diatribe reveals some of the key reasons for the association between actress and prostitute:

A woman who makes her mind public, or exhibits herself in any way, no matter how it may be dignified by the title of art, seems to me little better than a woman of a nameless class. [...] The stage is still worse [than authorship], for that is publishing both mind and body too. Every body may go to the theatre to see an actress, and may pass whatever gross comments on her they will; she has no protection, is open to every species of proposal, and that is not precisely the line of life from which one would choose one's wife. [...]

A public life must deteriorate women; [...] they lose all the beautiful ideal of their nature, all that is gentle, helpless, and confiding; they are obliged of necessity to keep a keen eye to their own interest, and, having no inherent force or strength, they are reduced to cunning [...]. In their dealings with men, they use their sex as a weapon; they play with the passions of men to some degree like courtesans.[11]

This view is confirmed and complemented by *An Appeal to the Women of England to Discourage the Stage*. This is a pamphlet published in 1855 by an anonymous lady, who asks her readers to consider

whether it is possible for a woman to become an actress, without suffering any moral deterioration. What is a woman's greatest charm? Does it not consist in a modest, retiring disposition, and if so, is the stage likely to foster and cherish it? Can it be right for a woman to *act* the best and holiest feelings of her nature [...] in order to excite public applause? Alas! How painful to know, as is too often the case, how completely at variance is the real, with the assumed character. [...] Though an actress may preserve an unblemished reputation notwithstanding the temptations which surround her, it is utterly impossible that she can so outrage her womanly feelings as to act before the public, without injuring her moral delicacy.[12]

It is against the background of such anti-theatrical prejudice and propaganda that I believe we have to read Vandenhoff's narrative, with its laboured insistence on Coralie's purity. Her prostitute mother, seen in this light, appears as the evil double onto whom the shamefulness of Coralie's profession is displaced in a way reminiscent of *Jane Eyre's* madwoman in the attic.[13] The mother functions here as the unacknowledged figure of shame who spawns an elaborate mechanism of projection and displacement within the narrative and the memoirs as a whole. For Coralie, this displacement exacts a terrible price: in order to expurgate her profession of its implicitly immoral duplicity, Coralie's hysterical identification with her characters collapses the distinction between fiction and reality to the extent that she is trapped by the tragic end of Shakespeare's slandered heroines:

> The mimic madness of Ophelia had been fatal to her; it had become a fearful reality! The circumstances of Ophelia's story, Hamlet's abandonment, and her despair, she had made her own; they had, in the earnestness of her acting, by a mysterious operation of the brain, been wrought up into a confused union with her own identity; and though she repeated the text of her part correctly, and sang the touching snatches of song that rise up in Ophelia's love-lorn memory, she had lost all distinction between herself and the character she was playing. It was no longer Ophelia, it was she herself who was forsaken; whose lover had fled beyond the sea; whose hopes were buried in the grave; whose heart was blighted; whose brain was maddened, and to whom nothing was left but to despair and die! Thus she rushed shrieking from the stage, and was borne home, a hopeless lunatic; henceforth,
> 'The queen of a fantastic realm!' (p. 159)

Tragically, at the very moment at which her identification with Ophelia is absolute and she no longer displays the variance between the real and the assumed character that the anonymous lady of the pamphlet deplores – at the very moment at which the purgation of her shame could seem complete – Coralie is also publishing her mind and body for all paying customers to enjoy. For Coralie there is no escape from the return of the repressed, whether in the shape of the repudiated prostitute mother or that of the self-publication of the theatre, except through death. Shakespeare, who provides the words for Coralie's self-defence, also provides the plot for her self-destruction.

All of this of course begs one central question: is the story fictional (at the core-a-lie, to borrow Peter Holland's apposite pun) or real?[14] And, if it is fictional, why is it told as part of Vandenhoff's supposedly factual memoirs? What sort of 'work' does it do? 'CORALIE WALTON; THE COUNTRY ACTRESS: An Episode from Real Life' is a four-chapter digression in Vandenhoff's memoirs, which cover the 17 years of his stage career, starting in Britain in 1839 and ending in America in 1856. The episode concerning Coralie is inserted as a kind of narrative 'buffer' between Vandenhoff's time in Britain and his emigration to America in August 1842, reaching both backwards to Coralie's love-affair in 1841, and forwards to Vandenhoff's conversation with Lionel Ransom in 1847.

While the Coralie chapters are thus integrated temporally and geo-graphically in Vandenhoff's life-writing, they are also strikingly de-tached from Vandenhoff's own life. The subject of the memoirs here suddenly withdraws to make room for another subject; the first-person narrator shares his task with two other male narrators, Mr Henderson (the company's manager) and Lionel Ransom. Information that is veri-fiable in Vandenhoff's earlier and later chapters here becomes impos-sible to check: although we are given vague dates and selected names, for the first time in the memoirs Vandenhoff deliberately leaves place-names blank and suggests that certain identities are protected through the use of pseudonyms. All that can be inferred about the location of the circuit theatres in which Coralie is employed is that they lie a six-hour railway journey to the North of London and are possibly part of the Preston, Manchester or Bolton circuits that Vandenhoff visited as a star in the months prior to his emigration. The few names that Vandenhoff provides are red herrings: nothing is known of a Coralie Walton or Wilton (she is not to be confused with Marie Bancroft, née Wilton, manager of the Prince of Wales' Theatre) or of her lover Lionel Ransom, and the only provincial theatre manager of the name of Henderson of whom there is a record was active in the 1850s, more than ten years after Coralie's supposed death.

While Vandenhoff obviously strives for a 'reality-effect' in his use of the subtitle 'an Episode from Real Life' and the protected identities and place-names, this effect is ultimately countered both by the unverifiable nature of the information and the stylistic distinctiveness of the digres-sion. Earlier and later chapters aim to provide the reader with biograph-ical facts about the author and a glimpse of back-stage arrangements and gossip about famous performers, all presented in the chatty, anecdotal, episodic style typical of Victorian actors' memoirs. Coralie Walton's story, by way of contrast, has unique narrative coherence, spans 52 pages, and is presented in a laboured 'literary' and not infrequently melodramatic style. All of these factors, combined with the implausibil-ity of Vandenhoff's American encounter with Lionel Ransom, lead me to suppose that the account is largely fictional. Michael Baker's unduly damning comment that Victorian theatrical memoirs in general are 'often [...] less than objective, self-indulgently anecdotal and factually incorrect' seems uncomfortably true in this instance.[15] Ultimately, I would maintain, it is precisely the subjective and anecdotal nature of these spuriously autobiographical texts that makes them a fascinating (and sadly neglected) source for a cultural history of the Victorian theatre. Actors' theatrical memoirs offer not only more or less fictionalised glimpses of back-stage dramas but also unique insights into social attitudes towards the theatre and its practitioners.

What is therefore important about the Coralie Walton narrative is not so much its doubtful claim to veracity, but rather the role it plays within Vandenhoff's published/public reminiscences as a whole. The story functions as a legitimising device in which Shakespeare is mobilised to voice and ultimately exorcise anxieties about the propriety and respectability of the acting profession in general. There is a double displacement at work, then: first, a projection of the shamefulness of the acting profession onto a female actor, followed by a second projection onto the actress' mother. The repressed returns only at the first level, that of Coralie, whose illness and self-destruction purge the blot on the profession as a whole. Portraying the actress/prostitute as diseased was, as Kerry Powell observes, a means repeatedly used by Victorian authors and commentators 'of controlling the public bodies and feigned emotions of these women who had exceeded the boundaries containing respectable wives and daughters'.[16] Displaced onto an actress and transposed into a Shakespearean idiom, Vandenhoff's unease about the low status of his profession and the actors' investment in the fictionalisation of the self can be 'outed' and dismissed. Coralie's death is the sacrifice necessary to purge the profession of its unsavoury associations, a purgation that is completed by Vandenhoff's emigration to America where, as Lionel Ransom suggests, past shame can be forgotten: 'Why did I not [...] carry her across the sea, where her name and her history could never have been guessed at?' (p. 177). The suspension of the narrative between Vandenhoff's British and American stage careers is thus structurally explicable as the device that allows him to construct an American identity which is unblemished and thoroughly honourable.

The necessity for this elaborate mechanism of projection and purgation becomes clear when we take into account that Vandenhoff's own father was a famous early nineteenth-century actor, John M. Vandenhoff, who had striven hard to keep his son from following in his footsteps by 'carefully educat[ing him] to the law'. It is evident from the memoirs that Vandenhoff senior could never really forgive his son for abandoning this respectable profession, with its 'secure position, and a handsome income' for the sake of a stage career (p. 2). In the Coralie Walton narrative, the father's disappointment with his son's emulation of his shameful profession is transformed into the daughter's shame at her mother's profession and her inability to escape from the parental blot on her own life.

As a consequence of the shamefulness of the parent's calling and the child's almost compulsive re-enactment of the parent's shame, the British part of Vandenhoff's autobiography shows a pervasive apprehension about the respectability of his professional vocation. In this, Vandenhoff's memoirs uncannily recall William Charles Macready's lifelong attempts to elevate his profession from its stigmatised status, which Macready connected with his actor father's moral and financial bankruptcy.[17] Almost the first thing Vandenhoff tells his reader is that he 'had no particular predilection for the stage', that he 'was anything but stage-struck' (p. 2). When talking about Madame Vestris' management of the Covent Garden theatre, where he had his first engagement, Vandenhoff takes care to record 'that she was not only scrupulously careful not to offend propriety by word or action, but she knew very well how to repress any attempt at *double-entendre* or doubtful insinuation, in others' (p. 50). The gentleman doth protest too much, methinks – his repeated insistence on the propriety of the theatre and the lack of its allure to him betrays a deep-seated unease at the profession's social status and respectability. This ambivalence is given further expression when, in a passage that ventriloquises his father's disapproval and anticipates the circumstances of Coralie's dramatic end, he claims

> that the Stage is the last occupation a young man of spirit and ambition should think of following, for this one reason, if for no other: that it seems to cut him off from the business of life, and from the great movements and practical working of the world – the objects of a worthy and legitimate ambition.
>
> The actor's individuality, as a citizen, seems lost in the fictitious world in which he lives and moves and has his being. He is king, governor, general, statesman, hero of a fantastic realm, but from the practical interests of this work-a-day world he seems to be segregated and apart. (p. 36)

If for a man, being 'cut off from the business of life' means little more than becoming the 'hero of a fantastic realm', for a woman losing herself and becoming the 'queen of a fantastic realm', specifically through identification with Shakespeare's tragic heroines, means death.

The Coralie Walton chapters are, then, the central site of Vandenhoff's engagement with a threat to the self that is rooted both in the social stigma of acting and in a more personal complex of filial shame. Is it overstretching my argument about the link between the parental prohibition of Vandenhoff senior and the necessity for Coralie's death to point back to the fact that Coralie's last words, '*Tell Hamlet not to forget*', identify her with the authority of Hamlet senior? It is certainly an intriguing coincidence, if it *is* a coincidence, that Coralie's last words, in the vague chronology of the memoirs, are spoken roughly at the same time as Vandenhoff's first and last stage engagement with his father and sister Charlotte in Liverpool. On this occasion, the twin complexes of family relations and theatrical display are brought together one last time:

> The plays selected were 'Romeo and Juliet,' 'As you like it,' 'Ion,' 'The Wife,' 'Love,' 'The Hunchback,' and 'The Bridals of Messina:' the latter we played four nights in succession. Our engagement created considerable interest, and drew fine houses; but my father, I was sorry to see, was very ill at ease in playing with me, and I felt no less *gêné* [*sic*] with him. He could not get over his feeling of disappointment at my having adopted the stage as a profession: this affected his acting, and I saw that it did: it was continually betraying itself, and destroying his abstraction, and his self-identification with his character, for the night. My sister was aware of this, too; and, of course, she was unpleasantly acted on by her consciousness of it. In fact, it threw us all off our balance; and we were very uncomfortable all round. (p. 123)

It certainly was not a happy occasion for the family, and Vandenhoff's emigration to America reads almost like an escape from his father's ghostly shadow.

By inserting the story of Coralie Walton at this point, Vandenhoff glosses over the discomfort caused by his father's disapproval. It is as if over Coralie Walton's fictional body Vandenhoff is finally able to turn his vocation into a reputable and socially useful profession. In her sacrificial body,[18] the stigma of acting and the parental disapproval are exposed and expurgated. Once Vandenhoff has left England, his father and Coralie behind, he is finally able to turn theatrical performance into a thoroughly estimable occupation that would do his father proud. After a few years in America, and having married the actress Mary Makeah, Vandenhoff gives up the stage proper to return to the law and become one of the first and most prominent public readers of Shakespeare's plays. It is as an orator, teacher of oral delivery and the author of several textbooks of elocution that Vandenhoff is mostly remembered today. In the end, George Vandenhoff's principal career relied on his ability to distinguish between his identity as a respectable citizen and his performance of Shakespeare's texts.

Notes

With thanks to Nicole Miller and Rosie Snajdr for their generous help and to the Swiss National Science Foundation and the Folger Shakespeare Library for funding this research.

1. Edmund Kean's collapse was witnessed and reported by J. R. Planché, *The Recollections and Reflections of J. R. Planché, A Professional Autobiography*, 2 vols (London: Tinsley Brothers, 1872), I, 195. For the urban legends about Booth and Aldridge, see Edward Pechter, *'Othello' and Interpretive Tradition* (Iowa City: University of Iowa Press, 1999) p. 12, and Herbert Marshall and Mildred Stock, *Ira Aldridge: the Negro Tragedian* (London: Camelot Press, 1958), pp. 268–9.
2. See Diana Henderson's discussion of Amy Robsart's sentimentalised and heroic portrayal in Sir Walter Scott's *Kenilworth*, Ch. 1 in this volume.
3. George Vandenhoff, *Leaves from an Actor's Notebook; with Reminiscences and Chit-Chat of the Green-Room and the Stage, in England and America* (New York: D. Appleton & Co., 1860), pp. 136–7. Further page references are provided after quotations in the text.
4. Arnold Hare, 'Shakespeare in a Provincial Stock Company', in *Shakespeare and the Victorian Stage*, ed. by Richard Foulkes (Cambridge: Cambridge University Press, 1986), pp. 258–70.
5. Leman Thomas Tertius Rede, *The Road to the Stage; or, the Performer's Preceptor* (London: Smith, 1927), p. ii.
6. For comments on the predominance of Shakespeare within the provincial theatre repertoire, see Jeremy Crump, 'The Popular Audience for Shakespeare in Nineteenth-Century Leicester', in *Shakespeare and the Victorian Stage*, ed. by Richard Foulkes (Cambridge: Cambridge University Press, 1986), pp. 271–82, and Douglas A. Reid, 'Popular Theatre in Victorian Birmingham', in *Performance and Politics in Popular Drama*, ed. by David Bradby, Louis James and Bernard Sharratt (Cambridge: Cambridge University Press, 1980), pp. 65–90.
7. See Francis O'Gorman's essay on Ruskin and Shakespeare, Ch. 12 in this volume.
8. The term is borrowed from Eric Trudgill, *Madonnas and Magdalens: the Origins and Development of Victorian Sexual Attitudes* (London: Heinemann, 1976), p. 101.
9. Mrs Jameson, *Shakespeare's Female Characters* (Bielefeld: Velhagen and Klasing, 1840), pp. 140 and 142. Vandenhoff invokes Mrs Jameson (or 'Jamieson', as he spells the name), in the very first sentence of his account of Coralie Walton's fate, setting up her idealising view of Shakespeare's female characters as a structuring paradigm for his own narrative.
10. See, for instance, Michael R. Booth, *Theatre in the Victorian Age* (Cambridge: Cambridge University Press, 1991), p. 113; Kerry Powell, *Women and Victorian Theatre* (Cambridge: Cambridge University Press, 1997), pp. 32–3 and *passim*; and especially Tracy C. Davis, *Actresses as Working Women* (London and New York: Routledge, 1991), pp. 78–86 and *passim*. Davis stresses that there is no hard evidence that large numbers of actresses ever did work as prostitutes in Victorian England (p. 78).

11. Geraldine Jewsbury, *The Half-Sisters* (Oxford: Oxford University Press, 1994), p. 214.
12. A Lady, *An Appeal to the Women of England to Discourage the Stage* (London: Masters, 1855), pp. 9–10.
13. See Sandra M. Gilbert and Susan Gubar's classic reading of the novel in *The Madwoman in the Attic: the Woman Writer and the Nineteenth-Century Literary Imagination*, 2nd edn (New Haven and London: Yale University Press, 2000). Gilbert and Gubar's argument is based on the premise that 'for every glowing portrait of submissive women enshrined in domesticity, there exists an equally important negative image that embodies the sacrilegious fiendishness of what William Blake called the "Female Will"' (p. 28).
14. Private conversation, 16 April 2002.
15. *The Rise of the Victorian Actor* (London: Croom Helm, 1978), p. 16.
16. Powell, p. 35.
17. The parallels between the careers and anxieties of the two men are pervasive enough to suggest that their reminiscences may be read as paradigms for the (self-)perceptions of actors and their profession in the period. Both men were born into families of actors, both had fraught relationships with their fathers which influenced their view of the respectability of their profession, and both were deeply concerned by the possibility and implications of over-identification of the performer with the character. Like Vandenhoff, Macready looked to America for refuge from the stigmatisation he suffered in Britain. There he found himself, as Alan S. Downer records, 'freely received by men of the best society without prejudices against his profession' (*The Eminent Tragedian William Charles Macready* (Cambridge, MA: Harvard University Press, 1966), p. 110). But the feud with his American rival Edwin Forrest which culminated in the Astor Place riot of 1849 put an end to the thought that he might settle there permanently. (For Forrest, see Lisa Merrill's essay in the companion volume.)
18. 'Sacrifice', Elisabeth Bronfen explains, 'works as a metonymic strategy, with one body killed as representative of an entire semantic realm. [...] One member of the community draws all the evil or pollution on to its body and purifies the city metonymically through her or his destruction.' (*Over Her Dead Body: Death, Femininity and the Aesthetic* (Manchester: Manchester University Press, 1992), p. 196)

12

'The Clue of Shakespearian Power Over Me': Ruskin, Shakespeare, and Influence

Francis O'Gorman

Ruskin read Shakespeare throughout his life. He began as a child by hearing the comedies and history plays read aloud by John James, his father.[1] In *Praeterita* (1885–89), he remembered listening to Shakespeare and Scott, the writer who was to exert more influence than any novelist on his later life, and Miguel de Cervantes. 'After tea,' he wrote, 'my father read to my mother what pleased themselves, I picking up what I could, or reading what I liked better instead. Thus I heard all the Shakespeare comedies and historical plays again and again, – all Scott, and all *Don Quixote*, a favourite book of my father's, and at which I could then laugh to ecstasy; now, it is one of the saddest, and, in some things, the most offensive of books to me.'[2] *Praeterita* linked Shakespeare and the once loved, now distasteful Cervantes in its account of childhood literary experience because Ruskin was faithfully memorialising John James's taste, but also because the deeper pattern of his own changes of heart, which I explore in this essay, underlay the memory.

Reading Shakespeare, and hearing him read 'again and again', made the plays an indelible part of Ruskin's childhood. When he was able to write himself, Shakespeare was in his blood. In his first letters to his father, references to the plays became common currency, expressing an element of the Ruskins' distinctive middle-class culture that his mother Margaret's Evangelical suspicion of theatre had not banished, and they helped bind Ruskin to John James's own intellectual interests. Indeed, also to his practical ones, for John James had had an early interest in actual theatrical performance: Ruskin would later recall his mother's fond memory of one of his costumes, despite her caution about the stage, and her never-wearying pleasure in reminding her son 'how beautiful my father looked in his Highland dress, with the high black feathers' (XXVIII, 347) [3] The filiation between John James and Shakespeare in Ruskin's correspondence was part of a life-long association between the 'greatest Master' (XX, 300) of the arts, whose works 'lay open on the table all day' (XXXV, 143) at Herne Hill and Ruskin's ambitious father, an 'absolutely beautiful reader' of the plays (XXXV, 61). The connection would give a personal energy to his long and changeful *pas de deux* with Shakespeare's legacy in his life.

In the Italian tour of 1845, the first Continental journey that Ruskin took unaccompanied by his parents, he was continuing his allusory habit in his letters home but was also reading more deeply, setting himself to study *Coriolanus* and *Julius Caesar* for the 'first time [...] seriously' (XXXV, 366). He admired the 'King love' of Shakespeare as 'very glorious',[4] making an association between monarchy and Shakespeare that would last, much reconfigured, to the end of his life. He also, perhaps, discussed Shakespeare with Anna Jameson in his evening walks, with important consequences for 'Of Queens' Gardens' (a text foregrounding a notion of moral monarchy).[5] But it was reading German Shakespearian criticism – Ruskin was normally no friend of German literature – in Italy in the winter of 1852 that prompted his most revealing early critical statement about the objects of the plays. Like so much of his thinking about the drama, this was directed to John James. Recently an admirer of Shakespeare's 'King love', Ruskin's reading of his pocket volume and Schlegel's *Dramatic Art and Literature* (first published in English in 1815) urged him, he told his father, to think of the plays' treatment of male error.

A. W. Schlegel regarded the plays more as 'elaborate pieces of art than as deep and natural expressions of a great man's mind', Ruskin wrote.[6] His treatment was 'shallow', he declared, setting out his own reading of the plays as unitary statements of a universalised intellectual conviction about the misfortunes of human life:

> I believe Shakespeare wrote with the most perfect ease – but had in each play – a simple and very grand purpose – which gives to it that consistency that the common critics think the result of laborious composition. I don't think this purpose has been at all noticed [...] I see that Shakespeare knew long ago what I am just beginning to find out – that the sorrow of the whole world is *all* the consequence of *Mistake*; and its chief miseries are brought about by small errors and misconceptions – trifles apparently – which our own evil passions leave us to be the prey of.[7]

Ruskin's words used Shakespeare to configure a reflection on art and morality and their relation with ease and labour that connected Schlegel's dramatic criticism to the ideas of 'The Nature of Gothic' (1853). They also identified the subject of accidents and mistake in the plays as central to Shakespeare's teaching: such a realisation would later metamorphose into a key motive behind his rejection of Shakespeare in the 1880s.

Ruskin was reading Shakespeare in 1852 for instruction. Like his approach to the architecture of Venice in *The Stones of Venice* (1851–53), in which he was immersed, he saw the plays scripting truths of moral fall that were generalisable. Ruskin's perception, against Schlegel's patient taxonomy of the literary identity of the plays, was characterised by an expectation of a single logic in textual statement. The 'whole of *Romeo and Juliet*', Ruskin said, 'is evidently written to show the effect of Heedless and unbridled passion – exposing men to infinite calamity from *accident only* – Every thing concurs to give this lesson'.[8] He perceived the play in unitary terms, where everything concurred, as a text dedicated to the articulation of consistent truth just as he was finding in Venice a dismally coherent statement of moral ruin.[9] Such a mode of reading was part of Ruskin's multiple Romantic inheritance, a result of his processing of the previous generation's legacy into a belief about the relationship between writers and texts that was to come under strain in his later decades. This practice of reading was also, so far as it concerned Shakespeare, distinctively paradoxical. Where Ruskin produced an assumption of consistent and sincere authorial intention from his transactions with Romanticism and brought that assumption to bear in his reading of Shakespeare, his response to his father's favourite playwright erased the complexity of actual Romantic interpretations of the dramatist half a century before. Keats's regard for Shakespeare's Negative Capability is only the most obvious of the early nineteenth-century conceptions of the playwright to generate friction with Ruskin's views in 1852. The Romantic genealogy of Ruskin's reading of Shakespeare, ironised by nothing less than Romanticism's own plural engagement with Shakespeare's writing, succinctly revealed one of the more complicated pathways of his literary inheritance of the kind he would endeavour to straighten out in *Praeterita*.

Ruskin did not consider gender implications in 1852, but his concentration was nonetheless on the calamities brought by male '*Mistake*'. In *Romeo and Juliet*, he perceived a catalogue of men behaving badly: 'Mercutio fights in a jest – Tybalt in a fury – both are slain [. . .] Capulet and Montague are *first* introduced calling for swords – and are *last* seen reconciled by the loss of all that is dear to them, the whole being a most profound teaching of the character of human passion – and its folly – and its punishment wrought out *by* its folly.'[10] Ruskin's meditation on Schlegel was a distant reflection of that grand narrative of moral caducity visible in the history of the Queen of the Adriatic but one in which a question of masculinity was becoming distinct.

Ruskin's next major statement on Shakespeare deepened his engagement with sexual/textual politics. Nina Auerbach comments in *Women and the Demon* (1982) that Ruskin's celebration of Shakespeare's female characters in 'Of Queens' Gardens', one of the two lectures delivered in Rusholme Town Hall in Greater Manchester in the winter of 1864, was commonplace. It was part, she said, of 'a well-known tradition of literary worship'.[11] In fact, Ruskin's praise was distinctive. His model, as Auerbach acknowledges, was the work of Anna Jameson, who herself drew on William Richardson's *Essays on Shakespeare's Dramatic Character* (1788). But this was not merely a case of shared viewpoints, for Ruskin was exceptional in his confidence in the moral self-possession of Shakespeare's heroines. Jameson, rather than seeing herself as part of a tradition, perceived opposition. She thought that 'the prevalent idea is, that Shakespeare's women are inferior to his men. This assertion is constantly repeated, and has been but tamely refuted.'[12] Jameson endeavoured to contest it, but not to deny those aspects in which the heroines were undoubtedly weaker than the heroes. Shakespeare's 'women are inferior in power to his men',[13] she agreed, suggesting that this feature of characterisation accurately mimicked the gender politics of his (and her own) society. But Ruskin had no doubt that Shakespeare's heroines, in their admirable moral qualities, were above the central male characters. As he put it to his Manchester audience in December 1864, only a few months after the death of John James, the central male character of his own life: 'In his laboured and perfect plays you have no hero,' (XVIII, 112).

Ruskin's reading of the plays in opposition to any neo-Aristotelian paradigm of heroism was a recognisable development from the views on male mistake in 1852, but he was now explicitly conscious of gender politics. 'Cordelia, Desdemona, Isabella, Hermione, Imogen, Queen Catherine, Perdita, Sylvia, Viola, Rosalind, Helena, and last, and perhaps loveliest, Virgilia, are all faultless;' he said, 'conceived in the highest heroic type of humanity,' (XVIII, 113). He had much to say, as has been substantially discussed, about the role and dignity of women in 'Of Queens' Gardens', guided by what he believed could be learned from Shakespeare. But this deliberation on women was revealing of, and partly an effect of, Ruskin's sharply troubled sense of the nature of manliness in 1864.

The shadow of *Unto this Last* (1860) lay on the Shakespeare of 'Of Queens' Gardens'. Ruskin's principal vexation in *Unto this Last* was with commerce and trade, and he was impatient of male failure to realise social responsibility in middle-class professions. He urged the re-conceptualisation of the merchant in terms of the heroic, aggregating to the man of trade the same forms of honour as those of the minister of religion and soldier. Commerce 'is an occupation which gentlemen will every day see more need to engage in, rather than in the businesses of talking to men, or slaying them' (XVII, 39), he said in the first instalment of *Unto this Last* in the *Cornhill*, insisting on the nobility and soldierly duty that should exist in the marketplace and lamentably did not. Aspiring to restore the plane of the heroic, Ruskin's economic writing was predicated on an acknowledgement of the hero's general absence from the social body, and his increasingly public resistance to the formal discourse of Ricardian thought, a practice akin to 'a science of gymnastics which assumed that men had no skeletons' (XVII, 26).

Shakespeare, whom Ruskin would later accuse of having no soul, played a significantly double role in this alternative political economy. He was imagined both as reflecting the absence of heroism in the contemporary domains of commercial activity and as offering examples of precisely the kind of manliness that characterised the ideal merchant. Declaring polemically in *Munera Pulveris* (1862) – like *Unto this Last*, a work of political economy – that 'The perfect type of manhood [. . .] involves the perfections [. . .] of his body, affections, and intelligence' (XVII, 150), Ruskin found modern economic man remarkably ignoble. In chapter 4 of *Munera*, in the heart of his debate about honesty and usury in modern financial transactions, it was Shakespeare who offered him a positive icon. Antonio from *The Merchant of Venice*, Ruskin said, taught a lesson that was not Shakespeare's but 'part of the old wisdom of humanity' (XVII, 223). In a modern world peculiarly lacking in commercial heroism, Shakespeare offered a glimpse of 'the true and incorrupt merchant' who was '*kind and free, beyond every other Shakspearian conception of men*' (XVII, 223, italic original). In Antonio, mercantile heroism took human form.[14] But in 'Of Queens' Gardens', two years later, Shakespeare obliquely reflected the gloomier diagnosis of the modern marketplace and the domains of male action. With its grave acceptance that there were no heroes even in his best plays, the lecture bore traces of Ruskin's vexation with the absence of those noble qualities that were both possible and necessary in the day-to-day of modern life, the failure of men to act heroically in labour.[15]

Ruskin's understanding up to 1864 of Shakespeare's plays as textual rather than theatrical was a familiar nineteenth-century assumption. This is not to say that Ruskin did not visit the theatre or see Shakespeare acted. He once complained publicly to his readers about 'the enthusiastic acceptance by an English audience of Salvini's frightful, and radically false, interpretation of Othello' (XXIX, 445), a perception partly expressive of an anxiety about Italian misconceptions of an English writer.[16] But as a reader of Shakespeare before the 1880s he was interested in character in terms of psychological unity just as, in 1852, he considered singleness of intellectual purpose as guiding the thematic organisation of the plays. There was, however, the beginning of a new uncertainty in Ruskin's mind about Shakespeare's purposes and the discernible coherence of his truths in the letters of *Fors Clavigera* (1871–84) that marked the starting point of his maturer reflections on Shakespeare, and the gradual withdrawal of admiration.

A clue to this is glimpsed in the late letter for September 1883 where Ruskin considered the intentions of the tragedies in relation to his overall expectation that great art should be part of a consistent moral scheme, affirming values associable with the eternal verities of religion and myth. Looking back on previous assumptions about the principles of Shakespeare's most theologically challenging plays, he remarked that he had overlooked the rootedness of the major tragedies in a religion of hope. 'I had not with enough care', he said, 'examined the spirit of faith in God, and hope in futurity, which, though unexpressed, were meant by the master of tragedy to be felt by the spectator what they were to himself, the solution and consolation of all the wonderfulness of sorrow,' (XXIX, 477). But, partly, he was trying to convince himself. Endeavouring to keep faith with the perceived integrity of Shakespeare's theological purposes in the great tragedies, he had nonetheless to admit that such faith was 'unexpressed', and that he could find no quotation that would adequately support his reading. He was obliged to fall back on his own assertions, to say that such views 'were *meant* by the master of tragedy' despite the absence of textual support. Aspiring to assimilate Shakespeare's tragedies into the fold of literature confident of the future life and the meaningful ways of God, Ruskin's Miltonic interpretation of the tragic plays as providential schemes betrayed signs of nervousness.

Elsewhere, Ruskin openly regretted what he found. In keeping with his shift of interest in the 1870s and 1880s, as political thinker, historian and biographer towards the lives of the ordinary and unregarded,

Ruskin was disappointed to realise that the class representations of the plays did not support any conception of the heroism of quotidian life, male or female. In 1868, he had declared that 'the intellectual measure of every man since born, in the domains of creative thought, may be assigned to him, according to the degree in which he has been taught by Shakespeare' (XVIII, 159). But two decades later, Ruskin's impatience with that teaching in class terms was becoming plain. 'In returning to my Shakespeare', he noted in 1888, 'after such final reading of the realities of life as may have been permitted me [...] it grieves me to find, in him, no laborious nor lowly ideal; but that his perfect shepherdess is a disguised princess; his Miracle of the White Island exultingly quits her spirit-guarded sands to be Queen of Naples; and his cottager Rosalind is extremely glad to get her face unbrowned again' (XXXII, 492). Sir Philip Sidney's work, Ruskin thought as he prepared the *Bibliotheca Pastorum* (1876–85), a collection of valuable texts for an ordinary labouring readership, could be placed at the service of ordinary men and women.[17] But, close to the end of his active life, Ruskin could only see Shakespeare at odds with his own matured politics of national rejuvenation. Such politics privileged laborious men and women who were customarily overlooked by official histories, who exemplified the 'Suffering Life, the rooted heart of native humanity, growing up in eternal gentleness, howsoever wasted, forgotten, or spoiled' (XXXIII, 59), as he phrased it in *The Bible of Amiens* (1880–85). As Ruskin's reading of Shakespeare intersected with these class preoccupations, his value as a teacher declined.

It was from this growing sense of Shakespeare's shortcomings that *Praeterita*'s final assessment emerged. In 1864, Ruskin's thoughts about Shakespeare's heroes had been bound up with his cultural critique of forms of modern, commercial, manliness. In the 'Macugnaga' chapter of *Praeterita*, he rebuked Shakespeare for what he now saw as moral failure to provide models of admirable manliness of general service, and his consequent negligence of prestigious literary authority. Sharply conscious that he had offered no heroes even in his laboured and perfect plays, Ruskin now conceived this a grievous error in the representation of masculinity in a writer of unparalleled cultural visibility:

> as I try to follow the clue of Shakespearian power over me [...], I cannot feel that it has been anywise wholesome for me to have the world represented as a place where, for that best sort of people, everything always goes wrong; or to have my conceptions of that best sort of people so much confused by images of the worst. To have

kinghood represented, in the Shakespearian cycle, by Richards II. and
III. instead of I., by Henrys IV. and VIII. instead of II.; by King John,
finished into all truths of baseness and grief, while Henry V. is only a
king of fairy tale; or in the realm of imagination, by the folly of Lear,
the cruelty of Leontes, the furious and foul guilt of Macbeth and the
Dane. (XXXV, 369)

Ruskin's search for the 'clue' of Shakespearean influence – in an autobiography dedicated generally to identifying the influences that helped
form his mind – was telling of the complexities that lay behind his final
views of the once-loved playwright. The word sprang from the dilemma
between moral principle and private enthralment in which he was now
caught. On the one hand, he needed to recognise a lifetime's reading of
the playwright who was admired by his family and inextricable from his
own past; on the other, he had to acknowledge his recent recognition of
Shakespeare's inadequacy as a teacher of men. In describing himself as
searching for a 'clue', in presenting himself embarking on the arduous
detection of an apparently hidden influence, he endeavoured to adjudi-
cate between these contrary feelings, allowing for the possibility that he
had learned from his father's favourite dramatist, while cagily implying
he had not.

In an autobiography that provocatively defined Ruskin's Toryism as a
'sincere love of kings, and dislike of everybody who attempted to dis-
obey them' (XXXV, 14), Shakespeare's characterisation of unadmirable
regal masculinity – Ruskin's link between Shakespeare and monarchy
reached its solemn climax – was neither instructive nor healthy in its
influence. The teaching on the role of women remained, and for that
Shakespeare continued silently valuable. But the book that lay open at
Herne Hill should have been symbolically closed long before the impov-
erished models of unheroic men seeped beyond its pages into the gender
expectations of the wider culture. Unadmirable in moral lessons and
bafflingly plural in dramatic intention, Ruskin could only admit in his
autobiography that Shakespeare's role among educated men of the
modern world had been wholly ineffective. Shakespeare's 'wisdom [is]
so useless,' he concluded, 'that at this time of being and speaking,
among active and purposeful Englishmen, I know not one who shows
a trace of ever having felt a passion of Shakespeare's, or learnt a lesson
from him' (XXXV, 369). If the responsibility of great writers was to
provide instruction that was historically durable, and to excite across
ages 'vital or noble emotion and intellectual action' (XVII, 157), as he
put it in *Munera Pulveris*, then Shakespeare's art, and the wisdom that

was the product of his peculiar knowledge of human beings, was without worth for the national culture and, more particularly, for its men. Matthew Arnold thought Shakespeare's work a poor model for modern poetic language: Ruskin, the *quondam* champion of his plays as the bearer of 'lesson[s]' to be disregarded only at peril, had come to see him as an inadequate textual model for a man's harmonious and morally successful life.

Praeterita emplotted the necessary sacrifice of Shakespeare. It recorded the movement from childhood pleasure to regret for his moral insufficiency, and his consequent exclusion from the canon of valuable national writers whose 'lesson[s]' could be profitably heeded. The symbolic economy of this narrative bears comparison with the sacrifice of Coralie Walton, the Shakespearian actress discussed by Pascale Aebischer in the previous chapter, which helped banish, through its own symbolic exchange, the moral taint of the stage from George Vandenhoff's *Leaves from an Actor's Notebook* (1860). In a reverse pattern from much of Ruskin's autobiography, which cherished home and the things of the past, Shakespeare was a prominent casualty. Significant shifts in Ruskin's thought came always from the confluence of multiple forces, public and private: even changes of heart that apparently concerned local issues were often complexly motivated and ample in suggestiveness or cultural significance. The narrative that finally saw Shakespeare abjured in *Praeterita* was, in this sense, no exception, either in the question of its origins or in the personal and cultural forces it suggested.

The plot of Shakespeare's fall is partly bound up, as I have already suggested, with Ruskin's persistent private negotiations with his paternal heritage that were always consequential for his public life. John James Ruskin, the central if contradictory personality of his son's career, was long associated with Shakespeare. Ruskin, honouring the man for whom the 'characters of Shakespearian comedy were all familiar personal friends' (XXXV, 366), had even commemorated him on his gravestone in 1864 in the terms he had applied two years earlier to the idealised mercantilism of *The Merchant of Venice*. John James, once a 'beautiful reader' of the plays, was, Ruskin wrote, 'an entirely honest merchant' (XVII, lxxvii). The criticism of Shakespeare in *Praeterita* belongs with the autobiography's regard for the memory of John James: partly memorial of the life of Herne Hill and Denmark Hill, the volume also invested heavily in forms of paternal distancing. In the case of Shakespeare, a writer bound to the paternal past, Ruskin staged a kind of ritual of personal maturation, a setting aside that signified something of his own intellectual independence from the formative powers of his youth. In marking out the limits of Shakespeare's teaching, Ruskin was silently opening up one of the many spaces between himself and the instruction of his ambiguous father, who, Ruskin said bitterly in the aftermath of his death, 'would have sacrificed his life for his son, and yet forced his son to sacrifice his life to him, and sacrifice it in vain' (XVIII, xxviii). Such bitterness was not characteristic and *Praeterita*'s tone was more measured. But Ruskin continued to identify the nature of his parental upbringing there as one of contraries, counting both the 'blessings' (XXXV, 43) he had enjoyed as a child and the 'equally dominant calamities' (XXXV, 44). Eschewing the teaching of Shakespeare in the autobiography was one of the many ways in which Ruskin could detach himself, though without any sense of triumph, from a father whose legacy was one of enabling/disabling polarity.

Inscribing a position of independence against the male authority of John James, Ruskin's narration of the loss of Shakespeare in *Praeterita* also complicated broader ideas about the gender politics of Ruskin's mid-career, which have been a topic of sustained scholarly interest for some thirty years. Critical concentration on 'Of Queens' Gardens' has repeatedly focused on Ruskin's delimitation of female virtues, including his appropriation of Shakespeare's female characters into his gender schemes. Indeed, all the recent references to his views on Shakespeare (Auerbach, Lootens, Marshall, Peterson) have dwelt on his interest in the heroines.[18] Yet the ampler narrative of Shakespeare's place in Ruskin's life reveals the imbalance of this: the troubled politics of masculinity it excludes.

The playwright's changing place in Ruskin's gender thinking reminds his readers, at the most general level, that masculinity, especially in the second half of his career, formed a sustained locus of his critical energies, and one involving disappointment greater than his considerations of femininity. More specifically, the narrative I have recounted suggests that, while the subject of Shakespeare and femininity has been prominent in Ruskin criticism, it was finally Shakespeare and masculinity that mattered more to Ruskin. His admiration of the heroines rather than the heroes of the dramas in 1864 found some cultural approval. The Shakespearian actress Helena Faucit, Lady Martin, writing to Ruskin on Beatrice from *Much Ado About Nothing* in *Blackwood's* in 1885, declared his ideas entirely in accordance with the 'lesson' she thought Shakespeare had taught about the place of women.[19] But the forces that helped shape Ruskin's views in 1864 were precisely those that would ultimately direct him away from the plays. Shakespeare's lessons of femininity, however much admired, were finally insufficient to compensate Ruskin for the playwright's weak teaching on men and to sustain him in the canon of valuable writing.

The lecture that had preceded the gender statements of 'Of Queens' Gardens' in 1864 – 'Of Kings' Treasuries' – was about reading practices, and the importance of remembering the unitary intention behind literary language. Even baffling statements in poetry or fiction, collocations apparently without sense in the work of writers of genius, would, when studied closely, Ruskin insisted, yield coherent meaning that was part of a great writer's consistent intentions. The substance of Ruskin's relationship with Shakespeare's plays – with coincidental symmetry – also reveals features of Ruskin's own practices of reading of consequence for the history of Shakespeare's reception in the period. For the dissatisfaction with Shakespeare marked by *Praeterita* was suggestively linked to a half-sensed perception of the inadequacy of the reading assumptions he had inherited for comprehending the generic specificity of the plays. In the first half of his career, Ruskin had thought Shakespeare's work unitary in its teaching, but in *Praeterita* he reluctantly sensed that this expectation was insecure, fretted with more obvious uncertainty than his hope that the tragedies affirmed the consolations of providential teleology. The plays are, he said in the 'Macugnaga' chapter of the autobiography, 'all [written] so inextricably and mysteriously that the writer himself is not only unknowable, but inconceivable' (XXXV, 369). The reading practices taught in 'Of Kings' Treasuries' that revealed sense even behind Milton's seemingly careless phrase 'blind mouths' in 'Lycidas' (XVIII, 72), could not, Ruskin implied, help in elucidating consistent and knowable intention in Shakespeare's drama. Ruskin in Venice in the winter of 1852 had proposed to his father the unitary meanings of the plays. But, in *Praeterita*, he disclosed a reluctant perception of ways in which they resisted such readings because of an 'inextricably and mysteriously' uncertain authorial presence.[20]

Jonathan Bate suggests in *The Genius of Shakespeare* (1997) that William Empson's grasp of emergent quantum physics facilitated his argument in *Seven Types of Ambiguity* (1930) that Shakespeare's texts were capable of meaning ambiguously, of including competing meanings, even of signifying opposite things at once. In dispensing with an 'either/or' reading, Empson allowed that Shakespeare, at the extreme, could mean 'and/both'. Quantum physics may have given direction to Empson's views of Shakespeare's embrace of semantic plurality at Cambridge in the 1920s, but Ruskin was too good a reader of literary texts not to perceive in the 1880s, however unwillingly, that Shakespeare's work could not be happily accommodated in a practice of critical reading –

even his own – that assumed unitary meaning and singleness of intellectual statement. The possibility that Shakespeare's texts could mean conflicting things, that deep ambiguity of meaning characterised his work, even that he could be, perhaps, at the extreme point, a practitioner of what Empson would name the seventh type of ambiguity, lurked behind Ruskin's dissatisfaction with a non-unitary authorial personality whose coherence could not be grasped and whose work was resistant to the hermeneutic strategies of 'Of Kings' Treasuries'. Ruskin's nervousness about Shakespeare's 'inconceivable' mind in the 1880s marked a moment when an important early assumption about the relation between a cherished author and his texts was visibly under pressure.

Under particular scrutiny in Ruskin's last years, if not under pressure, was the question of literary writing – in all genres – and its relation to schemes of moral instruction and cultural profit; Shakespeare's fate in *Praeterita* was involved in this too. Ruskin's literary career had begun with poetry – *Marcolini: a Dramatic Fragment* (1836) imitated Shakespeare – and, though he swiftly relinquished hopes of distinction there, literature remained a constant source of reference throughout his writing. But in the 1870s and 1880s, literature, and its identity as cultural effect as well as guide, began to assume additional significance. The moral power of the literary, particularly its capacity to speak to ordinary men and women, was increasingly politicised in these decades across the whole cultural spectrum; for Ruskin, it acquired a value that was sufficient to urge a shift in his public mode. Once a poet, and the early author of a fairytale (*The King of the Golden River*, which he later deemed 'totally valueless' (XXXV, 304)), he now began to edit fictional texts himself. The story of Hansli in *Fors Clavigera* (begun in June 1873)[21] or the narratives of *The Story of Ida* (1883) or Gotthelf's *Ulric the Farm Servant* (1886–88) indicated his investment in Continental tales, both Protestant and Catholic, ample in domestic teaching.[22] Ruskin envisaged such texts as directly helpful to a readership able more easily to absorb lessons embodied in the affective medium of fictional language than those embedded in discursive prose. Ruskin's sense of writerly identity now included a literary midwifery through which he facilitated the transmission of other's fictional work into the wider community.

In keeping with this increasing attention, the early 1880s also saw Ruskin's first and only publication of literary criticism. *Fiction, Fair and Foul* (1880–81) was a trenchant, unexpected, and demanding series of essays. Although surprising in their impatience with writers whom Ruskin had previously admired (chiefly Wordsworth), they were built around a determining opposition in Ruskin's thinking which had characterised his entire intellectual life between the noble productions of the past and the ethically indigent present. Walter Scott was celebrated as a particular touchstone of value; modern fiction was excoriated. Even Dickens, whom Ruskin had in other respects admired, was assailed for the cheapness of a sensationalism that endeavoured to satisfy desires born of the deprivations of city life. In fulfilling an unnatural 'craving [...] for some kind of excitement' (XXXIV, 271), novels like *Bleak House* (1852–53), Ruskin declared, arose only from:

> The monotony of life in the central streets of any great modern city, but especially in those of London, where every emotion intended to be derived by men from the sight of nature, or the sense of art, is forbidden, for ever[.] (XXXIV, 270)

Fiction, Fair and Foul was an outcome of Ruskin's increasing emphasis on literature as cultural effect and on his own role as its guardian through the periodical press. The essays were also part of his aim to identify the core components of a national canon of texts for differently classed readerships that would legitimately edify a benighted age. In the formation of the *Bibliotheca Pastorum* from 1876, Ruskin had endeavoured to provide the germ of a national library for the working class. In the early 1880s, literary criticism – however much the corrupt forces of the fiction it denounced paradoxically energised it – became a further mode for policing, in middle-class culture, the circulation of texts expressive only of 'the Divinity of Decomposition' (XXXIV, 270). The demise of Shakespeare in *Praeterita* is explicable within these dynamics, with canon-making for the middle classes of modern England, and with the increasing sense of literature's circulation as a matter of national consequence.

Shakespeare became a peculiarly difficult figure for Ruskin in the last years partly because he recognised the poverty of his teaching at the same time as the ideological identity of literature in national culture was his growing concern.[23] But it would be unfaithful to the elegiac temper of Ruskin's autobiography and its dealings with Shakespeare to end here. For what was finally most memorable about Shakespeare's loss in *Praeterita* was its personal nature. Many of the chapters in the present book and its companion consider forms of Shakespearian celebration, and Ruskin is peculiar among these as a writer for whom Shakespeare's cultural status did not, in the end, avail against a perception of his failure of moral duty and his abnegation of responsibility as a teacher.

But, unlike Hal's spurning of the companion of his youth in *2 Henry IV*, the eschewal of Shakespeare in *Praeterita* was, however necessary, a matter of felt personal loss. Tolstoy, whose patterns of thought variously corresponded to Ruskin's, had banished the 'trivial and immoral works of Shakespeare' in his famously 'wrongheaded'[24] 1906 *Shakespeare and the Drama* partly on the grounds of their 'evil' teaching, but in doing so he was aware only of the absurdity of the playwright's popular reputation. Tolstoy lost nothing of himself in disputing with what he pathologised as 'the epidemic suggestion about the greatness of Shakespeare'.[25] Ruskin's investment had been different. His tone was far from neutral, neither did he speak with the accents of the public moralist, as he lamented the failure of providential schemes in Shakespeare's plays and continued to regret the influence that was not in 'anywise wholesome for me' in a lifetime's reading:

> Why must the persons of Iago and Iachimo, of Tybalt and Edmund, of Isabel's brother and Helena's lord, pollute, or wither with their shadows, every happy scene in the loveliest plays; and they, the loveliest, be all mixed and encumbered with languid and common work, – to one's best hope spurious, certainly, so far as original, idle and disgraceful? (XXXV, 369)

Such words were shaped first by private bafflement and personal disappointment, however much the public issue of a writer's responsibility was at stake.

The period charted by the present volumes witnessed the emergence of Shakespeare as public property, as a highly marketable literary commodity, whose works circulated increasingly through the national culture as an embodiment of culture itself. The sustained and multiform Victorian celebration of Shakespeare surveyed here became a part of the country's self-definition: he was, in Richard Foulkes's words, solidly 'enshrined [. . .] in the institutions of national life'.[26] But where celebration, and memorialisation in the public arena, determined leading features of Shakespeare's Victorian afterlife in general terms, Ruskin's Shakespeare was, at the last, caught up with private memories and meshed in a subdued elegy for a dear possession of former times that, like *Don Quixote*, had proved no lasting value. Shakespeare, Ruskin had once said in an earlier, more buoyant mood, was not a national but an international writer, 'rather the world's than ours' (XX, 77). In the farewell to Shakespeare in *Praeterita*, a plangent moment in the context of the present study's investigation of the dramatist's enchanting power, it was the extent to which he had been his family's and his own that gave most torsion to Ruskin's words. The long-enduring personal attachment, and the memory of a lifetime's reading, made the pain of that final frustration peculiarly deep.

Notes

My thanks to Dinah Birch, Peter Holland, Gail Marshall, Adrian Poole and John Whale.

1. As is customary, 'Ruskin' in this essay refers to John Ruskin; 'John James' to his father.
2. *The Library Edition of the Works of John Ruskin*, ed. by E. T. Cook and Alexander Wedderburn, 39 vols (London: Allen, 1903–12), XXXV, 61: all future references to this edition in the main text.
3. For sensitive discussion of this memory, see Dinah Birch, 'Fathers and Sons: Ruskin, John James Ruskin, and Turner', *Nineteenth-Century Contexts*, 18 (1994), 147–62.
4. *Ruskin in Italy: Letters to his Parents, 1845*, ed. by Harold I. Shapiro (Oxford: Clarendon, 1972), p. 184.
5. See Linda H. Peterson, 'The Feminist Origins of Ruskin's "Of Queens' Gardens"', in *Ruskin and Gender*, ed. by Dinah Birch and Francis O'Gorman (Basingstoke: Palgrave – now Palgrave Macmillan, 2002), pp. 86–106. Another overlap between Ruskin's and Jameson's thought is suggested by Clara Thomas, *Love and Work Enough: the Life of Anna Jameson* (London: Macdonald, 1967), p. 167.
6. *Ruskin's Letters from Venice 1851–1852*, ed. by J. L. Bradley (New Haven: Yale University Press, 1955), p. 167.
7. *Letters from Venice*, p. 167.
8. *Letters from Venice*, p. 167.
9. For more on the Romantics' use of Shakespeare, see Jonathan Bate, *Shakespeare and the English Romantic Imagination* (Oxford: Clarendon, 1986).
10. *Letters from Venice*, p. 167.
11. Nina Auerbach, *Woman and the Demon: the Life of a Victorian Myth* (Harvard: Harvard University Press, 1982), p. 210.
12. Mrs [Anna] Jameson, *Characteristics of Women, Moral, Poetical, and Historical*, 2 vols (London: Saunders & Otley, 1832), p. xxii.
13. Jameson, p. xxx.
14. Cf. Francis O'Gorman, '"Suppose it were your own father of whom you spoke": Ruskin's *Unto this Last* (1860)' in *Review of English Studies*, 51 (2000), 230–47.
15. For more discussion of Ruskin, Shakespeare, and economics, see David Everett Blythe, 'A Stone of Ruskin's Venice' in *New Approaches to Ruskin: Thirteen Essays*, ed. by Robert Hewison (London: Routledge, 1981), pp. 157–73.

218 Victorian Shakespeare: Literature and Culture

16. Some of Ruskin's experiences with the theatre, including Shakespeare, are discussed in Sharon Aronofsky Weltman, 'Pantomime Truth and Gender Performance' in *Ruskin and Gender*, ed. by Birch and O'Gorman, pp. 159–76.
17. Ruskin edited *'Rock Honeycomb': Broken Pieces of Sir Philip Sidney's Psalter* as part of his 'shepherd's library', the *Bibliotheca Pastorum*, in 1877.
18. See Nina Auerbach, *Woman and the Demon*; Tricia Lootens, *Lost Saints: Silence, Gender, and Victorian Literary Canonization* (Charlottesville: University Press of Virginia, 1996); Gail Marshall, 'Helena Faucit: Shakespeare's Victorian Heroine', in *Translating Life: Studies in Transpositional Aesthetics*, ed. by Shirley Chew and Alistair Stead (Liverpool: Liverpool University Press, 1999), and Linda H. Peterson, 'The Feminist Origins of Ruskin's "Of Queens' Gardens"'.
19. Helena Faucit, Lady Martin, 'On Some of Shakespeare's Female Characters: By One who has Personated Them: VIII: Beatrice', *Blackwood's*, 137 (1885), 203.
20. For different, earlier doubts about Shakespeare's purposes, see the incident narrated in Derrick Leon, *Ruskin: the Great Victorian* (London: Routledge, 1949), p. 379.
21. Adapted from *Der Besenbinder von Rychiswyl*, first published in 1852.
22. The domestic principle of Gotthelf was privately accented by the fact that he was admired by John James, and read to the family in the Alps on their tour in 1854.
23. The most recent discussion of debates about literature and ideology at the end of the period is Patrick Brantlinger, *The Reading Lesson: the Threat of Mass Literacy in Nineteenth-Century British Fiction* (Bloomington: Indiana University Press, 1998).
24. Leo Tolstoy, *Shakespeare and the Drama* in *Shakespeare in Europe*, ed. by Oswald LeWinter (Harmondsworth: Penguin, 1970), pp. 274, 214 (the view of Oswald LeWinter).
25. *Shakespeare in Europe*, p. 272.
26. Richard Foulkes, 'Introduction', in *Shakespeare and the Victorian Stage*, ed. by Richard Foulkes (Cambridge: Cambridge University Press, 1986), p. 1.

Selected Bibliography

Primary works

By Authority of the Royal Commission: Official Catalogue of the Great Exhibition of the Works of Industry of All Nations, 1851, Third Corrected and Improved Edition, 1 August 1851 (London: Spicer Brothers, 1851)

[Bayne, Peter], 'Shakespeare and George Eliot', *Blackwood's*, 133 (April 1883), 524–3

Bradley, A. C., *Shakespearean Tragedy* (London: Macmillan, 1904)

Browning, Robert, *Robert Browning: the Poems*, ed. by John Pettigrew, 2 vols (Harmondsworth: Penguin, 1981; repr. 1996)

Bunn, Alfred [and Thomas John Dibdin], *Kenilworth: an Historical Drama, in Two Acts* (London: J. Duncombe [1832])

Carlyle, Thomas, 'The Hero as Poet' (Lecture III), in *On Heroes and Hero-Worship and the Heroic in History* (1841), from *Past and Present and Heroes and Hero-Worship* (London: Chapman and Hall, 1893), pp. 1–232

Clarke, Mary Cowden, *The Girlhood of Shakespeare's Heroines*, 5 vols (London: W. H. Smith & Son, Simpkin, Marshall & Co., 1850–2); condensed version by Sabilla Novello (London: Bickers & Son, 1879)

Cole, Henry, *Fifty Years of Public Work of Sir Henry Cole, K.C.B.*, 2 vols (London: George Bell & Sons, 1884)

Coleridge, Samuel Taylor, *Coleridge's Shakespearean Criticism*, ed. by Thomas Middleton Raysor, 2 vols (London: Constable, 1930)

Collins, Wilkie, *The Frozen Deep and Mr Wray's Cash-box* (Stroud, Gloucestershire: Alan Sutton Publishing, 1996)

Dickens, Charles, *David Copperfield* (1849–50)

—— *Great Expectations* (1860–1)

Eliot, George, *The Mill on the Floss* (1860)

—— *Silas Marner* (1861)

—— *Middlemarch* (1871–2)

—— *Daniel Deronda* (1876)

—— *The George Eliot Letters*, ed. by G. S. Haight, 9 vols (New Haven: Yale University Press, 1954–74)

Emerson, Ralph Waldo, 'Shakspeare; or, the Poet', in *Representative Men* (1850), in *Essays and Lectures*, The Library of America (New York, 1983), pp. 710–26

Faucit, Helena, Lady Martin, *On Some of Shakespeare's Female Characters*, 6th edn (Edinburgh: William Blackwood & Sons, 1899)

Hardy, Thomas, *The Complete Poetical Works of Thomas Hardy*, ed. by Samuel Hynes, 5 vols (Oxford: Clarendon Press, 1982–95)

James, Henry, *The Tragic Muse* (1890; rev. version 1908), ed. by Philip Horne (London: Penguin Classics, 1995)

—— *The Scenic Art: Notes on Acting and the Drama 1872–1901*, ed. by Allan Wade (London: Rupert Hart-Davis, 1949)

Jameson, Anna, *Characteristics of Women: Moral, Political, and Historical*, 2 vols (London: Saunders & Otley, 1832: later known as *Shakespeare's Heroines*)

Lamb, Charles, 'On the Tragedies of Shakespeare, Considered with Reference to their Fitness for Stage Representation' (1811), in *Romantic Critical Essays*, ed. by David Bromwich (Cambridge: Cambridge University Press, 1987), pp. 56–70

Lewes, G. H., *On Actors and the Art of Acting* (London: Smith Elder, 1875)

Macready, William Charles, *Reminiscences and Selections from his Diary and Letters*, ed. by F. Pollock (London: Macmillan, 1875)

—— *The Diaries of William Charles Macready 1833–1851*, 2 vols, ed. by William Toynbee (New York: Putnams, 1912)

Maynard, John, *Browning's Youth* (Cambridge, MA: Harvard University Press, 1977)

Newman, John Henry, *University Sermons*, ed. by D. M. MacKinnon and J. D. Holmes (London: SPCK, 1970)

—— *An Essay on the Development of Christian Doctrine*, ed. by Ian Ker (Notre Dame, Indiana: University of Notre Dame Press, 1989)

Oxberry, W. 'Kenilworth, A Melo-drama', *The New English Drama, with Prefatory Remarks, Biographical Sketches, and Notes, Critical and Exploratory*, vol. 19 (London: W. Simpkin and R. Marshall, and C. Chapple, 1824)

Ruskin, John, *The Complete Works*, ed. by E. T. Cook and Alexander Wedderburn, 39 vols (London: Allen, 1903–12)

Scott, Sir Walter, *Kenilworth; a Romance* (1821), ed. by J. H. Alexander (Edinburgh: Edinburgh University Press, 1993)

Shaw, George Bernard, *Shaw on Shakespeare*, ed. by Edwin Wilson (London: Cassell, 1962)

Tennyson, Alfred Lord, *The Poems of Tennyson*, ed. by Christopher Ricks, 2nd edn, 3 vols (Harlow: Longman, 1987)

—— *The Letters of Alfred Lord Tennyson*, ed. by Cecil Y. Lang and Edgar F. Shannon, Jr., 3 vols (Oxford: Clarendon Press, 1987)

Tennyson, Hallam, *Materials for a Life of A. T.: Collected for My Children*, 4 vols (London: Macmillan [limited run], 1895)

—— *Alfred Lord Tennyson: a Memoir by His Son*, 2 vols (London: Macmillan, 1897)

Thompson, Ann, and Sasha Roberts (eds) *Women Reading Shakespeare 1660–1900: an Anthology of Criticism* (Manchester and New York: Manchester University Press, 1997)

Trollope, Anthony, *He Knew He Was Right* (1869)

Vandenhoff, George, *Leaves from an Actor's Notebook; with Reminiscences and Chit-Chat of the Green-Room and the Stage, in England and America* (New York: D. Appleton & Co., 1860)

Wells, Stanley (ed.) *Nineteenth-Century Shakespeare Burlesques*, 5 vols (London: Diploma Press, 1977–8)

—— (ed.) *Shakespeare in the Theatre: an Anthology of Criticism* (Oxford: Oxford University Press, 2000), pp. 67–178

Secondary works

Adler, John (ed.) *Responses to Shakespeare*, vols 6, 1830–1859 and 7, 1861–1898 (London: Routledge/Thoemmes Press, 1997)

Alexander, J. H. and David Hewitt (eds) *Scott and his Influence* (Aberdeen: Association for Scottish Literary Studies, 1983)

Arac, Jonathan, 'Hamlet, *Little Dorrit*, and the History of Character', in *Critical Conditions: Regarding the Historical Moment*, ed. by Michael Hays (Minneapolis: University of Minnesota Press, 1992), pp. 82–96

Auerbach, Jeffrey A., *The Great Exhibition of 1851: a Nation on Display*, (New Haven and London: Yale University Press, 1999)

Auerbach, Nina, *Woman and the Demon: the Life of a Victorian Myth* (Harvard: Harvard University Press, 1982)

——*Ellen Terry: Player in Her Time* (New York: Norton, 1987)

——*Private Theatricals: the Lives of the Victorians* (Cambridge, MA: Harvard University Press, 1990)

Baker, Michael, *The Rise of the Victorian Actor* (London: Croom Helm, 1978)

Bate, Jonathan, *Shakespeare and the English Romantic Imagination* (Oxford: Clarendon, 1986)

Booth, Michael R., *English Melodrama* (London: Jenkins, 1965)

——*Theatre in the Victorian Age* (Cambridge: Cambridge University Press, 1991)

Bradby, David, Louis James and Bernard Sharratt, *Performance and Politics in Popular Drama* (Cambridge: Cambridge University Press, 1980)

Brewer, Wilmon, *Shakespeare's Influence on Sir Walter Scott* (Boston: Cornhill Publishing Co., 1925)

Carroll, David (ed.) *George Eliot: the Critical Heritage* (London: Routledge, 1971)

Davis, Philip, 'Nineteenth-Century Juliet', *Shakespeare Survey*, 49 (1996), pp. 131–40

——*Sudden Shakespeare* (London: Athlone Press, 1996)

Davis, Tracy C., *Actresses as Working Women* (London and New York: Routledge, 1991)

Desmet, Christy, and Robert Sawyer (eds) *Shakespeare and Appropriation* (London and New York: Routledge, 1999)

Disher, Maurice Willson, *Blood and Thunder: Mid-Victorian Melodrama and its Origins* (London: Muller, 1949)

Douglas-Fairhurst, Robert, *Victorian Afterlives: the Shaping of Influence in Nineteenth-Century Literature* (Oxford: Oxford University Press, 2002)

Downer, Alan S., *The Eminent Tragedian: William Charles Macready* (Cambridge, MA: Harvard University Press, 1966)

Elliott, G. R., 'Shakespeare's Significance for Browning', *Anglia. Zeitschrift für Englische Philologie*, 32 [N.S. 20] (1909), 90–161

Foulkes, Richard, *The Shakespeare Tercentenary of 1864* (London: Society for Theatre Research, 1984)

——*Shakespeare and the Victorian Stage* (Cambridge: Cambridge University Press, 1986)

——*Performing Shakespeare in the Age of Empire* (Cambridge: Cambridge University Press, 2002)

Gager, Valerie L., *Shakespeare and Dickens: the Dynamics of Influence* (Cambridge: Cambridge University Press, 1996)

Hankey, Julie (ed.) *Othello: Plays in Performance* (Bristol: Bristol Classical Press, 1987)

Hayden, John O. (ed.) *Scott: the Critical Heritage* (London: Routledge, 1970)

John, Juliet, *Dickens's Villains: Melodrama, Character, Popular Culture* (Oxford: Oxford University Press, 2001)

222   Selected Bibliography

Jump, John D. (ed.) *Tennyson: the Critical Heritage* (London: Routledge & Kegan Paul, 1967)

Lootens, Tricia, *Lost Saints: Silence, Gender, and Victorian Literary Canonization* (Charlottesville and London, University Press of Virginia, 1996)

Marsden, Jean I. (ed.) *The Appropriation of Shakespeare: Post-Renaissance Reconstructions of the Works and the Myth* (New York and London: Harvester Wheatsheaf, 1991)

Marshall, Gail, 'Helena Faucit: Shakespeare's Victorian Heroine', in *Translating Life: Studies in Transpositional Aesthetics*, ed. by Shirley Chew and Alistair Stead (Liverpool: Liverpool University Press, 1999)

Meisel, Martin, *Realizations: Narrative, Pictorial, and Theatrical Arts in Nineteenth-Century England* (Princeton, NJ: Princeton University Press, 1983)

Millgate, Michael, *Testamentary Acts: Browning, Tennyson, James, Hardy* (Oxford: Clarendon Press, 1992)

Novy, Marianne, *Engaging with Shakespeare: Responses of George Eliot and Other Women Novelists* (Iowa City: University of Iowa Press, 1998)

——(ed.) *Women's Re-Visions of Shakespeare* (Urbana and Chicago: University of Illinois Press, 1990)

Odell, George C. D., *Shakespeare from Betterton to Irving*, 2 vols (New York: Benjamin Blom, 1966)

Poole, Adrian, 'The Shadow of Lear's "Houseless" in Dickens', *Shakespeare Survey*, 53 (Cambridge: Cambridge University Press, 2000), pp. 103–13

——'Northern Hamlet and Southern Othello? Irving, Salvini and the Whirlwind of Passion', in *Shakespeare and the Mediterranean: Proceedings of the Seventh World Shakespeare Congress*, ed. by Tom Clayton, Susan Brock and Vicente Forès (Newark: University of Delaware Press, 2003)

——*Shakespeare and the Victorians* (London: Arden Shakespeare, 2003)

Powell, Kerry, *Women and Victorian Theatre* (Cambridge: Cambridge University Press, 1997)

Price, Leah, *The Anthology and the Rise of the Novel from Richardson to George Eliot* (Cambridge: Cambridge University Press, 2000)

Richards, Thomas, *The Commodity Culture of Victorian England: Advertising and Spectacle* (London and New York: Verso, 1990)

Ricks, Christopher, 'Tennyson Inheriting the Earth', in *Studies in Tennyson*, ed. by Hallam Tennyson (Basingstoke: Macmillan – now Palgrave Macmillan, 1981), pp. 66–104

Schoch, Richard W., *Shakespeare's Victorian Stage: Performing History in the Theatre of Charles Kean* (Cambridge: Cambridge University Press, 1998)

——*Not Shakespeare: Bardolatry and Burlesque in the Nineteenth Century* (Cambridge: Cambridge University Press, 2002)

Schoenbaum, Samuel, *Shakespeare's Lives*, rev. edn (Oxford: Oxford University Press, 1991), Part V: Victorians, and Part VI: Deviations, pp. 273–454

Shannon, Edgar Finley, Jr., *Tennyson and the Reviewers: a Study of His Literary Reputation and of the Influence of the Critics upon His Poetry 1827–1851* (Cambridge, MA: Harvard University Press, 1952)

Stavisky, Aron Y., *Shakespeare and the Victorians: Roots of Modern Criticism* (Norman, Oklahoma: University of Oklahoma Press, 1969)

Taylor, George, *Players and Performances in the Victorian Theatre* (Manchester: Manchester University Press, 1989)

Vaughan, Virginia Mason, *Othello: a Contextual History* (Cambridge: Cambridge University Press, 1994)

Wells, Stanley, *Shakespeare For All Time* (Basingstoke: Macmillan – now Palgrave Macmillan, 2002)

White, Henry Adelbert, *Sir Walter Scott's Novels on the Stage* (New Haven: Yale University Press, 1927)

Wood, Sarah, *Robert Browning: a Literary Life* (Basingstoke: Palgrave – now Palgrave Macmillan, 2001)

Woolford, John and Danny Karlin, *Robert Browning* (Harlow: Longman, 1996)

Index